# DICK VITALE'S

## Fabulous 50 Players & Moments in College Basketball

# DICK VITALE'S

## Fabulous 50 Players & Moments in College Basketball

**By Dick Vitale**

**Co-authored by Dick Weiss**

**Foreword by Patrick Ewing**

ASCEND BOOKS

www.ascendbooks.com

Photographs courtesy of AP Images, unless otherwise
noted.  Every reasonable attempt has been made to
determine the ownership of copyright.  Please notify the
publisher of any erroneous credits or omissions, and
corrections will be made to subsequent editions/future
printings.

Requests for permission should be addressed
to Ascend Books, LLC, Attn: Rights and
Permissions Department.

Printed in China
ISBN-13: 978-0-9836952-4-0  (Pbk)
Originally published in hardcover ISBN 978-0-9817166-2-6
©2008 by Dick Vitale and Dick Weiss
Library of Congress Cataloging-in-Publications
Data Available Upon Request.

Editor: Laurie Bollig
Cover Design and Book Design: Lynette Ubel
Project Manager: Meggan Cowan

# Dedications

I want to dedicate this book to all the beautiful people I've had the opportunity to work with at ESPN.

It starts up on top with our president, George Bodenheimer, and people in the executive office such as John Skipper and Norby Williamson. I can't imagine where I would be without the aid of Jed Drake, David Miller and Dan Steir. They have all been an integral part of my career in broadcasting.

And I can't forget to mention the guy who gave me my first big break in the business, Scotty Connal. Scotty came from NBC and was in charge of production, and, along with Chet Simmons, ESPN's first president, started the ball rolling in the world of 24-hour sports on TV.

When I was asked to do my first college game for ESPN, I had no idea what would happen. The Detroit Pistons had just fired me on November 8, 1979, and I was desperately trying to get back into coaching college basketball. Little did I know that November 8, 1979, would be the turning point in my professional life.

Along the way, I've had a lot of help and support.

I can't say enough about the play-by-play people with whom I have shared the booth. I've been blessed to sit next to broadcasting giants Jim Simpson, Keith Jackson and Brent Musburger. Currently, I am thrilled to work with ESPN stars like Mike Patrick, Dan Shulman and Brad Nessler. Also, on the sidelines and reporting at various game sites it has been fun working with Doris Burke and Erin Andrews. They are all first-class pros who have allowed me to be in my comfort zone, talking about a game I deeply love.

I have worked in the studio with brilliant hosts Bob Ley, John Saunders, Chris Fowler, Mike Tirico and Rece Davis. It's also been fun trading comments with basketball analysts like the late Jimmy V – that's right, Jimmy Valvano – Digger Phelps, Jay Bilas and, recently, the General, Robert Montgomery Knight.

I also want to thank all the people who make each television broadcast so special – all the sports anchors, the cameramen, the graphics operators, producers, directors and the many other people behind the scenes. Hey, I can't forget radio baby, *The Mike and Mike Show*. These guys have been absolutely fantastic to me, as well as all of the people at ESPN.com. I am so grateful to our public relations office, specifically Mike Soltys and Josh Krulewitz, who have assisted me over the years.

One last thing: Where would I be without our research department, especially my guy, Howie Schwab, who has been so dedicated to helping me prepare for each broadcast?

To put it in Vitalese, if I were doing a game, I would simply say, "All these people are Awesome, baby, with a capital A."

*Dick Vitale*

I'd like to dedicate this book to my mother, Barbara Weiss; and to my wife, Joan Williamson, who has been a constant source of help and inspiration with just about every major project I have undertaken since we attended Temple University together, including editing my copy for the student newspaper.

*Dick Weiss*

# Acknowledgements

A special note of thanks to my wife, Joan, who did the preliminary edits on this manuscript; Dick and Lorraine Vitale, who have always been so kind to Joan and me; and their daughters, Terri and Sherri; Patrick Ewing and Joel Glass of the Orlando Magic for writing the foreword; and our research expert, Howie Schwab.

I couldn't have done this without Pat Plunkett, who supplied the players' statistics and has the potential to become the second coming of the late, great Larry Donald; his wife, Trish, and their daughter, Mairead.

Dick Vitale and I owe a great deal of gratitude to Bob Snodgrass, Meggan Cowan, Kate Hegarty, and Laurie Bollig of Ascend Media, who made this project happen.

No list would be complete without mentioning Adam Berkowitz, Leon Carter, Teri Thompson, Delores Thompson, Bill Price, Eric Barrow, Jim Rich, Roger Rubin and the rest of the staff at the New York Daily News.

In addition, I'd like to mention Bob and Elaine Ryan, Kenny Denlinger, John Feinstein, Steve Richardson, John Akers and Nanci Donald of Basketball Times, Joe, Betty Ann, Tyler and Devon Cassidy, Mike Tranghese, Sam Albano, Jerry McLaughlin, Allen Rubin, Steve Miller from Fox Sports.com, Joe Timony, Rick Troncelliti, Frank Morgan, Mike Flynn, John Salvo, Robyn Norwood, Brian Morrison, Tom Healy, Dr. Dave Raezer, Mike Sheridan, Clark Francis, Joe Mitch, Howard Garfinkel, Larry Pearlstein, John Paquette, Al Featherston, David Pauley, Saul Frankel, Bill Brill and the staff at New Heights for the many enjoyable conversations we've had on college basketball over the years.

And, of course, The Guys.

*Dick Weiss*

# Foreword *by* PATRICK EWING

Every now and then you get some news that causes you to pause, to stop and reflect.

Such was the case when I received the call from Dick Vitale telling me he had selected me number one on his list of the 50 greatest players he has covered over the last 30 years.

"Numero uno, Babeeee! Are you kidding me? Are YOU kidding me?!"

Yes, there's a little Dickie V in all of us.

I am completely honored and feel privileged to be among this group. And to be selected number one left me momentarily speechless, as Dick has covered thousands of players.

I look back at my time at Georgetown with great fondness. It was a privilege to put on the Hoya uniform and play for and learn from legendary coach John Thompson. The foundation for my Hall of Fame career was set at Georgetown. I can't tell you how many life lessons I was fortunate enough to experience.

I clearly remember the times Dick and ESPN broadcast our games. The energy, enthusiasm and passion he brought to the gym were certainly tangible. We all knew he was in the house, and we were all hoping we were going to be a PTPer or Diaper Dandy that night.

I am also proud to have joined Dick as part of the Class of 2008 elected into the Naismith Memorial Basketball Hall of Fame.

I've always admired what Dick has brought to this great game and how he has used his platform to promote college basketball and worthy causes far beyond the baseline.

Thank you, Dickie V. I am touched and I sincerely appreciate this accolade.

You are Awesome with a capital A.

*Patrick Ewing*

*Photo Courtesy of Georgetown Sports Information.*

## Introduction *by* DICK VITALE

I can't believe that over 50 years have passed since I became a big fan of college basketball. During that time, I was able to serve as a high school, college and NBA coach as well as a broadcaster for ESPN. My friends, I can honestly say, I have been living a dream!

It started when I was a teenager and I used to go to the old Madison Square Garden in New York City. I was all excited just to sit up in the third deck and watch all the superstars as they'd come through the Big Apple. That's back when the NIT was big. It was back when I first laid eyes on the General – Robert Montgomery Knight – when he was in his early days, coaching at Army.

My love for the game has only gotten stronger over the years. I've been lucky enough to work as an analyst for ESPN, sitting courtside in the best seat in the house, over the last 30 years.

So when I got a call from Bob Snodgrass at Ascend Books, challenging me to select my fabulous 50 players and moments during my three decades on TV, I was absolutely thrilled.

The list starts in 1979, when I had the opportunity and the privilege to broadcast ESPN's first-ever major college basketball game, between DePaul and Wisconsin, from Chicago. Little did I know at the time, ESPN would grow to be a giant in the sports world. I feel so proud to be a little spoke in the big wheel it has created.

Hey baby, let me get back to my world. Oh, this was fun. Remember, this is nothing more than my opinion. That's right, just my views. It's not etched in stone. I respect the opinion of any fan who may feel differently about my choices. Remember, this is purely subjective, baby. Purely subjective.

The following criteria were utilized in determining the players and moments selected:

1. NBA careers were not a factor.
2. Consistency as a collegiate superstar was vital.
3. Ability to make teammates better was essential.
4. Players that were one and done were not eligible for consideration under our standards.
5. Players that were crucial in their team's success were certainly taken into consideration.

Yes, basketball fans, I can't wait to receive your feedback as to who would have been your choices for NUMBER ONE player and moment!

Obviously, when you talk about the NBA, you would immediately say Michael Jordan is the best player of all time. But in this book, we're talking about how he compared to the other great ones when he played for North Carolina.

Don't get me wrong. Michael was sensational in college. He always had my heart racing whenever I watched him play.

But was he number one on my list?

Remember this. He played on a great team – with All-Americans James Worthy and Sam Perkins – during his days under Dean Smith in Chapel Hill, so he wasn't nearly as dominant as when he won six NBA titles with the Chicago Bulls.

So, here we go, baby. Let me lay on you my fabulous 50, the players and moments from my three decades with ESPN. It will be interesting to see how you feel as I give you my crème de la crème.

Wow, I've had a blast doing this book. I hope you have a super time reading it.

*Dick Vitale*

**I know, I am just a shy, introverted broadcaster who used to serve as a teacher in New Jersey. I am living a dream, baby!**

*Photo courtesy of Dick Vitale.*

# GEORGETOWN:

PLAYER NUMBER

## Patrick Ewing

7' 0"

245 pounds

Center

1981-1985

*Profile:* When Georgetown coach John Thompson played for the NBA Boston Celtics, he had the privilege of being on the same team as the great Bill Russell, who set the standard for excellence at his position.

When Thompson signed Patrick Ewing out of Cambridge (Mass.) Rindge and Latin High, he found a clone.

The seven-foot tall, 245-pound Ewing was a dominant force in the modern era, a physically imposing defensive presence who, under Thompson's tutelage, led Georgetown to three appearances in the Final Four and a national championship in 1984. Ewing averaged 15.3 points and 9.2 rebounds, shot 62 percent and left an indelible imprint when the Big East was in its infancy.

He was a consensus first-team All-American three straight years, 1983-85. He was a star on the U.S. Olympic team, which won a gold medal at the 1984 games in Los Angeles and won the AP and Naismith National Player of the Year awards in 1985.

Ewing was born in Kingston, Jamaica, and grew up playing soccer and cricket. He did not touch a basketball until he moved to the United States to join his family when he was 12 years old. Six years later, he had led Rindge and Latin to three state titles and was the most sought-after prospect in the country.

Thompson first saw Ewing play as a high school sophomore – by accident. He was in town to visit his former coach, Red Auerbach, when he stopped off at the old Boston Garden to watch the Massachusetts state title game and saw Ewing warming up. "Get me him," Thompson told Auerbach, "and I'll win the national championship."

How prophetic.

Ewing could have jumped right from high school to the pros; but like so many other players on our list, he promised his late mother, Dorothy, that he would become the first member of his family to graduate from college.

Thompson, who became a protective father figure for Ewing, made sure his star got a degree in fine arts in 1985. He also maximized Ewing's massive defensive skills. Ewing helped lead the Hoyas to the national championship game against North Carolina as a freshman. Although the Tar Heels won the game, 63-62, at the New Orleans Superdome, Ewing gave the Tar Heels something to think about, swatting away four Carolina shots – all of them goal tends – in the first eight minutes.

Two years later, he completed his mission as the Hoyas swept through the Final Four, holding mighty Kentucky to just three-for-33 shooting with suffocating defense during the second half of a 53-40 victory in the national semis at the Seattle Kingdome, then methodically dispatching Houston and 7' 0" Akeem Olajuwon, 84-75, in the finals. Ewing, who finished with 10 points and nine rebounds, was selected the Most Outstanding Player of the NCAA Tournament.

In his senior year, Ewing was once again the dominant player in the game. Georgetown was ranked No. 1 in the AP poll. The Hoyas were heavily favored to beat unranked Big East rival Villanova in the national title game, but were beaten by the Cats, 66-64, in a huge upset in Lexington.

Ewing was the first player selected in the NBA draft that spring. The New York Knicks, who won the league's first draft lottery, chose him.

*Dickie V's View:* Bob Knight once told me his all-time MVP in basketball would be Bill Russell. He loved winners and Russell led the Boston Celtics to nine world championships as a player. That thought popped into my mind when I was picking my number one player since I've been covering college basketball at ESPN.

Wow, was this a tough call, but I finally decided on Patrick Ewing because of his incredible competitive winning spirit that was a major factor in Georgetown becoming dominant from 1981 through 1985. Remember, Ewing was the major reason why Georgetown celebrated as national champs in 1984. Also, don't forget that the big fella was the central

**Patrick Ewing had a tremendous wingspan that made him a true defensive dynamo. The Georgetown center proved that the lane was his place to dominate.**

reason why the Hoyas made three journeys to the Final Four in his four years.

Some guys are all about stats.

Patrick didn't have to score to be effective. He was all about winning, all about the team concept.

Just win, baby.

Ewing made Georgetown the beast of the young Big East. He was the league's best player ever. He was a dominator from the day he arrived. He was worth 20 points to his team just by walking onto the court because of his ability to intimidate the Georgetown opposition with his incredible shot-blocking ability.

In 1984, when Georgetown won the national championship, Ewing was the catalyst for a suffocating defense that took down Kentucky, 53-40, in the national semifinals. Kentucky failed to score on its first 14 possessions of the second half and its five starters shot a combined zero for 21.

There were stories that Joe B. Hall, the Kentucky coach, was so upset he sent his manager over to the arena afterwards to measure the rims to make sure they were 10-feet tall. It was this type of Hoya paranoia Ewing created for opposing coaches.

And the type of performance to be expected from a player whose First Commandment was: Thou Shalt Not Enter the Lane. Ewing sent that message loud and clear to Houston's "Phi Slamma Jamma" and its celebrated superstars Akeem Olajuwon and Clyde Drexler. Ewing controlled the game with his physical presence right from the start and the Hoyas were on their way to winning the big prize.

I remember one time, coming in to do a Georgetown game and John Thompson grabbing me and saying, "I want you to talk to Patrick about what you've been saying on TV, that he has to work on his post moves so he can be more effective offensively."

So I ended up going into the locker room. There was Patrick Ewing sitting down. And I found out what a great guy this young kid was as he listened intently as I spoke to him about the need to work on his drop step moves. I also told him what a big plus it was playing for a coach like Thompson, who had been an All-American center at Providence.

Afterwards, I received a big hug and a thank you from the Hall of Famer, Mr. Thompson.

Mission accomplished, baby.

## #1. PATRICK EWING, GEORGETOWN

|  | MIN | FG% | 3P% | FT% | RPG | APG | TPG | BPG | SPG | PPG |
|---|---|---|---|---|---|---|---|---|---|---|
| 81-82 | 28.8 | 63.1 |  | 61.7 | 7.5 | 0.6 | 2.0 | 3.2 | 1.1 | 12.7 |
| 82-83 | 32.0 | 57.0 |  | 62.9 | 10.2 | 0.8 | 2.5 | 3.3 | 1.5 | 17.7 |
| 83-84 | 31.9 | 65.8 |  | 65.6 | 10.0 | 0.8 | 2.4 | 3.6 | 1.0 | 16.4 |
| 84-85 | 30.6 | 62.5 |  | 63.8 | 9.2 | 1.3 | 2.2 | 3.6 | 1.1 | 14.6 |
| **TOTALS** | 30.8 | 62.0 |  | 63.5 | 9.2 | 0.9 | 2.3 | 3.4 | 1.2 | 15.3 |

**P**atrick Ewing, my number
one player over the last 30
years, cut down the nets
as a national champion for
Georgetown in 1984.

# DUKE:

**PLAYER NUMBER 2**

# Christian Laettner

6' 11"

245 pounds

Center

1988-1992

*Profile:* Christian Laettner got his name from Hollywood. His mother named him after Christian Diestl, the German soldier played by Marlon Brando in the 1958 movie, *The Young Lions.*

Although he looked like he had just come off the set of "Beverly Hills 90210," and had attended the prestigious Nichols School in Buffalo, the 6' 11" center was hardly the pretty boy type. Laettner was the son of a printer for the *Buffalo News* and his family lived in the lower-middle-class community of Angola, 30 miles south of the city. He was on scholarship at Nichols and got up at 6 every morning to make the 45-minute bus trip to school. He had a blue-collar soul and the most competitive heart of any player in the history of Duke basketball. With ice water running through his veins, Laettner demanded excellence from himself and his teammates. He was both confident and cocky – personality traits that combined to make him a three-time All-American and the 1992 National Player of the Year.

He was the poster child for a proud program that won two national championships and made four consecutive Final Four appearances at the height of the Mike Krzyzewski era.

Laettner, whose superb face-up game combined a soft touch with tremendous range on his jump shot, averaged 16.6 points and 7.8 rebounds and made 48.5 percent of his three-pointers during his career. But he is best known for making so many big shots when it mattered most – during March Madness.

As a freshman, Laettner scored 24 points, grabbed nine rebounds and outplayed 6' 10" Alonzo Mourning as the Blue Devils defeated Georgetown, 85-77, in the East Regional finals at the Meadowlands.

As a sophomore, he drained a 15-foot game-winning shot at the buzzer to give the Blue Devils a 79-78 overtime win over Connecticut in another regional final game at the same arena. Duke advanced to the championship game, only to lose to UNLV, 103-73, in Denver.

The bitter memory of that loss helped motivate the Dukies when they played the top-ranked, 34-0 Runnin' Rebels in the national semifinals the next year. Laettner came up huge again, scoring 28 points and making a pair of free throws with five seconds left to break a 77-77 tie. Duke held on for a stunning victory that propelled the Blue Devils to their first national championship.

Laettner was selected Most Outstanding Player of the Final Four.

But his most dramatic shot occurred during the East Regional finals in his senior year and helped keep Duke's hopes for back-to-back titles alive. Laettner caught a long looping pass from teammate Grant Hill, spun and then shot an 18-foot jumper that ripped through the net at the buzzer as the Blue Devils defeated Kentucky, 104-103, in double overtime at the Philadelphia Spectrum. Laettner averaged a career-high 21.5 points and 7.9 rebounds as a senior, shooting 57.5 percent and making 55.7 percent from three-point range.

He was selected by Minnesota with the third pick in the NBA draft. USA Basketball honored him by selecting him as the only college player on the immortal 1992 Olympic "Dream Team," ahead of Shaquille O'Neal of LSU and Alonzo Mourning of Georgetown.

## #2. CHRISTIAN LAETTNER, DUKE

|  | MIN | FG% | 3P% | FT% | RPG | APG | TPG | BPG | SPG | PPG |
|---|---|---|---|---|---|---|---|---|---|---|
| 88-89 | 16.9 | 72.3 | 100.0 | 72.7 | 4.7 | 1.2 | 1.6 | 0.8 | 1.0 | 8.9 |
| 89-90 | 29.9 | 51.1 | 50.0 | 83.6 | 9.6 | 2.2 | 2.7 | 1.1 | 1.6 | 16.3 |
| 90-91 | 30.2 | 57.5 | 34.0 | 80.2 | 8.7 | 1.9 | 3.1 | 1.1 | 1.9 | 19.8 |
| 91-92 | 32.2 | 57.5 | 55.7 | 81.5 | 7.9 | 2.0 | 3.3 | 0.9 | 2.1 | 21.5 |
| **TOTALS** | *27.4* | *57.4* | *48.5* | *80.6* | *7.8* | *1.8* | *2.7* | *1.0* | *1.6* | *16.6* |

**Dickie V's View:** When Christian Laettner was a freshman, Duke played Arizona at the Meadowlands and he had a chance to be a hero. Duke was trailing 77-75, but Laettner was at the line with a shot to force overtime if he converted both ends of a one-and-one. He missed and had to be consoled by his teammates.

Then Richard Nixon – that's right, the former president of the United States who was a Duke law school graduate and was at the game – asked to speak to him in the locker room. He told Laettner: "I know you feel badly but everything will be fine. I've won a few and lost a few myself."

That was the last big shot Laettner missed in his Duke career.

He made two huge ones in two NCAA Tournament games in 1991 and 1992 when Duke won back-to-back championships – hitting dramatic game winners against Connecticut and Kentucky in the regional finals each year. He was a guy who loved the pressure squarely on his shoulders at the end of a big game.

He knew he could deliver, baby.

Laettner had a rare combination of confidence and arrogance. He had that arrogance, that cockiness, that made him special and he also had that confidence in his ability and talent. And he was so competitive. He'd battle his teammates in everything – ping pong, pool, air hockey – you name it.

He just hated to lose.

Especially in practice. Just ask his teammates. It's what drove him to become one of the great players in ACC history.

Before Laettner left Duke, he had his number retired. But Mike Krzyzewski, who has always been a big believer in academics, warned that Laettner's jersey and the 1992 national championship banner would come down from the rafters in Cameron if Laettner did not get his degree by July. Laettner took a psychology course to complete his undergraduate work in the first session of summer school before he joined the 1992 Olympic "Dream Team," which struck gold in Barcelona.

Christian Laettner helped lead Duke to back-to-back championships in 1991 and '92. I always felt he was a fierce competitor for Mike Krzyzewski's squad.

# VIRGINIA:

PLAYER NUMBER

## Ralph Sampson

7' 4"

230 pounds

Center

1979-1983

*Profile:* When the University of Virginia beat out North Carolina, Kentucky and Virginia Tech for Ralph Sampson, giddy undergrads immediately painted the words "Ralph's House" on the roof of old University Hall in bold, black letters.

It was hard to know whether Sampson was ready for this type of adulation when he drove up from nearby Harrisonburg, Va., to enroll at the Charlottesville campus in a pickup truck with his eight-foot-long bed in tow.

Sampson was a private person and did not like the idea of being the object of so much curiosity. He spent much of his time sleeping in the basement of coach Terry Holland's house to avoid the fans and tourists.

But he was hard to miss on the basketball court. Sampson was a towering presence in the ACC. He was a three-time national player of the year, three-time consensus All-American and three-time ACC Player of the Year. "Stick," as he was known, was not a prolific scorer, but he did average 16.9 points and 11.4 rebounds despite double and triple man-to-man defenses that surrounded him. He dominated every aspect of the game with his size and surprising face-the-basket versatility. He finished his college career with 2,225 points and 1,511 rebounds.

He led Virginia to an NIT championship as a freshman in 1980, scoring 15 points and grabbing 15 rebounds in a 58-55 victory over Minnesota. He took the Cavs to a Final Four as a sophomore, No. 1 rankings in 1982 and 1983 and a 112-23 record in four seasons. Three times, Sampson and Virginia – previously thought to be a middle-of-the-pack team

in the conference – either won or tied for first place in the ACC regular season during the Michael Jordan era at North Carolina.

Sampson could have left for the NBA at any time. He was offered $400,000 from the Boston Celtics following his freshman year and $800,000 from both the Detroit Pistons and the Dallas Mavericks following his junior year. But he stayed all four years, participating in one of the most memorable games in college basketball history when the Cavs defeated a Patrick Ewing-fueled Georgetown team in the most hyped game of the decade before a nationally syndicated TV audience at the Capital Centre in Landover, Md.

Sampson never achieved his dream of winning a national title. The Cavs fell one game shy of the Final Four in his senior year when they lost to Cinderella North Carolina State, 63-62, in the NCAA West Regional finals when Virginia couldn't get the ball to Sampson on the final play.

But he gave the Cavs a national address before moving on to the NBA and was selected by Houston with the first overall pick in the 1983 draft.

*Dickie V's View:* Ralph Sampson lived in a fish bowl when he went to Virginia. From the time he arrived on campus as a freshman, he became the local tourist attraction. He tried to live on the Lawn on campus one year, but students and fans were constantly trying to peek into his room to get a look.

That happens when you're 7' 4" and the most dominant center in college basketball. Sampson was the national player of the year three times at Virginia

If you judge him strictly on his college career, he belongs in the Hall of Fame.

He was brilliant from the first day he arrived in Charlottesville.

In a way, it's unfortunate that Sampson doesn't get the credit and recognition he deeply deserves for his collegiate career, especially when it comes to consideration for the Naismith Memorial Basketball Hall of Fame in Springfield, Mass. People have a tendency to remember his last days as a player on the professional level and unfortunately forget about the greatness he achieved at the University of Virginia. Sampson had an above-average career with the Houston Rockets.

## #3. RALPH SAMPSON, VIRGINIA

|         | MIN  | FG%  | 3P%   | FT%  | RPG  | APG | TPG | BPG | SPG | PPG  |
|---------|------|------|-------|------|------|-----|-----|-----|-----|------|
| 79-80   | 29.9 | 54.7 |       | 70.2 | 11.2 | 1.1 | 3.1 | 4.6 | 0.8 | 14.9 |
| 80-81   | 32.0 | 55.7 |       | 63.1 | 11.5 | 1.5 | 2.7 | 3.1 | 0.8 | 17.7 |
| 81-82   | 31.3 | 56.1 |       | 61.5 | 11.4 | 1.2 | 1.9 | 3.1 | 0.6 | 15.8 |
| 82-83   | 30.2 | 60.4 | 60.0  | 70.4 | 11.7 | 1.0 | 2.6 | 3.1 | 0.6 | 19.1 |
| **TOTALS** | **30.8** | **56.8** | ***60.0** | **65.7** | **11.4** | **1.2** | **2.6** | **3.5** | **0.7** | **16.9** |

*ACC used the three-point shot on an experimental basis starting in the 1982-83 season.*

But whenever you're that big and you get that kind of interest, the fans and media are going to get on you if you don't win a national college championship or an NBA title. Expectations, expectations and expectations were a problem for Sampson as fans expected an NCAA championship.

After a while, people started to judge Sampson by his NBA career and they forgot about what he did in college. People remember your last dance, the last shot. When you're Goliath, they can't wait to put a little hole in your armor and they'll jump on it like you can't believe.

Sampson was always sensitive about his place in the basketball universe. After doing the North Carolina-Virginia game in 1983 when Carolina came back on the strength of a brilliant performance by Michael Jordan, I remember screaming out, "America, this is the best player in college basketball. It's not Mr. Sampson. It's Mr. Jordan."

Well, wouldn't you know, I had a journey coming up to see Virginia play in Charlottesville. As soon as I walked in, Ralph said to me, "Here comes Michael Jordan's PR agent."

**V**irginia's Ralph Sampson was a dominant big man. He was a three-time national player of the year who scored more than 2,000 points while grabbing more than 1,500 rebounds.

# NORTH CAROLINA:

PLAYER NUMBER

## Michael Jordan

6' 6"

190 pounds

Forward

1981-1984

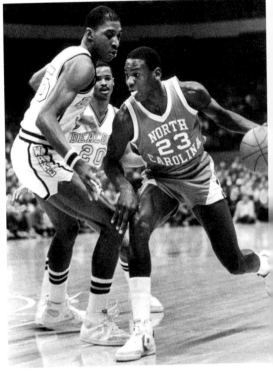

*Profile:* The player who would one day become the shining star of the NBA grew up with an intense dislike for his future alma mater.

When Michael Jordan was a youngster, he was a huge fan of North Carolina State's sky-walker, David Thompson. He even rooted for Marquette when the Warriors played North Carolina in the 1977 NCAA championship game.

But he had a change of heart after he visited the University of North Carolina campus to participate in Carolina's basketball camp the summer before his senior year in high school.

It took a little longer for Dean Smith to determine how good Jordan could be. Jordan had been cut from his junior high team and couldn't even make varsity at Laney High in Wilmington, N.C., as a sophomore. But he sprouted up from 5' 11" to 6' 3" as a junior and his game blew up.

Smith and his assistant coach, Roy Williams, arranged for Jordan to participate in Howard Garfinkel's famed Five Star camp in the Poconos to make a final determination whether they would offer Jordan a scholarship. It almost backfired. Jordan was the best player in the camp and suddenly Carolina, which thought Jordan would fly under the radar, was a national name and the Tar Heels had to battle NC State, Maryland and South Carolina for his signature on a letter of intent.

Eventually, Jordan chose North Carolina over South Carolina because of Smith's reputation for transforming in-state stars like Phil Ford and Walter Davis into pros.

Then he proceeded to create his own legend.

Jordan averaged a modest 17.7 points and 5.0 rebounds during his three-year career in Smith's balanced offense, but he helped lead Smith's 1982 team to the national championship as a freshman. He then went on to become a first-team All-American the next two years. Jordan averaged 20 points as a sophomore and led the ACC in scoring with a 19.6-point average as a junior while grabbing 5.3 rebounds and shooting 55.1 percent. He was selected consensus National Player of the Year that season and went on to become the star of the 1984 U.S. Olympic team that won a gold medal in Los Angeles.

Along the way, Jordan developed a reputation for creating dramatic endings, beginning with the game-winning shot from the left wing with just 16 seconds to play to give the Tar Heels a 63-62 victory over Georgetown in the 1982 national title game. He punctuated his junior year with a steal and a

ast-second jumper to force overtime in a victory
ver Tulane; he blocked a last-second shot by
Chuckie Driesell to preserve a one-point victory
ver Maryland; and he led the Heels on a 16-point
ally against Ralph Sampson and top-ranked Virginia,
vinning the game with a steal off Rick Carlisle and a
breakaway dunk.

Jordan turned pro after Indiana upset the Tar
Heels in the 1984 Sweet 16. He was selected by
Chicago with the third pick overall in the draft.

And the rest is history.

*Dickie V's View:* When Michael Jordan was a
freshman at Carolina, I was doing one of the Tar
Heels' games at Carmichael Auditorium. This lady
an down to courtside before tipoff. Security tried to
keep people away, but she made it up to the table and
he said to me, "Dick Vitale, you don't know me, but
'm Michael Jordan's mother and I want to give you
big kiss for all the beautiful things you say about
ay son."

Then she did just that.

It was hard not to gush all over the microphone.

I started singing his praises and became enam-
red of him. I called him Michael "The Magnificent"
ordan after his game-winning dunk against Ralph
ampson and Virginia in 1983. I knew he'd be a great
player, but I never knew he'd become the mega mega
uperstar he was. When I catch one of his college
ames on ESPN Classic, I am absolutely mesmerized
y his magical talents.

Howard Garfinkel, who ran the Five-Star camp,
ells it the best. Jordan went there to camp the
ummer before his senior year in high school.

He played on those outside courts, up in the
mountains in Honesdale, Pa.

All the preseason basketball magazines were about
to go to print in July with their superstars – including
the top five players in the country. Not many people
had heard of the kid from Wilmington Laney High
School, but Garf couldn't wait for me to see Jordan
as I was visiting the camp to be a guest lecturer.
"Hurry up," Garf said. "You've got to see this kid."
We watched him a little bit, and you could see his
great elevation and his undeniable talent in the camp
games.

Then Garfinkel ran to the phone and called the
late Bob Lapidus of Street & Smith's. "Who's in your
top five," he starts screaming and yelling. "They can't
compare to this guy."

Leave it to Garf to try to stop the presses.

The Garf strikes gold. The Garf strikes gold.

Michael Jordan went on to become the ultimate,
possibly the best ever to play the game if you
evaluate his NBA career. However, I think he would
agree that playing in the North Carolina system
helped him grow as a player. Remember, basketball
fans, he had the honor of playing under one of the
best minds to ever work the sidelines in solid gold
Hall of Famer Dean Smith. Jordan, a keen student
of the game, listened intently to every word that
Dean Smith preached about the game he loved.

**I** loved the way Michael Jordan would attack the basket. Here a young Mr. Jordan makes his move against Wake Forest back in 1982.

## #4. MICHAEL JORDAN, NORTH CAROLINA

|  | MIN | FG% | 3P% | FT% | RPG | APG | TPG | BPG | SPG | PPG |
|---|---|---|---|---|---|---|---|---|---|---|
| 81-82 | 31.7 | 53.4 | | 72.2 | 4.4 | 1.8 | 1.7 | 0.2 | 1.2 | 13.5 |
| 82-83 | 30.9 | 53.5 | 44.7 | 73.7 | 5.5 | 1.6 | 2.1 | 0.8 | 2.2 | 20.0 |
| 83-84 | 29.5 | 55.1 | | 77.9 | 5.3 | 2.1 | 2.2 | 1.1 | 1.6 | 19.6 |
| **TOTALS** | *30.8* | *54.0* | *\*44.7* | *74.8* | *5.0* | *1.8* | *2.0* | *0.7* | *1.7* | *17.7* |

*\*ACC used the three-point shot on an experimental basis starting in the 1982-83 season.*

## KANSAS:

PLAYER NUMBER 5

# Danny Manning

6' 10"

230 pounds

Forward/
Center

1984-1988

*Profile:* Danny Manning may have had a bigger impact on Kansas basketball than any player in the program's storied history, including Clyde Lovellette or the late Wilt Chamberlain.

The versatile 6' 10" center, who averaged 24.8 points and nine rebounds as a senior and helped change the way coaches looked at big men, led Kansas to an unlikely NCAA Tournament title in 1988. He did it by scoring 31 points and grabbing 18 rebounds as a patchwork sixth-seeded, 23-11 Jayhawk team rallied from a disappointing 12-8 start to defeat Oklahoma, 83-79, in the 50th anniversary celebration of the championship game at Kemper Arena in Kansas City. He was named the tournament's Most Outstanding Player.

It was the crowning achievement for this shining star, who is Kansas' all-time leading scorer and rebounder, piling up 2,951 points and 1,187 rebounds and averaging 20.1 points and 8.1 rebounds during a brilliant four-year career. Manning, the ninth all-time leading scorer in NCAA Division I history, was named a consensus first-team All-American selection in 1987 and 1988, the National Player of the Year in 1988, and was a three-time Big Eight Conference Player of the Year.

Larry Brown must have realized Manning's enormous potential when he left the NBA's New Jersey Nets to take the Kansas job in 1983. He immediately offered Manning's father, Ed – who had played for Brown with the ABA Carolina Cougars and spent time as a college assistant before becoming a truck driver – a spot on his staff. Manning, a junior in high school at the time, had just led Greensboro Page to the North Carolina state title but moved to Lawrence with his family and then signed with Kansas.

Manning became an immediate starter as a freshman and was named the MVP of the NCAA Midwest Regional in 1986 and 1988. He played a key role on the 1986 KU team that finished 35-4 and advanced to the Final Four in Dallas, but scored only four points in a foul-plagued national semifinal loss to Duke.

Manning's averages jumped to 23.9 points and 9.5 rebounds as a junior, and he looked ready for the NBA. But he came back for a last hurrah, taking his game to a new level in the Final Four with 68 points, 28 rebounds and nine steals in the final two games.

The Los Angeles Clippers selected Manning with the first overall pick in the 1988 NBA draft.

*Dickie V's View:* Oklahoma's All-American center Stacey King put it in the proper perspective when he said that Danny Manning changed the way college basketball fans looked at big men because he was more than just a low post player. Manning was 6' 10". He never showed any expression when he played, but he was skilled enough to handle the rock against pressure, pass it and shoot the trifecta. He was also incredibly unselfish. I think there were times when he had to be prodded by Larry Brown and his teammates to become a superstar.

And what a superstar.

He could definitely have gone pro after his junior year, but we hadn't yet reached the point in college basketball when there was a tidal wave of players who still had eligibility leaving early.

When Manning was a senior, 22 of the first 25 players taken in the NBA draft were seniors. Today, we're lucky if there are three or four seniors who go in the first round.

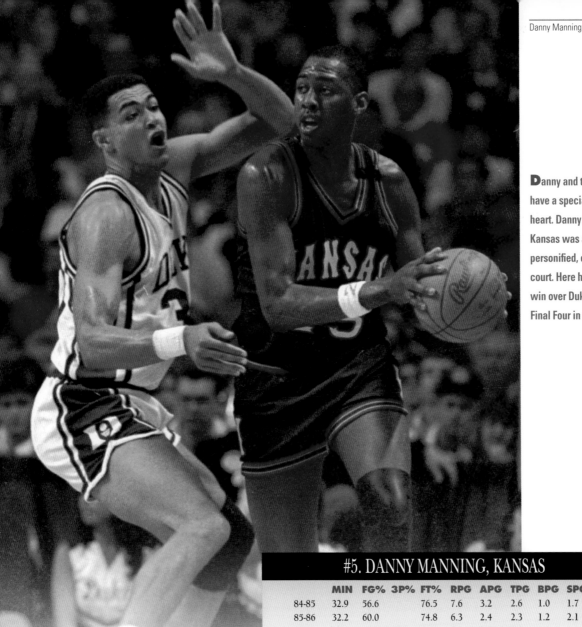

## #5. DANNY MANNING, KANSAS

|         | MIN  | FG%  | 3P%  | FT%  | RPG | APG | TPG | BPG | SPG | PPG  |
|---------|------|------|------|------|-----|-----|-----|-----|-----|------|
| 84-85   | 32.9 | 56.6 |      | 76.5 | 7.6 | 3.2 | 2.6 | 1.0 | 1.7 | 14.6 |
| 85-86   | 32.2 | 60.0 |      | 74.8 | 6.3 | 2.4 | 2.3 | 1.2 | 2.1 | 16.7 |
| 86-87   | 34.7 | 61.7 | 33.3 | 73.0 | 9.5 | 1.8 | 2.8 | 1.3 | 1.2 | 23.9 |
| 87-88   | 35.2 | 58.3 | 34.6 | 73.4 | 9.0 | 2.0 | 3.0 | 1.9 | 1.8 | 24.8 |
| **TOTALS** | **33.7** | **59.3** | **34.5** | **74.0** | **8.1** | **2.3** | **2.7** | **1.4** | **1.7** | **20.1** |

But Manning still had some unfinished business. He wanted to get back to the Final Four, wanted to wipe that bitter taste of his first experience there – when he had scored just four points and fouled out against Duke in the 1986 semifinals – out of his mouth.

And, my friends, Kansas' semifinal opponent that year was none other than Duke. This time, however, Manning got 25 points, 10 rebounds, six blocked shots and four assists as the Jayhawks took out the ACC's finest, setting the stage for his golden performance against Oklahoma in the finals.

It was a stellar performance by "Danny and the Miracles".

# WAKE FOREST:

PLAYER NUMBER

# Tim Duncan

6' 11"

245 pounds

Center

1993-1997

*Profile:* Tim Duncan excelled in the 50-, 100- and 400-meter freestyle swimming events as a teenager in the Virgin Islands. He was attempting to follow in the footsteps of his sister, Tricia, and become a member of the U.S. Olympic swim team. Then Hurricane Hugo destroyed St. Croix's only Olympic-sized pool in 1989. A fear of sharks kept Duncan from swimming in the ocean. It was at this point that his athletic career took an unexpected turn.

Disappointed, the 6' 11" Duncan turned his misfortune into triumph, taking up the sport of basketball and eventually becoming a two-time first-team All-American at Wake Forest. He was also a two-time ACC Player of the Year, a three-time NABC Defensive Player of the Year and the National Player of the Year his senior season in 1997.

Duncan will always be known as Demon Deacon, coach Dave Odom's greatest discovery.

Odom was looking for a big man to complement his two stars – Randolph Childress and Rodney Rogers. He flew to the Caribbean on the advice of one of his former players, Chris King, who had scrimmaged against Duncan when a group of NBA players stopped on St. Croix and arranged to play a pickup game against the locals on an outdoor court. According to King, Duncan, then only 16 and with just two years of organized basketball at St. Croix Country Day School, played Alonzo Mourning to a draw.

Odom was concerned about the level of competition in the islands, but he loved what he had seen in that game the summer before Duncan's senior year in high school and thought he had found arguably the greatest sleeper in the history of the ACC.

Duncan averaged 25 points that year but was still largely unknown when he signed with Wake, choosing the Deacs – the smallest school in the ACC – over Providence and Delaware State.

His anonymity changed quickly.

The stoic Duncan was almost gone before he had a chance to make an impact. He averaged 16.8 points, 12.5 rebounds and 4.2 blocked shots as a sophomore, leading his team to the ACC title and a Sweet 16 appearance when Los Angeles Lakers GM Jerry West suggested that he could be the first pick in the 1995 draft. Duncan, a good student who promised his dying mother he would get his college degree, stayed, even though he knew the NBA was ready to implement a salary cap the next season.

Duncan averaged 19.1 points and 12.3 rebounds as a junior, leading the conference in scoring, rebounding, field goal percentage and blocked shots. He was selected MVP of the 1996 ACC Tournament, which Wake won again, and led the Deacs to another Sweet 16. Duncan was rumored to be entering the draft again following that season, but he stayed for his senior year, when he averaged 20.8 points, 14.7 rebounds, 3.2 assists and 3.3 blocks for an NCAA second-round team.

Duncan never got to a Final Four, but he graduated that spring with a degree in psychology, then was selected by San Antonio with the first pick overall in the 1997 NBA draft.

*Dickie V's View:* What do you think might have happened if Hurricane Hugo hadn't destroyed the swimming pool on Tim Duncan's island of St. Croix?

He might have gone on to represent the U.S. swimming team in the 1996 Olympic games at Atlanta. And basketball might have been robbed of one of its greatest players ever.

It still amazes me how coaches discover some of these international players. But at Wake, you always have to be resourceful. It's not as though you're going to win a lot of recruiting battles with ACC giants like North Carolina and Duke. Here's a kid who came in without a big reputation. He picked Wake Forest over Delaware State. He didn't really know the difference.

He was kind of an add-on recruit for Wake. The school's big names were Ricardo Peral and Makhtar Ndiaye. But Dave Odom wound up getting a gem.

Duncan just got better and better and better in a very quiet way. Nothing spectacular, just fundamentally solid. He played with great feeling and was a complete player, a team-oriented guy who was so skilled in the low post. He really knew how to get offensive position and defensively he was a terror blocking shots.

Dave Odom always reminded me of Duncan's work ethic and his pride as a player. Duncan wanted to prove without a doubt he was as good as any of the McDonald's All-Americans.

My friends, he not only proved he was as good as them; he was the crème de la crème.

And he made a big difference. Wake Forest hadn't won an ACC Tournament championship in 33 years before Duncan arrived. By the end of his junior year, the Deacons were the first team in 14 years to win back-to-back titles.

**If it wasn't for a problem with a swimming pool in the Virgin Islands, Tim Duncan might have been an Olympian in a different sport. Wake Forest was happy he ended up on the basketball court.**

## #6. TIM DUNCAN, WAKE FOREST

|  | MIN | FG% | 3P% | FT% | RPG | APG | TPG | BPG | SPG | PPG |
|---|---|---|---|---|---|---|---|---|---|---|
| 93-94 | 30.2 | 54.5 | 100.0 | 74.5 | 9.6 | 0.9 | 1.2 | 3.8 | 0.4 | 9.8 |
| 94-95 | 36.5 | 59.1 | 42.9 | 74.2 | 12.5 | 2.1 | 2.8 | 4.2 | 0.4 | 16.8 |
| 95-96 | 37.3 | 55.5 | 30.4 | 68.7 | 12.3 | 2.9 | 3.3 | 3.8 | 0.7 | 19.1 |
| 96-97 | 36.7 | 60.8 | 27.3 | 63.6 | 14.7 | 3.2 | 3.2 | 3.3 | 0.7 | 20.8 |
| **TOTALS** | 35.1 | 57.7 | 32.1 | 68.9 | 12.3 | 2.3 | 2.6 | 3.8 | 0.5 | 16.5 |

# INDIANA:

PLAYER NUMBER

# Isiah Thomas

6' 1"

180 pounds

Guard

1979-1981

*Profile:* Isiah Thomas was the only NBA All-Star ever to play for Bob Knight at Indiana. Knight thought enough of his talent to call him the best player of his size in the history of the sport.

Calvin Murphy and Tiny Archibald might disagree, but there can be no argument about the impact the baby-faced Thomas had on the Hoosiers during his two years on campus. He made first-team All-American as a sophomore when he averaged 16 points and 5.8 assists and led the 26-9 Hoosiers to the 1981 national championship. Thomas – whose nickname was "The Smiling Assassin" – was selected Most Outstanding Player in the NCAA Tournament after scoring 23 points during a 63-50 victory over North Carolina in the title game.

Thomas was the youngest of nine children, seven of them sons, who grew up in a Chicago west side ghetto. His house often had no heat during the cold Chicago winters. His mother, Mary, raised all nine children on her own. On one occasion when gang members approached the Thomas residence to recruit the boys, Mary responded by pulling a shotgun on the gang members and threatening to kill them. Isiah's older brothers protected him, allowing him to focus on basketball at a young age.

Thomas was a CYO star as a fourth grader, playing on a team with seventh and eighth graders,

but there was a fear he might be too small to play because he was only 5' 6" when he entered high school. Thomas attended St. Joseph's High in Westchester, getting up at 5:30 a.m. to make the 90-minute trip to play for Gene Pignatore. Thomas led St. Joe's to a state title as a junior. He was recruited nationally, but signed with Indiana because he wanted to attend school close to home.

Thomas made a big splash on the international stage before he ever enrolled in college, playing for the 1979 U.S. Pan Am team coached by Bob Knight. He scored 23 points with five steals and four assists as the U.S. won the gold medal in Puerto Rico.

Thomas did not take long to adjust to the college game, becoming the first freshman ever to make first-team All-Big Ten after he combined with Mike Woodson to lead the Hoosiers to the first of two conference titles and a spot in the Sweet 16. He was a strong-willed point guard who was selected for the 1980 Olympic team, but never got a chance to participate because of the American boycott of the Moscow games.

Thomas was the first Knight-coached player to leave early for the NBA. Ignoring advice from Knight and former IU star Quinn Buckner to remain in school, he declared for the draft and was selected by the Detroit Pistons with the second pick overall in the 1981 draft. But he has always remained close to Knight.

*Dickie V's View:* I want to make a case here that Isiah Thomas – pound for pound, inch for inch – might have been the best ever.

## #7. ISIAH THOMAS, INDIANA

|  | MIN | FG% | 3P% | FT% | RPG | APG | TPG | BPG | SPG | PPG |
|---|---|---|---|---|---|---|---|---|---|---|
| 79-80 | 34.0 | 51.0 |  | 77.2 | 4.0 | 5.5 |  |  |  | 14.6 |
| 80-81 | 35.0 | 55.4 |  | 74.2 | 3.1 | 5.8 |  |  | 2.2 | 16.0 |
| **TOTALS** | 34.5 | 53.4 |  | 75.6 | 3.5 | 5.7 |  |  |  | 15.4 |

when the game was on the line. When Thomas was a sophomore, Indiana struggled out of the gate to a 7-5 start, but the Hoosiers got on a roll in the 1981 NCAA Tournament and looked like they were all set to win their second national championship in Philadelphia, the same place where Bob Knight had won his first in 1976.

But six hours before Indiana was to play North Carolina for the title, President Ronald Reagan was shot and wounded by would-be assassin John Hinckley in Washington, D.C. The NCAA went ahead with the third-place game, but it didn't make a decision to play the title game until 30 minutes before the scheduled tipoff. Once word arrived that the president was out of danger, the game went on. Thomas took a while to get going, but he was on fire in the second

**P**ound for pound, Isiah Thomas was one of the toughest players I have seen on the college hardwood. He led the Hoosiers of Indiana to the national championship in 1981.

He certainly would rate as one of the best little men ever to play the game. Thomas grew up in a tough neighborhood in Chicago, and it showed whenever he played for Bob Knight at Indiana. Talk about street tough. He had a competitive drive that separated him from most players. He had so much skill. The ball was an extension of his hand.

And he loved the big moment. He wanted the ball

half when he scored 19 of his 23 points in a 63-50 victory over Dean Smith's gang. Thomas was an easy choice for the NCAA Tournament's Most Outstanding Player and he was a key reason why Indiana was celebrating. Thomas had such a special intensity and desire to win, win, and win. And that, my friends, is why he was admired so much by Hall of Famer Bob Knight.

# HOUSTON:

PLAYER NUMBER 8

## Akeem Olajuwon

7' 0"

250 pounds

Center

1981-1984

*Profile:* University of Houston center Akeem "The Dream" Olajuwon is the realization of the American dream.

He was born in Lagos, Nigeria, and never played organized basketball until he was 15, concentrating instead on soccer and handball, which helped give him the footwork and agility to go with his size and strength.

After emigrating from Africa to play basketball for Guy V. Lewis, he began a path that would eventually make him one of the top centers ever to play the game.

He was not highly recruited and was merely offered a visit to the university to work out for the coaching staff, based on a recommendation from a friend of Lewis, who had seen Olajuwon play for the national team. When he arrived at the airport, no one was there to greet him; and when he called the basketball staff, they told him to take a taxi to the gym.

Hopefully, they reimbursed him.

Olajuwon, who averaged 13.3 points and 10.7 rebounds during his career, played sparingly as a redshirt freshman. But his game jumped a level after the staff hooked him up that summer with local resident and multiple NBA MVP Moses Malone, who took him under his wing during pickup games at famed Fonde Recreation Center. Olajuwon emerged as a different, dominant player.

After his redshirt season, Olajuwon helped lead the Cougars to three straight Final Fours. Olajuwon and forward Clyde Drexler were charter members of "Phi Slamma Jamma," Houston's famed slam-dunking fraternity.

He went off for 21 points and 22 rebounds in a 94-81 victory over Louisville in the fabled 1983 national semifinal dunkathon and was selected Most Outstanding Player in the Final Four even though his team lost to NC State in the championship game.

Olajuwon was a consensus first-team All-American as a junior. He averaged 16.8 points, 13.5 rebounds and 5.6 blocked shots. He led the country in rebounding, field goal percentage (.675) and blocked shots while leading UH back to the 1984 championship game, where the Cougars lost to Patrick Ewing and Georgetown in a foul-plagued title game in Seattle.

After the Georgetown loss, Olajuwon had to decide whether to stay in college or enter the NBA draft. He gambled that the Houston Rockets would win the coin flip and select him with the number one pick in the draft. They did, two picks ahead of Michael Jordan.

**A**keem Olajuwon (center), battling for a rebound with teammate Larry Micheaux and opponent Thurl Bailey of NC State, was one of the first foreign stars in college basketball during my tenure behind the microphone.

I remember calling Akeem Olajuwon, "The Dream" during his days with Phi Slamma Jamma. Olajuwon was so tough in the paint, opponents often had to double-team him.

*ickie V's View:* Olajuwon was the first big international star I covered for ESPN. When he was a freshman, he was just learning how to play. I remember being with him in the elevator – just he and I – and I said to him, "Son, one day you will be special. You've got things that people can't teach. You've got size, strength and your agility." You could see it. He was just loaded with potential.

This guy had a great attitude for a superstar. He was always smiling. He was a man-child when he started in basketball. And he became such a force in the low box where he really learned how to dominate defensively.

But what else would you expect from a player whose name means "always being on top?"

Let's fast-forward to 2008 in San Antonio at the Final Four when Olajuwon and I were being introduced by the head of the Hall of Fame, John Doleva, as members of the Class of 2008. Olajuwon was telling many of his friends and people gathered in the room that, "Dickie V was the one who gave me the nickname 'The Dream' when I played for the Cougars." To be honest, I don't remember the situation, but I was absolutely thrilled that he would give me credit for laying on him a name that fit him to perfection. Olajuwon and I were standing in a room that had many of the past superstars and Hall of Fame greats, such as Bob Cousy, Rick Barry, Denny Crum, Jerry Colangelo and John Thompson. The list went on and on as it was filled with greatness. In fact, to be honest, I felt like getting out my pad of paper and asking for autographs. One of the first I would've asked for would have been from "The Dream."

That day, my friends, the dream came true for both of us as I couldn't help but shed a tear, being in the company of such basketball icons.

## #8. AKEEM OLAJUWON, HOUSTON

|  | MIN | FG% | 3P% | FT% | RPG | APG | TPG | BPG | SPG | PPG |
|---|---|---|---|---|---|---|---|---|---|---|
| 80-81 |  |  | *Did Not Play* |  |  |  |  |  |  |  |
| 81-82 | 18.2 | 60.7 |  | 56.3 | 6.2 | 0.4 | 1.4 | 2.5 | 0.9 | 8.3 |
| 82-83 | 27.4 | 61.1 |  | 59.5 | 11.4 | 0.9 | 2.3 | 5.1 | 1.4 | 13.9 |
| 83-84 | 34.1 | 67.5 |  | 52.6 | 13.5 | 1.3 | 1.6 | 5.6 | 1.6 | 16.8 |
| **TOTALS** | 27.2 | 63.9 |  | 55.5 | 10.7 | 0.9 | 1.8 | 4.5 | 1.3 | 13.3 |

University of Houston's Akeem Olajuwon pulls in the basketball as Wake Forest's Anthony Teachey defends during semi-final game in the NCAA Midwest Regionals in St. Louis, March 25, 1984.

# UNITED STATES NAVAL ACADEMY:

PLAYER NUMBER

## David Robinson

7' 1"

250 pounds

Center

1983-1987

*Profile:* When David Robinson was growing up, he had his heart set on attending the U. S. Naval Academy. But the towering center had no idea that he would one day become known as "The Admiral" – one of the most admired college players ever during his time in Annapolis.

Robinson, the son of a retired naval engineer, became the Middies' first consensus first-team All-American since 1933 and the school's first-ever National Player of the Year during his senior year in 1987. He averaged 21 points, 10.3 rebounds and 4.1 blocks during an inspirational four-year career, scoring 2,669 points, grabbing 1,314 rebounds while shooting 61.3 percent from the field.

But he had little interest in basketball at the start of high school. He participated in tennis, gymnastics and baseball and was an excellent student who was more inclined toward music, science and mathematics.

He never played organized basketball until his senior year at Osbourn Park High School in Manassas, Va. Robinson was 6' 7" at the time, and the school's basketball coach pleaded with him to give the sport a try. Robinson received several scholarship offers, but he enrolled in the Academy to study mathematics.

His development as a player began slowly. Robinson averaged just 7.6 points as a Plebe; and his first coach, Paul Evans, often complained that Robinson was too laid back and practiced only when he had to. But Robinson, who grew six inches in college, began to dominate as a sophomore, averaging 23.6 points, 11.6 rebounds and 4 blocks while leading the Middies to the first of three Colonial Athletic Association titles and three NCAA Tournament bids.

Robinson quickly became the poster child for Navy athletics: a smart, clean-cut, high-profile athlete cut along the same lines as Roger Staubach.

After his sophomore year, sensing he might be an NBA prospect, he thought about transferring, which would have freed him from a five-year military obligation. But he honored his commitment after being told his active service requirement would be reduced to two years.

Robinson had a monster final two seasons. He averaged 22.7 points and led the country in rebounding (13.0) and blocked shots (5.9) while leading Navy to the NCAA East Regional finals. Then, playing for Pete Herrmann, he averaged 28.2 points, 11.8 rebounds and 4.5 blocks as a senior and finished off his career with a 50-point performance during an NCAA first-round loss to Michigan.

Robinson was drafted by San Antonio with the first pick overall in 1987 but the Spurs had to wait until he completed his tour of duty. He spent two years supervising the building of a submarine base in Georgia, but did get time off to play for the 1988 Olympic team, the first of three appearances on the U.S. national team in the Summer Games.

*Dickie V's View:* I love everything that David Robinson is about. He is the NCAA's definition of a student-athlete. I used to call him "The Admiral."

I spoke at the Naismith banquet in Atlanta when he was being honored as the National Player of the Year in 1987. I was sitting next to Robert Montgomery Knight, who was being honored as the National Coach of the Year.

I got up and said a few words. Then David gets

p, gets his award, talks about his family, talks about he Naval Academy. He looked like a million bucks n his dress uniform. As he was talking, Knight lbowed me and said – I'll never forget it – "How ould you like to coach that kid?"

Robinson was a coach's dream for both Paul vans and, later, Pete Herrmann at Navy. He came o the Academy without much hype. Like Duncan, e wasn't part of all the hullabaloo in recruiting and ever thought of himself as America's guest.

Believe it or not, when he first arrived, he was a etter student than a basketball player. But he just orked and worked on his game and utilized his size nd quickness in such a positive way to become as ood as it gets as a collegian. Over the years, I have eveloped a friendship with David Robinson's former ommate and teammate, Carl Liebert. Today, Liebert erves as a member of the Board of Directors with he V Foundation and is also currently the CEO of 4-Hour Fitness. Liebert has told me, on numerous ccasions, about David's intense work ethic and his ompetitive drive to be the best he possibly can be. iebert said he marveled at his teammate's loyalty, ntegrity and character.

I will never forget doing a Kentucky game versus Javy at Rupp Arena, one of the shrines of college asketball. Nobody gave Navy much of a shot. ut Robinson had an amazing game: 45 points, 20 ebounds and 10 blocked shots, a triple double. All f a sudden, whistles are blowing out of the blue – nd the kid fouled out. I jumped out of my chair and ave him a standing ovation. In fact, many of the entucky faithful who are so passionate about ollegiate basketball also paid tribute to The Admiral.

I know it violated all the rules of journalism, but that's how I felt at the moment.

And guess what? If I had to do it over, I'd stand again, man. I'll tell you, if the NCAA wanted a true definition of the term 'student-athlete,' they would simply have to place the picture of David Robinson as he epitomized all that was good about intercollegiate competition.

The Admiral (50) was one of the hardest working players that I covered. He made great improvement from the day he started at the Naval Academy until the day he left.

## #9. DAVID ROBINSON, NAVY

|        | MIN  | FG%  | 3P% | FT%  | RPG  | APG | TPG | BPG | SPG | PPG  |
|--------|------|------|-----|------|------|-----|-----|-----|-----|------|
| 83-84  | 13.3 | 62.3 |     | 57.5 | 4.0  | 0.2 |     | 1.3 | 0.2 | 7.6  |
| 84-85  | 33.6 | 64.4 |     | 62.6 | 11.6 | 0.6 |     | 4.0 | 0.8 | 23.6 |
| 85-86  | 33.9 | 60.7 |     | 62.8 | 13.0 | 0.7 |     | 5.9 | 1.7 | 22.7 |
| 86-87  | 34.6 | 59.1 |     | 63.7 | 11.8 | 1.0 |     | 4.5 | 2.1 | 28.2 |
| **TOTALS** | 29.5 | 61.3 |     | 62.7 | 10.3 | 0.6 |     | 4.1 | 1.3 | 21.0 |

# MARYLAND:

PLAYER NUMBER

## Len Bias

6' 8"

220 pounds

Forward

1982-1986

*Profile:* Perhaps it was only fitting that the late Len Bias wore a gold necklace with a Superman insignia around his neck when he played for the University of Maryland.

The 6' 8", 220-pound forward, who grew up close to the Terps' College Park campus in nearby Hyattsville, Md., and used to sell popcorn at the Maryland home games in high school, had a superhero quality to his game for much of the four seasons he spent in the ACC.

Bias, blessed with exceptional leaping ability and great upper body strength, scored 2,149 points and averaged 16.4 points and 5.7 rebounds during his career for a team that made four straight NCAA Tournament appearances. He averaged only 7.2 points as a freshman, but blossomed into the most dominant player in college basketball's premier league by the end of his sophomore year when he scored 56 points on 26-for-43 shooting and had 18 rebounds as the Terps won their first ACC Tournament title since 1958. Bias scored 26 points when Maryland defeated North Carolina, 74-62, in the championship game at Greensboro.

Then he took his game to a Jordanesque level, winning the conference's MVP award in his junior and senior seasons.

Bias led the league in scoring both years, improving his game to a point where he averaged 23.2 points and 7 rebounds, shooting 54.4 percent from the field and 86.4 percent from the line. He was a first-team All-American as a senior.

His career was filled with special moments, but none better than the time he scored 35 points in an overtime victory over North Carolina – the Tar Heels' first loss in the Smith Center. Late in the game, Bias stole an inbounds pass and scored on a dunk, then blocked a driving layup by guard Kenny Smith to preserve the upset.

Tragically, the aura he cast over Tobacco Road didn't last.

Bias appeared headed for a spectacular NBA career when the Boston Celtics selected him with the second pick in the 1986 draft. He met with Celtics officials the next day and also signed a $1.6 million endorsement contract with Reebok. Less than 24 hours later, in the early morning hours of June 19, 1986, Bias, who was never known as a drug user, was dead from an overdose of cocaine.

We will always be left to wonder how good he might have been.

*Dickie V's View:* Len Bias was as good as it gets. I'll never forget him. I didn't pick him preseason first-team All-American in my magazine before his senior year. I had him second team. As the season was going on, he was just dominating the ACC.

Bias became a scoring and rebounding machine. Think about these numbers, as he scored 41 against Duke and 35 against North Carolina in an overtime victory at the Dean Dome. I will never forget doing a Maryland game. As we were getting ready to do our opening, Maryland was warming up in front of us and I received a tap on my shoulder; Bias said, "Dickie V, let me ask you, am I still second team?"

I looked at him and said, "Lenny, you are flat out number one, my friend. First team, Rolls Royce, All-American."

His career ended much too quickly. I will never forget driving on the Lodge Parkway in Southfield, Mich., when breaking news came across the radio that Lenny Bias's life had ended due to a drug overdose. I pulled over and could not believe what I was hearing. He seemed like such a level-headed youngster who knew where he wanted to go with his life. Remember, Red Auerbach, the architect of the Boston Celtics, had just drafted him and was looking forward to him becoming a superstar on the professional level.

My personal feeling is that Bias would have become one of the premier players ever to play in the NBA. I think we would be talking about Bias in a special manner like we do about Michael Jordan, Kobe Bryant, and LeBron James. I think you get the picture. I was a big, big fan of Lenny Bias. He had that special bounce off the floor, a superb first step, and he was physical, strong and explosive. To put it bluntly, he had the entire package that would make you simply marvel at his talents.

Wow, I can't even imagine what it would have been like to watch Bias play together with Larry Bird, one of my favorite players of all time. Can you believe B Squared – Bird and Bias? That, my friend, would have been a dynamic duo.

Len Bias goes up for a shot against UNLV's Armon Gilliam. Bias' passing was such a tragedy; I really enjoyed calling his games while he was at Maryland.

## #10. LEN BIAS, MARYLAND

|         | MIN  | FG%  | 3P%   | FT%  | RPG | APG | TPG | BPG | SPG | PPG  |
|---------|------|------|-------|------|-----|-----|-----|-----|-----|------|
| 82-83   | 22.0 | 47.8 | 27.3  | 63.6 | 4.2 | 0.7 | 1.1 | 0.5 | 0.3 | 7.2  |
| 83-84   | 34.5 | 56.7 |       | 76.7 | 4.5 | 1.5 | 1.5 | 0.8 | 0.4 | 15.3 |
| 84-85   | 36.5 | 52.8 |       | 77.7 | 6.8 | 1.8 | 3.1 | 0.9 | 0.9 | 18.9 |
| 85-86   | 37.0 | 54.4 |       | 86.4 | 7.0 | 1.0 | 2.8 | 0.4 | 0.8 | 23.2 |
| **TOTALS** | 32.8 | 53.6 | *27.3 | 79.5 | 5.7 | 1.3 | 2.2 | 0.7 | 0.6 | 16.4 |

*ACC used the three-point shot on an experimental basis starting in the 1982-83 season.

# LOUISIANA STATE UNIVERSITY:

## Shaquille O'Neal

7' 1"

290 pounds

Center

1989-1992

*Profile:* Shaquille Rashaun O'Neal's first two names mean "Little Warrior" in Arabic. But O'Neal was anything but little.

When he was just five years old, his mother had to carry his birth certificate with her to prove to bus drivers that he was not eight or nine years old because he was so tall. By the time he was a teenager, he had grown to 6' 8". He was an Army brat living on a military base in Wildflecken, West Germany, with his father, drill sergeant Phillip Harrison, when LSU coach Dale Brown, who was conducting a clinic for the troops, spotted him.

"Where you from, soldier?" Brown asked.

"I'm not a soldier," O'Neal replied. "I'm 13 years old."

Brown began recruiting him then and his persistence paid off. O'Neal, who moved back to the states before his junior year in high school after his father was transferred to San Antonio, was an overpowering force of nature by the time he signed with the Tigers. O'Neal averaged 32.1 points, 22 rebounds and eight blocks for a 36-0 Texas state championship team as a senior and was selected MVP of the McDonald's All-American game.

The extroverted, playful O'Neal, who averaged 21.6 points, 13.5 rebounds and 4.6 blocked shots during a three-year career at LSU, was a two-time consensus first-team All- American, a two-time SEC Athlete of the Year and the AP National Player of the Year as a sophomore. During that season, he averaged 27.6 points, grabbed 14.7 rebounds, had 5.0 blocks and shot 62.8 percent from the field to lead the SEC in all four categories.

His individual statistics as a junior were almost as dominant. O'Neal averaged 24.1 points, 14 rebounds and 5.2 blocks and shot 61.5 percent while leading the Tigers to a ninth straight NCAA appearance.

O'Neal led the SEC in rebounding and blocked shots for three straight years. Ironically, his team never made it to a Final Four, even though he played his freshman year with two-time All-American guard Chris Jackson and the 7' 0" center Stanley Roberts.

But his best days as a player were ahead of him.

O'Neal was selected by Orlando with the first pick overall in the 1992 NBA draft. He then went on to become a movie star and best-selling rap artist while leading the Lakers and Miami to a combined four world championships.

*Dickie V's View:* I will never ever forget doing Shaquille O'Neal's debut on national TV – the 1989 McDonald's All-American game. He ripped a rebound off the glass, went the length of the court in traffic, and then threw down a monster slam dunk I went bananas – throwing around adjectives – and I was surprised to read in a book about Shaq's life when he referred to that moment and me singing his praises. Shaq claimed that was his introduction to the nation. In fact, it is featured on YouTube as one of the highlights when you Google the name Shaquille O'Neal.

At 7' 1", 290 pounds, he was hard to miss – another Wilt who just dominated the SEC for three years as well as anyone else who got in his way. He was a big, tough guy on the court but he was like a big teddy bear off it. He was ag-ile, mo-bile, but not frag-ile.

**S**haq put on an incredible display of power during his time at LSU. He averaged a double-double during each of his three seasons with the Tigers.

## #11. SHAQUILLE O'NEAL, LSU

| | MIN | FG% | 3P% | FT% | RPG | APG | TPG | BPG | SPG | PPG |
|---|---|---|---|---|---|---|---|---|---|---|
| 89-90 | 28.2 | 57.3 | | 55.6 | 12.0 | 1.9 | 2.9 | 3.6 | 1.2 | 13.9 |
| 90-91 | 31.5 | 62.8 | | 63.8 | 14.7 | 1.6 | 3.5 | 5.0 | 1.5 | 27.6 |
| 91-92 | 32.0 | 61.5 | | 52.8 | 14.0 | 1.5 | 3.4 | 5.2 | 0.9 | 24.1 |
| **TOTALS** | *30.5* | *61.0* | | *57.5* | *13.5* | *1.7* | *3.3* | *4.6* | *1.2* | *21.6* |

When O'Neal was a sophomore at LSU, the Tigers ayed second-ranked Arizona at the Deaf Dome wn in Baton Rouge in December 1990. I had been mping Shaquille up as the number one center in e country, and the Arizona coaches were using it as otivation. Before the game, Wildcat assistant Jessie ans came strolling up to me and said their big guys players like Brian Williams, Sean Rooks and Chris ills – would be ready.

But they weren't ready for this. Shaq was esome with 29 points, 16 rebounds and six ocked shots. He tore apart a big-time front line,

giving the No. 2-ranked team in the country its first loss after seven straight wins.

I remember doing the game with Keith Jackson – Mr. "Whoa, Nellie" of college football fame – for ABC. I was going bonkers: "America, get ready for the next great big guy."

Well, Keith Jackson was trying to calm me down. "Richard," he said, "he's only 18 years old. Let him grow." And I simply said, "Mr. Jackson, you can't hide it. This is a unique, unique talent."

# OKLAHOMA:

PLAYER NUMBER

## Wayman Tisdale

6' 9"

250 pounds

Center

1982-1985

*Profile:* Wayman Tisdale's first love was music. When he was young, his father, the late Rev. Louis Tisdale, who served as the pastor of the Tulsa Friendship Baptist Church for more than 20 years, bought each of his three sons a Mickey Mouse guitar with the hope that one of them would take an interest. Wayman, the youngest, became mesmerized listening to the bass players at the church and began to teach himself how to play guitar and bass.

Tisdale might have settled for a spot in the school band had he not undergone a 24-inch growth spurt during junior high school that left him towering over his older brothers and pushed him into a career in basketball.

By the time he was a senior at Tulsa's Booker T. Washington High, he was 6' 9" and one of the most highly recruited players in the country. When the left-handed Tisdale decided to stay close to home and play for Billy Tubbs at Oklahoma, it was a decision that changed the face of the basketball program at what had always been considered a football school.

Tisdale was the first Big Eight player ever to make first-team All-American in each of his first three years. He led the Big Eight in scoring three times, averaging 24.5, 27.0 and 25.2 points, and set a school single-game scoring record with 61 points against Texas-San Antonio in 1984. Tisdale scored 2,661 points in his career – a school record – and led the Sooners to conference titles as a sophomore and junior. He averaged 25.6 points, 10.1 rebounds and

shot a torrid 57.8 percent for his career. Tisdale was selected to play on the 1984 Olympic team that won a gold medal in Los Angeles after his sophomore year.

He took the Sooners to previously unheard of heights as a junior, leading the team to a 31-6 record and a spot in the NCAA Tournament regional finals. OU fans desperately attempted to get him to stay for his senior year, even erecting three billboards near campus to voice their plea.

However, Tisdale felt it was time to move on. He was selected by Indiana with the second pick overall in the 1985 draft.

But he had set the stage for OU's No. 1 ranking in 1988 and a run to the national championship game. Tisdale was the first OU player to have his jersey number, 23, retired.

After playing in the NBA for 12 years, he began a highly successful music career as a jazz guitarist and has released numerous albums that have been ranked in the Top 10 on the Billboard charts.

*Dickie V's View:* Wayman Tisdale has made the successful transition from basketball star to contemporary jazz musician. He plays bass guitar with his group, the Fifth Quarter Band, and has released eight albums for the MoJazz label since 1995.

His latest, "Rebound," deals with a subject that is dear to my heart – the fight against cancer. Tisdale was diagnosed with bone cancer in his right knee

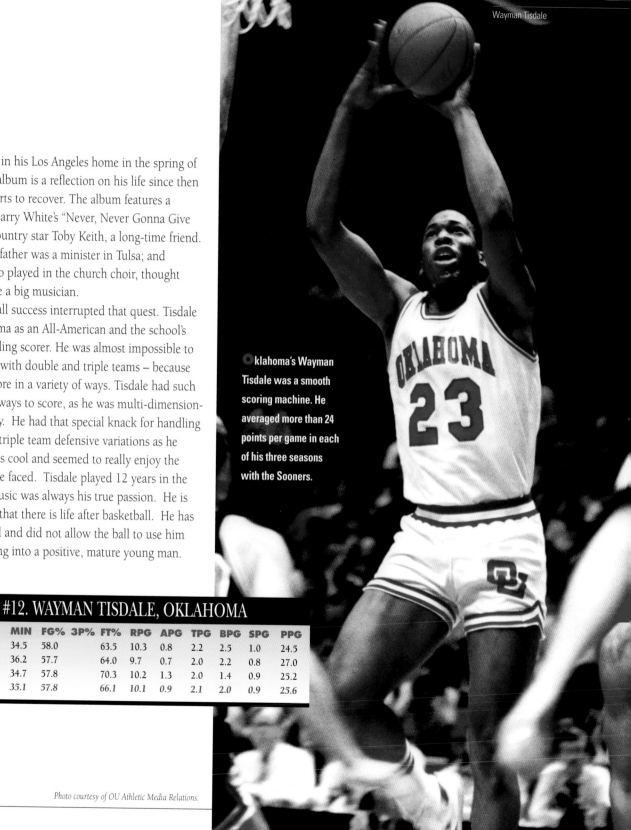

Wayman Tisdale

after he fell in his Los Angeles home in the spring of 2007. The album is a reflection on his life since then and his efforts to recover. The album features a version of Barry White's "Never, Never Gonna Give Up" with country star Toby Keith, a long-time friend.

His late father was a minister in Tulsa; and Tisdale, who played in the church choir, thought he would be a big musician.

Basketball success interrupted that quest. Tisdale left Oklahoma as an All-American and the school's all-time leading scorer. He was almost impossible to stop – even with double and triple teams – because he could score in a variety of ways. Tisdale had such a variety of ways to score, as he was multi-dimensional offensively. He had that special knack for handling double and triple team defensive variations as he never lost his cool and seemed to really enjoy the challenges he faced. Tisdale played 12 years in the NBA, but music was always his true passion. He is living proof that there is life after basketball. He has used the ball and did not allow the ball to use him while growing into a positive, mature young man.

Oklahoma's Wayman Tisdale was a smooth scoring machine. He averaged more than 24 points per game in each of his three seasons with the Sooners.

## #12. WAYMAN TISDALE, OKLAHOMA

|  | MIN | FG% | 3P% | FT% | RPG | APG | TPG | BPG | SPG | PPG |
|---|---|---|---|---|---|---|---|---|---|---|
| 82-83 | 34.5 | 58.0 | | 63.5 | 10.3 | 0.8 | 2.2 | 2.5 | 1.0 | 24.5 |
| 83-84 | 36.2 | 57.7 | | 64.0 | 9.7 | 0.7 | 2.0 | 2.2 | 0.8 | 27.0 |
| 84-85 | 34.7 | 57.8 | | 70.3 | 10.2 | 1.3 | 2.0 | 1.4 | 0.9 | 25.2 |
| **TOTALS** | 35.1 | 57.8 | | 66.1 | 10.1 | 0.9 | 2.1 | 2.0 | 0.9 | 25.6 |

*Photo courtesy of OU Athletic Media Relations.*

# DUKE:

**PLAYER NUMBER 13**

# Johnny Dawkins

6' 2"

165 pounds

Guard

1982-1986

*Profile:* You could say that Johnny Dawkins was Mike Krzyzewski's most important recruit – maybe even the savior of the Duke program at a time when the Blue Devils were struggling to tread water in the powerful ACC.

Krzyzewski was just entering his third year at Duke, and the boosters were starting to become impatient with the fact that the Blue Devils were 27-30 and falling behind rival Tobacco Road powers North Carolina and NC State, schools that had recently won national championships in 1982 and 1983. They were concerned with the fact Krzyzewski was building a track record for frustration – finishing second in the running for blue chip recruits like Chris Mullin and Bill Wennington, who went to St. John's; and Uwe Blab, who signed with Indiana.

Dawkins' presence on the court at Cameron changed everything.

The slender 6' 2" McDonald's All-American from Mackin High in Washington, D.C., took a chance on the Blue Devils, and it paid off in a big way. He was the biggest talent in a recruiting class that also included starters Mark Alarie, Jay Bilas and David Henderson. That group plus Tommy Amaker went to three NCAA Tournaments and advanced to the 1986 national championship game, losing to Louisville in the finals. Krzyzewski-coached Duke teams reached the Final Four nine times in 14 years from 1986 to 1999.

Dawkins was a first-team All-American his junior and senior years, averaging 19.2 points and 4.2 assists. His 2,556 career points – made without the benefit of the three-point line – was Duke's scoring record until 2006 when it was broken by J. J. Redick.

Dawkins started to make his presence felt with his consistency as a freshman, scoring in double figures in all but one of 28 games during an 11-win season. He never averaged less than 18.1 points a season as the Duke program took off.

Dawkins saved his best work for his senior year when he led the Blue Devils to 37 victories, the preseason NIT championship, the ACC regular-season and tournament championships (in a year where three ACC teams – North Carolina, Duke and Georgia Tech – were all ranked No. 1 at one point), and a trip to the Final Four.

Dawkins was the MVP of the ACC Tournament, scoring 60 points and making two critical free throws as the Devils dusted off Georgia Tech, 68-67, in the finals. Then he went wild in the NCAA

| | MIN | FG% | 3P% | FT% | RPG | APG | TPG | BPG | SPG | PPG |
|---|---|---|---|---|---|---|---|---|---|---|
| 82-83 | 35.8 | 50.0 | 35.2 | 68.2 | 4.1 | 4.8 | 3.7 | 0.4 | 0.9 | 18.1 |
| 83-84 | 38.4 | 48.1 | | 83.1 | 4.1 | 4.1 | 3.4 | 0.1 | 1.1 | 19.4 |
| 84-85 | 36.0 | 49.5 | | 79.5 | 4.5 | 5.0 | 2.9 | 0.2 | 1.6 | 18.8 |
| 85-86 | 33.1 | 54.9 | | 81.2 | 3.6 | 3.2 | 2.7 | 0.1 | 1.3 | 20.2 |
| **TOTALS** | **35.7** | **50.8** | ***35.2** | **79.0** | **4.0** | **4.2** | **3.1** | **0.2** | **1.3** | **19.2** |

*ACC used the three-point shot on an experimental basis starting in the 1982-83 season.

...urnament, averaging 23.7 points in six games. ...awkins personally bailed out Duke in the ...urnament opener against Mississippi Valley State, ...oring 16 points in five minutes as the Devils rallied ...the final 10 minutes for an 85-78 victory. He was ...lected the Most Outstanding Player of the East ...gional after scoring 28 points during a 71-50 ...ctory over David Robinson and Navy at the ...eadowlands, and he scored 24 points against ...uisville in the championship game.

Dawkins was a deserving choice for the Naismith ...ational Player of the Year.

He was selected by the San Antonio Spurs in the ...st round of the NBA draft and played nine years ...the league. He came back to Duke in 1997 and ...ached on Krzyzewski's staff for 11 years before ...ecoming head coach at Stanford in 2008.

*ickie V's View:* Johnny Dawkins was the first ...eat player in the Mike Krzyzewski era. He helped ...art the Duke dynasty.

Dawkins was the best young player in ...ashington, D.C., when Krzyzewski was ...cruiting him. He knew the impact a player like ...awkins could make on his program so he or a ...ember of his staff saw every game Dawkins played ...om the time he was a sophomore at Mackin High.

Some more established programs like ...eorgetown, Maryland and Notre Dame were also ...cruiting Dawkins. But he built up a trust factor ...ith Krzyzewski and was willing to take a chance ...en though he knew there would be backlash from ...e local community.

Dawkins turned an ACC also-ran into a national contender and turned himself into a leading candidate for national player of the year during one special weekend in mid-February of his senior year in 1986. Duke had back-to-back games against North Carolina State in Raleigh Saturday and against Notre Dame in Cameron Indoor Stadium the next afternoon at 1 p.m.

Dawkins scored 24 points and made two free throws in the closing seconds to give the Blue Devils a 72-70 victory over the Wolfpack, then came up huge against the Irish less than 24 hours later.

Dawkins was forced to play the point for much of the game after Tommy Amaker got into early foul trouble. He also managed to score 18 points and made a game-saving play at the end. Duke was hanging on to a 75-74 lead with six seconds left but Notre Dame had the ball at midcourt.

Irish guard David Rivers got the ball and went up for a shot from the corner with time running out. But Dawkins blocked it. The buzzer sounded, sending Cameron into a frenzy.

It seemed like Dawkins was always throwing life-savers during Duke's journey to the Final Four that year. The Blue Devils could have easily lost in the first round of the tournament against Mississippi Valley State from the SWAC. They were behind for 30 minutes. Then Dawkins scored 16 points in five minutes to help Duke survive and advance.

**Johnny Dawkins was one of the first true superstars at Duke under coach Mike Krzyzewski. He was always a consistent scoring threat, making big baskets as the Blue Devils made it to the 1986 championship game.**

# NORTH CAROLINA:

## James Worthy

6' 9"

225 pounds

Forward

1979-1982

*Profile:* The first time North Carolina coach Dean Smith saw James Worthy play, he knew he would someday be a college and NBA star.

Worthy was just a gangly eighth grader from Gastonia, N.C., at the time, and Smith once joked that he wished Worthy could go hardship out of high school so he could help the Heels.

Worthy certainly lived up to his potential, becoming the dominant force on Smith's first national championship team in 1982. Worthy – whose nickname was "Big Game James" – came up huge in the biggest game of his career, shooting 13 for 17 and scoring 28 points as a junior when the Tar Heels defeated intimidating Georgetown, 63-62, in the national championship game in New Orleans.

Precocious freshman Michael Jordan may have nailed the game-winning jump shot with 16 seconds left, but the 6' 9" Worthy sealed the deal when he stepped in front of a pass by Freddie Brown on the next possession, stealing the ball as time ran out.

Worthy, a Hall of Famer who is one of the great fast break finishers in the history of the game, averaged 14.5 points and 7.4 rebounds while shooting 54.1 percent during his three-year career. He averaged what looked to be a modest 15.6 points and 6.3 rebounds as a junior on a balanced team that also included Jordan and Sam Perkins. But that did not stop him from making first-team All-American and being selected Most Outstanding Player of the Final Four and the Helms' National Player of the Year.

When he declared early for the NBA, Worthy was selected by the Los Angeles Lakers with the number one pick in the 1982 draft and went on to win three NBA titles, becoming the MOP of the 1988 playoffs.

Ironically, Worthy hated the sport when he first started playing at age four. But he knew that his father, a minister, was struggling to pay college tuition for his brothers and decided to get a scholarship to help out.

Worthy had plenty of offers after leading Ashbrook High to the state championship game his senior year in high school. But Smith won his parent over by promising them that their son would go to class and church unless he had a letter from them excusing him.

Worthy was a man among boys. He became an instant starter and double-figure scorer for the Tar Heels, but his freshman year was cut short when he slipped on the ice and shattered his ankle. He missed 14 games and returned the next year after doctors implanted two screws and a six-inch metal plate to repair the damage. Worthy wasn't sure he would be able to come back with the same type of intensity after the injury, but in his sophomore year, with the screws still intact, he combined with Al Wood to lead the Tar Heels to the 1981 national championship game where they lost to Indiana.

*Dickie V's View:* Dean Smith – the Michelangelo of coaching – sculpted that 1982 title team perfectly, using the brilliant talents of his stars like James Worthy, Michael Jordan and Sam Perkins – the great trifecta – to bring home the gold trophy for North Carolina.

James Worthy

Worthy was from Gastonia, N.C., the same town as Sleepy Floyd, who attended a rival high school and went on to become an All-American at Georgetown. After missing out on Cornbread Maxwell who went to UNC-Charlotte and became the biggest star on that surprise 1977 Final Four team, Smith wanted to make sure he didn't miss on any more in-state talent.

Recruiting Worthy was a no-brainer, man. Worthy attended Smith's camp the summer after eighth grade and just dominated the 11th and 12th graders there.

The trend continued at UNC, where he became one of the most talented baseline players you'll ever see. Worthy was one of those players who had just an unbelievable offensive ability – those swooping dunks, his ability to get into transition and then square up and make the long-range shot.

He was The Man at Carolina before Michael Jordan.

And he was at his best in big games, which is where he got his nickname – "Big Game James." Worthy lost just one of 10 games in NCAA play and scored 28 against Georgetown – and Floyd – in the 1982 NCAA championship game, helping Dean Smith capture the NCAA gold trophy after six previous trips to the Final Four.

## #14. JAMES WORTHY, NORTH CAROLINA

|  | MIN | FG% | 3P% | FT% | RPG | APG | TPG | BPG | SPG | PPG |
|---|---|---|---|---|---|---|---|---|---|---|
| 79-80 | 28.3 | 58.7 |  | 60.0 | 7.4 | 1.9 | 3.4 | 1.6 | 1.2 | 12.5 |
| 80-81 | 33.7 | 50.0 |  | 64.0 | 8.4 | 2.8 | 3.1 | 1.0 | 1.3 | 14.2 |
| 81-82 | 34.6 | 57.3 |  | 67.4 | 6.3 | 2.4 | 2.8 | 1.1 | 1.5 | 15.6 |
| TOTALS | 33.2 | 54.1 |  | 65.2 | 7.4 | 2.5 | 3.0 | 1.1 | 1.4 | 14.5 |

# DUKE:

**15**

PLAYER NUMBER

## Grant Hill

6' 8"

225 pounds

Forward

1990-1994

*Profile:* Grant Hill grew up in the shadow of two celebrity parents. His father, Calvin, was an All-American running back at Yale and a star with the Dallas Cowboys. His mother, Janet, was a suitemate of Hillary Rodham Clinton at Wellesley College, worked for the secretary of the army and went on to become a highly successful lawyer in D.C.

They became his biggest fans when he played for Duke.

The versatile 6' 8" Hill was widely traveled as a youngster when he took educational trips with his mother to Asia, South America and most of Europe.

He built his own level of celebrity at that ACC program, where he was a four-year starter and a consensus first-team All-American as a senior. He became the first ACC player to finish with more than 1,900 points, 700 rebounds, 400 assists, 200 steals and 100 blocked shots. Hill has two NCAA championship rings – from 1991 and 1992 – and played in a third championship game in 1994 before he graduated and was selected by Detroit with the third pick overall in the NBA draft.

Calvin Hill originally had planned to have his son follow in his footsteps in football. But Grant Hill abandoned that sport in ninth grade to concentrate on basketball – where he went on to become a McDonald's All-American and choose Duke over North Carolina.

Hill averaged 14.9 points on 53.2 percent shooting, 6.0 rebounds and 3.6 assists during his career. He may not have been spectacular, but he had a history of memorable plays. There was the one-handed dunk off a high-arching alley-oop pass

from Bobby Hurley that set the tone for Duke's 72-65 national championship victory over Kansas in 1991. Then there was the 70-foot pass he threw to Christian Laettner to set up the miracle shot that beat Kentucky, 104-103, in the 1992 East Regional finals at the Philadelphia Spectrum.

Hill was part of two great teams in 1991 and 1992. He personally made Duke a great team his senior year when he averaged 17.4 points and 6.9 rebounds and filled up his line every game. He was the catalyst for a team that had no true point guard, no power forward and limited depth, yet still made it back to the national title game before losing to Arkansas in the final moments.

Hill, the National Defensive Player of the Year, made his biggest statement when the Devils played Purdue in the NCAA South Regional finals. Purdue's All-American forward Glenn Robinson had gone off for 44 points in a Sweet 16 victory over Kansas. Hill seemed unfazed. He held the "Big Dog" to just 13 points on six-of-22 shooting during a 69-60 victory.

*Dickie V's View:* Mike Krzyzewski hates to compare one Duke player with another. However, if you really press the issue with Coach K as to who has been the best overall player at Duke, the answer would be Grant Hill.

But when Hill first arrived on campus, he actually had no idea how good he was. A week before freshman registration, in fact, Hill remembers calling assistant coach Tommy Amaker and asking him, "Do you think I can play here?"

Coach K knew what Hill could do.

When you talk about Duke's back-to-back titles,

ey didn't happen without Grant "The Velvet Man"
ill. He had a great all-around game that fit in
erfectly with the size and skill of Christian Laettner
d point guard extraordinaire, Bobby Hurley. Hill
d that great transition ability – and the heart to go
ith it.

I mean, you talk about class. He had it all. Great
arents, terrific academics, great skills. He could play
ree positions, handle the rock and penetrate.

Grant started at Duke all four years, moving
om small forward to the point his senior year. As a
eshman, he set the tone for the Blue Devils' 72-65
ctory over Kansas in the 1991 national title game
ith a vicious one-hand dunk off an alley-oop pass
at made it to the cover of *Sports Illustrated*. Some-
dy asked him about the picture, and he said he was
mbarrassed by the awful haircut he had at the time.

After Laettner and Hurley moved on, Hill became
e Man at Duke. He was everybody's All-American.
uring his senior year, he got to go up against Glenn
obinson, the National Player of the Year, in the 1994
CAA Southeast Regional finals at Knoxville.

Hill drew the assignment of covering Robinson.
here is a story that goes around
ith the Duke faithful that the
ght before the game in his hotel
om, his teammate Cherokee
rks kept calling out, "Big Dog,
g Dog" and Hill would jump
t of bed and do defensive
des across the floor.

The next day, Hill shut Robinson down during a
-60 victory as Duke made another journey to the
nal Four.

### #15. GRANT HILL, DUKE

| | MIN | FG% | 3P% | FT% | RPG | APG | TPG | BPG | SPG | PPG |
|---|---|---|---|---|---|---|---|---|---|---|
| 90-91 | 24.6 | 51.6 | 50.0 | 60.9 | 5.1 | 2.2 | 2.1 | 0.8 | 1.4 | 11.2 |
| 91-92 | 30.3 | 61.1 | 0.0 | 73.3 | 5.7 | 4.1 | 2.4 | 0.8 | 1.2 | 14.0 |
| 92-93 | 31.6 | 57.8 | 28.6 | 74.6 | 6.4 | 2.8 | 2.4 | 1.4 | 2.5 | 18.0 |
| 93-94 | 35.7 | 46.2 | 39.0 | 70.3 | 6.9 | 5.2 | 3.0 | 1.2 | 1.9 | 17.4 |
| **TOTALS** | 30.4 | 53.2 | 37.6 | 69.8 | 6.0 | 3.6 | 2.5 | 1.0 | 1.7 | 14.9 |

I always loved Grant Hill's versatility on the court. The son of former NFL star running back Calvin Hill shoots against Marquette big man Jim McIlvaine in this NCAA Tournament game.

**34**

# ST. JOHN'S:

PLAYER NUMBER

# Chris Mullin

6' 7"

215 pounds

Forward

1981-1985

*Profile:* Chris Mullin had the perfect pedigree to become Lou Carnesecca's biggest star at St. John's.

He was born in Brooklyn, where he played basketball at St. Thomas Aquinas grammar school and attended Carnesecca's basketball camp from the time he was in the sixth grade. He played for fabled Power Memorial and then transferred to Xavierian High in Bay Ridge as a junior because he wanted to be closer to the neighborhood. Mullin led Xavierian to the New York state championship. He became a McDonald's All-American, then signed to attend school at St. John's – a commuter school in nearby Queens – spurning overtures from both Virginia and Duke so he could play in the recently formed Big East.

Mullin averaged 16.6 points as a freshman, then became the Big East Player of the Year and an All-American in his final two years. He played for the 1984 U.S. Olympic team that won a gold medal in the Los Angeles Olympics before leading the Red Storm to their first Final Four since 1952.

The versatile 6' 7" left-handed Mullin averaged 19.5 points, 4.1 rebounds, 3.6 assists and 1.7 steals in 37.4 minutes a game during his career and left as St. John's all-time leading scorer with 2,440 points. He is currently second all-time behind the late Malik Sealy.

Mullin was strictly old school, a textbook player who used trademark jab steps and crossover dribbles to free himself up for open looks.

He was a classic gym rat who was given the key to Alumni Hall by athletic director Jack Kaiser and had a reputation of going home for dinner, doing his homework, before driving back to campus to shoot

hoops until 1 a.m.

Practice made near perfect. Mullin shot 55 percent from the floor and 84.8 percent from the line for his career. He was the driving force behind a team that was ranked No. 1 for most of the 1985 season. Mullin scored 30 points against Kentucky and 25 against North Carolina as the Johnnies won the West Regional before losing to powerful conference rival Georgetown in the national semifinals. After the season, Mullin was selected as the winner of the Wooden Award as the National Player of the Year.

The Golden State Warriors selected Mullin with the seventh pick in the 1985 NBA draft.

*Dickie V's View:* Here's a kid out of New York City who used to sneak into the gym on the high school level, just to shoot by himself. Then he got the keys to Alumni Hall when he was at St. John's. I remember the late Katha Quinn, the former sports information director at St. John's, telling me how Chris Mullin was such a fanatic, he would stay there until Looie Carnesecca chased him out. One time, there was this huge blizzard that buried the city and he stayed in the gym for two days, just working on his game. He was this typical gym rat who made himself a great shooter.

Without a doubt, throughout my tenure at ESPN I thought he was the best pure shooter I'd ever seen. And he had the luxury of playing with a great point guard, Mark Jackson, who got him the ball.

His St. John's team in 1985 could have won the national championship. Mullin played on the same team with Walter Berry, Bill Wennington and Jackson

ere was a lot of New York flavor on that team.
And that was good, baby. When you think about
rnesecca and his personality and Chris Mullin and
jump shot, they were such fan favorites in the
rden and became a vital part of the landscape of
city.

Right now, that's what's missing from big-time
college basketball in the Big Apple – and it's needed
so much. They need to get the Garden rockin' again,
and the only way that's going to happen is by
convincing the local superstars to stay home.

And create a New York state of mind again.

**C**hris Mullin was one of my favorite shooters to watch. He was the epitome of a gym rat, a guy who always worked on his shooting. Looie Carnesecca loved his work ethic as Mullin and company reached the Final Four in 1985.

## #16. CHRIS MULLIN, ST. JOHN'S

|  | MIN | FG% | 3P% | FT% | RPG | APG | TPG | BPG | SPG | PPG |
|---|---|---|---|---|---|---|---|---|---|---|
| 81-82 | 35.4 | 53.4 |  | 79.1 | 3.2 | 3.1 | 3.2 | 0.2 | 1.4 | 16.6 |
| 82-83 | 36.7 | 57.7 |  | 87.8 | 3.7 | 3.1 | 2.8 | 0.2 | 1.2 | 19.1 |
| 83-84 | 39.6 | 57.1 |  | 90.4 | 4.4 | 4.0 | 3.7 | 0.4 | 2.1 | 22.9 |
| 84-85 | 37.9 | 52.1 |  | 82.4 | 4.8 | 4.3 | 2.6 | 0.5 | 2.1 | 19.8 |
| **TOTALS** | 37.3 | 55.0 |  | 84.8 | 4.1 | 3.6 | 3.0 | 0.3 | 1.7 | 19.5 |

# LOUISVILLE:

## Darrell Griffith

6' 4"

190 pounds

Guard

1976-1980

*Profile:* His name was Darrell Griffith but most rabid Louisville fans simply referred to him as "Dr. Dunkenstein" because of his 48-inch vertical leap (reminiscent of David Thompson), his hang time and penchant for spectacular dunks.

Griffith picked up the nickname from his friends in his Louisville neighborhood when he was younger. It was a spin-off of the George Clinton "Dr. Funkenstein" character in the group "Funkadelic Parliament."

"Nobody could fly like Darrell," former Memphis State coach Dana Kirk once said. "He could dip his wings twice in salute as he passed over the rest of u...

The 6' 4" high-flying guard was much more tha... a dunkaholic. He led Louisville to four straight NCA appearances. He averaged 18.2 points, 4.6 rebound... and 2.9 assists during his career and was the first Cards' player to surpass 2,000 points, finishing his career with 2,333.

Griffith could have turned pro and been a top five draft pick after his junior year in 1979. But he

### #17. DARRELL GRIFFITH, LOUISVILLE

|        | MIN  | FG%  | 3P% | FT%  | RPG | APG | TPG | BPG | SPG | PPG  |
|--------|------|------|-----|------|-----|-----|-----|-----|-----|------|
| 76-77  | 23.6 | 50.1 |     | 36.4 | 3.9 | 1.7 | 2.7 |     |     | 12.8 |
| 77-78  | 33.2 | 52.2 |     | 70.9 | 5.4 | 3.5 | 3.8 | 0.7 | 1.6 | 18.6 |
| 78-79  | 31.3 | 49.7 |     | 70.9 | 4.4 | 2.8 | 2.8 | 0.9 | 1.9 | 18.5 |
| 79-80  | 34.6 | 56.3 |     | 71.3 | 4.8 | 3.8 | 3.6 | 0.8 | 2.4 | 22.9 |
| **TOTALS** | 30.9 | 51.8 |     | 69.7 | 4.6 | 2.9 | 3.2 |     |     | 18.2 |

omised his hometown he would bring Louisville a
ational championship.

The 1979-80 team had its work cut out for it.
riffith was the lone senior on a team that had been
iminated early in the tournament the three previous
ears and had three sophomores and one freshman in
e starting lineup.

Griffith stepped up in a big way all season. He
as a consensus first-team All-American and National
ayer of the Year in 1980. He led the 33-3 Cardinals
a perfect 12-0 season in the Metro Conference and
en the national championship when he averaged
2.9 points, shot a torrid 56.3 percent, scored in
ouble figures 34 straight times and led the "Doctors
Dunk" in steals and assists.

Griffith scored 34 points against Iowa in the
ational semis, then got 23 against four different
efenders as the Cardinals flew past UCLA, 59-54,
the championship game. Ironically, none of them
ere dunks. But with the 'Ville trailing by four with
ast four minutes left, Griffith ignited a game-winning
lly, hitting sophomore lead guard Jerry Eaves for
vo field goals and nailing a jumper from the top of
e key to break a 54-54 tie with 2:21 remaining to
lfill the promise he made to his fans and one of his
hildhood friends.

Griffith dedicated the game to Jerry Stenger, who
as dying of cancer. The next day the team visited
enger, who was bedridden at his home, and draped
rands of the net around his head.

Griffith was eventually selected by the Utah Jazz
ith the second pick overall in the NBA draft later
at spring.

*Dickie V's View:* Darrell Griffith was a local kid
from Louisville Male High School who helped the
Cardinals fly into the stratosphere, turning them into
one of the elite programs in the country.

He started it off.

Griffith was the most complete player ever to
play for Denny Crum. He really knew how to operate
in outer space. He just floated in the air. He was
David Thompson and Michael Jordan in terms of
being a high riser. He was so explosive – with an
unbelievable 48-inch vertical leap. He was in another
world, igniting the Cards with his monster jams.

He was the star of the 1980 team that was known
as "The Doctors of Dunk," a team filled with high
fliers that won the national championship. They'd
throw down two or three dunks in a row and you
were so intimidated. It was lights out, the party was
over.

Kentucky was still the big program in the
Commonwealth at the time and the Wildcats
wouldn't play Louisville. Kentucky fans used to
call the Cards "little brother."

But "little brother" grew up, man.

And Darrell made the whole country sit up
and take notice, leading the 'Ville to the national
championship game against UCLA and Kiki
Vandeweghe. The Cardinals had to go up against
Larry Brown, a great coach who got the most out of
his teams in terms of scouting and creating matchup
problems for other teams. But the Bruins had no
matchup to contain Griffith that night.

Louisville won, 59-54, and Griffith was an ESPN
*SportsCenter* highlight film, going off for 23 points.

**D**arrell Griffith was
the main member of
the Doctors of Dunk at
Louisville. He helped the
Cardinals cut down the
nets when they won the
national championship
in 1980.

DUKE:

PLAYER NUMBER

# Danny Ferry

6' 10"

235 pounds

Center

1985-1989

*Profile:* When Duke coach Mike Krzyzewski beat out North Carolina and Maryland for Danny Ferry in 1985, it was considered a major coup. Carolina had always been Ferry's dream school, and Maryland was located just two miles from his home.

But there was something about Krzyzewski, a young coach with a talented young team on the rise in the ACC that intrigued Ferry.

"I saw greatness," Ferry said.

Krzyzewski saw the same qualities in Ferry.

Ferry, a versatile 6' 10" center with Larry Bird-like skills, was considered the number one prospect in the country at fabled DeMatha Catholic High School just outside Washington, D.C. Ferry set the standard for future big men Coach K recruited because of his ability to take his game outside and become a playmaker.

Ferry learned the game at a young age from his father, Bob, a former NBA player who was the GM with the Washington Bullets, and polished it by playing for Hall of Famer Morgan Wooten in high school. He was destined to become a college star and helped Krzyzewski bridge the gap after the Johnny Dawkins era ended, when Duke was starting to establish itself as a Final Four regular.

Ferry was a sixth man on the first Krzyzewski-coached team to make a Final Four in 1986. He stepped into the spotlight as a sophomore when Krzyzewski allowed him to spread his wings offensively, leading the Blue Devils in scoring, rebounding and assists.

He was the dominant player in the ACC his junior and senior years when Duke made two consecutive trips to the Final Four. Ferry led the ACC in scoring as a junior and senior, averaging 19. and 22.6 points. He was twice selected ACC Player of the Year, was a two-time All-American as well as National Player of the Year in 1989.

Ferry set the ACC single-game scoring record his senior year with 58 points in a road game against the University of Miami. He still remembers celebrating the fact that the trainer finally allowed the team to have pancakes for breakfast that morning by shootin a near-perfect 23 for 26.

Ferry, who averaged 15.1 points and 7.0 rebounds during his career while shooting 48.4 percent and demonstrating the ability to step outside and consistently make threes, was the first player in ACC history to score at least 2,000 points, grab 1,00 rebounds and contribute 500 assists.

He was selected by the Los Angeles Clippers with the second pick in the draft, but opted not to play there, going to Italy for a year before the Clippers traded his rights to Cleveland.

*Dickie V's View:* Danny Ferry's father, Bob, was a basketball lifer. He played in the NBA and was the general manager of the Washington Bullets and scouted for many years when Danny was growing up

Danny was 6' 10" and the number one player in America his senior year at DeMatha. Duke, North Carolina and Maryland recruited him heavily.

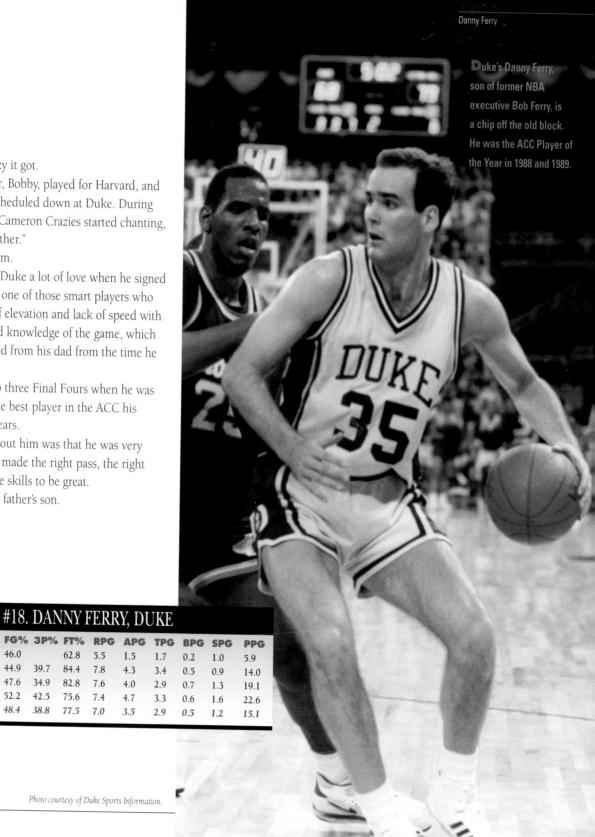

Danny Ferry

Duke's Danny Ferry, son of former NBA executive Bob Ferry, is a chip off the old block. He was the ACC Player of the Year in 1988 and 1989.

Here's how crazy it got.

Danny's brother, Bobby, played for Harvard, and they had a game scheduled down at Duke. During introductions, the Cameron Crazies started chanting, "We want your brother."

And they got him.

Danny showed Duke a lot of love when he signed with them. He was one of those smart players who made up for lack of elevation and lack of speed with great awareness and knowledge of the game, which he obviously learned from his dad from the time he was in the crib.

Duke made it to three Final Fours when he was here and he was the best player in the ACC his junior and senior years.

What I loved about him was that he was very cerebral. He always made the right pass, the right play. And he had the skills to be great.

He was truly his father's son.

## #18. DANNY FERRY, DUKE

|  | MIN | FG% | 3P% | FT% | RPG | APG | TPG | BPG | SPG | PPG |
|---|---|---|---|---|---|---|---|---|---|---|
| 85-86 | 22.8 | 46.0 |  | 62.8 | 5.5 | 1.5 | 1.7 | 0.2 | 1.0 | 5.9 |
| 86-87 | 33.2 | 44.9 | 39.7 | 84.4 | 7.8 | 4.3 | 3.4 | 0.5 | 0.9 | 14.0 |
| 87-88 | 32.5 | 47.6 | 34.9 | 82.8 | 7.6 | 4.0 | 2.9 | 0.7 | 1.3 | 19.1 |
| 88-89 | 33.2 | 52.2 | 42.5 | 75.6 | 7.4 | 4.7 | 3.3 | 0.6 | 1.6 | 22.6 |
| **TOTALS** | *30.1* | *48.4* | *38.8* | *77.5* | *7.0* | *3.5* | *2.9* | *0.5* | *1.2* | *15.1* |

*Photo courtesy of Duke Sports Information.*

# GEORGETOWN:

## Alonzo Mourning

6' 10"

261 pounds

Center

1988-1992

*Profile:* Alonzo Mourning was the most heavily recruited prospect in the country during his senior year at Indian River High in Chesapeake, Va., when he averaged 22 points, 15 rebounds and 12 blocked shots for a team that won 51 consecutive games and a Virginia state title.

But there was little question where "Zo" – who once blocked 27 shots in an AAU game – was going to attend college.

The 6' 10" Mourning had become enamored with Georgetown when he watched the 1982 national championship game and saw Patrick Ewing swat away North Carolina's first four field goal attempts – all goaltending. Mourning even had posters of Ewing plastered all over his bedroom wall.

Some viewed Mourning as a younger version of Kareem Abdul-Jabbar. And after Mourning signed with the Hoyas, he was the first high school player ever invited to participate in the U.S. Olympic basketball trials in Colorado Springs.

Mourning did not make the team, but he was one of the final two players cut and showed he could compete with anyone on the next level.

Mourning, who wore Ewing's No. 33, helped perpetuate his legacy, averaging 16.7 points, 8.6 rebounds and 3.8 blocked shots during his four-year career. Mourning was Big East Rookie of the Year and led the country in blocked shots his freshman year when the Hoyas advanced to the NCAA East Regional finals.

Unlike Ewing, he never played on a Final Four or national championship team, but he did leave his mark. Mourning, who spent three years playing power forward in the same frontcourt as 7' 2" center Dikembe Mutombo, was selected as second- or third-team All-American, then put together one of the most dominant senior years ever.

Mourning, who had been plagued by an injured arch that forced him to miss nine games as a junior, spent the following summer working out with Ewing and Mutombo at Georgetown's McDonough Arena.

Then he took out his frustrations on the rest of college basketball.

Mourning averaged 21.3 points, 10.7 rebounds and five blocks. He was a consensus first-team All-American and the first player ever to be selected Big East Player of the Year, Defensive Player and MVP of the Big East Tournament. He scored in double figures every game and grabbed double-figure rebounds 22 times, despite getting limited touches in the post.

Mourning's career ended prematurely in the second round of the NCAA Tournament when Florida State held him to seven shots and three rebounds during a 78-68 loss.

But he struck it rich in the draft, signing a $2.1 million contract after being selected by the Charlotte Bobcats with the second pick overall.

*Dickie V's View:* Georgetown coach John Thompson has always had a legacy of great big men, beginning with Patrick Ewing and continuing through Alonzo Mourning, Dikembe Mutombo and Othella Harrington.

Mourning was a slightly smaller version of Ewing, who had been his hero in high school. Mourning wanted to follow in Ewing's footsteps.

was as tough as they come. The great thing about
hn Thompson's big men is that they played with
ch passion. Just like Patrick, Alonzo never took a
ossession off and, like Patrick, he had great instincts
d timing as a shot blocker.

Mourning was a terrific rejecter – a human eraser
who led the country in blocked shots as a freshman
d was the first Big East player ever to win the
gular season MVP, defensive player of the year and
VP of the conference tournament his senior year.

He and Patrick stayed close after he graduated.
hey would work out together in the summer.
trick is the godfather of Alonzo's daughter. In 2000,
er he helped lead the U.S. to Olympic glory as a
ember of the Miami Heat, Mourning suffered a life-
reatening kidney disease, and Patrick volunteered
donate one of his kidneys to him if it was needed.

People, that is truly the definition of the word
iend."

As it turned out, on November 25, 2003,
ourning's cousin and a former U.S. Marine,
son Cooper, was visiting Mourning's seriously ill
andmother in the hospital. Mourning's father was
ere and explained the situation. Cooper asked if
ere was anything he could do for his cousin, who
had not seen in 25 years and knew only by reputa-
on. Cooper was tested for compatibility and, ironi-
lly, during his grandmother's funeral, Mourning
ceived the good news that Cooper was a match.

Mourning received Cooper's left kidney December
, 2003. He eventually returned to play in the NBA.
ourning has since established Zo's Fund for Life,
charity seeking funds for research, education and
sting to fight kidney disease.

### #19. ALONZO MOURNING, GEORGETOWN

|        | MIN  | FG%  | 3P%  | FT%  | RPG  | APG  | TPG  | BPG  | SPG  | PPG  |
|--------|------|------|------|------|------|------|------|------|------|------|
| 88-89  | 28.3 | 60.3 | 25.0 | 66.7 | 7.3  | 0.7  | 2.0  | 5.0  | 0.4  | 13.1 |
| 89-90  | 30.2 | 52.5 | 0.0  | 78.3 | 8.5  | 1.2  | 2.8  | 2.2  | 0.5  | 16.5 |
| 90-91  | 29.6 | 52.2 | 30.8 | 79.3 | 7.7  | 1.1  | 2.5  | 2.4  | 0.4  | 15.8 |
| 91-92  | 32.8 | 59.5 | 25.0 | 75.8 | 10.7 | 1.7  | 2.6  | 5.0  | 0.6  | 21.3 |
| **TOTALS** | 30.3 | 56.6 | 26.1 | 75.4 | 8.6  | 1.2  | 2.5  | 3.8  | 0.5  | 16.7 |

Alonzo Mourning was a physical presence, one of many impressive big men under John Thompson at George-town. He battles against Pittsburgh's Brian Shorter and Darrelle Porter here.

# UNLV:

**PLAYER NUMBER 20**

# Larry Johnson

6' 7"

235 pounds

Forward

1989-1991

*Profile:* Larry Johnson was one of the lucky ones. He escaped from the crime and poverty of his poor Dallas neighborhood. His mother found a refuge for him in the PAL gymnasiums, where he mastered boxing and basketball. He became the relentless cornerstone of Jerry Tarkanian's greatest teams at UNLV.

The powerful 6' 7" Johnson had developed into the best prospect in the country his senior year at Skyline High and initially signed to play at SMU in his hometown. But problems with his SAT scores forced him to attend Odessa (Texas) Junior College for two years. Tarkanian got him the second time around, outrecruiting Georgetown for the best junior college prospect in the country, and then turning him into the perfect inside complement to future NBA players Greg Anthony and Stacey Augmon.

Johnson was a beast who made an immediate impact. He was a two-time first-team All-American who averaged more than 20 points and 10 rebounds as a junior and senior when the Runnin' Rebels – who routinely scored more than 100 points – won a national championship in 1990. They made a return trip to the Final Four the following year when Johnson was selected the consensus National Player of the Year.

Johnson was too much for Duke to handle in the 1990 championship game, scoring 22 points and grabbing 11 rebounds as the Rebels – who won 21 of their last 22 games – blew away the Blue Devils, 103-73, in a game that could have been much worse if Tarkanian hadn't pulled his starters. As it was, the Rebels set simultaneous NCAA records for both the largest margin of victory and the highest score in an NCAA championship game.

Before Johnson's senior year, it looked like the Rebels would be even more dominant. They were 34-0, scored more than 100 points 16 times and were beating their regular-season opponents by an average of 26.1 points. A talented Duke team stunned the Rebels with a 79-77 upset win in the national semifinals.

It was the end of the golden age of UNLV basketball. Tarkanian resigned under pressure amidst speculation of numerous violations and fought the NCAA for years before receiving a $2.5 million settlement from the U.S. Supreme Court.

Johnson was chosen by Charlotte with the number one pick overall in the 1991 draft.

Some 16 years later, after a long NBA career, he walked down the aisle with his college degree in social studies – something he had promised his mother when he entered school. He is now coaching at the middle school he attended.

*Dickie V's View:* Larry Johnson was a man playing with kids when he was at UNLV. He was 6' 7" and weighed 235 pounds. As a kid, he would box in the PAL and he looked like he could have given Mike Tyson a run for his money if he had continued to pursue the sport seriously.

He was the maximum force behind a club that won a national title in 1990 and won 45 straight games before losing to Duke in the 1991 NCAA semifinals.

Jerry Tarkanian has said on numerous occasions, that he probably wouldn't have gotten Johnson had he not gone to Odessa Junior College first. People thought he would be staying home and going to SMU, but to the delight of many Runnin' Rebel fans, he became a solid gold all-American for UNLV.

He turned out to be that imposing figure every great club needs, a physically intimidating talent. If he got the ball inside, you had no chance to stop him. As strong as he was, he also had the great bounce and agility.

I loved going to Vegas to do their games, but I'll tell you what impressed me the most was watching practice. Tark had the unique ability to get his players to play as hard in practice as they did in games – with emotion and intensity.

And Larry Johnson bought right into it. The rest of the team did, too. If Vegas had finished the season undefeated in 1991, we would have been talking about the Rebels as one of the great teams of all time.

Larry Johnson enjoys a slam dunk while Loyola Marymount's Bo Kimble looks on. Johnson helped lead the Runnin' Rebels to the 1990 national championship in convincing fashion.

### #20. LARRY JOHNSON, UNLV

|  | MIN | FG% | 3P% | FT% | RPG | APG | TPG | BPG | SPG | PPG |
|---|---|---|---|---|---|---|---|---|---|---|
| 89-90 | 31.5 | 62.4 | 34.2 | 76.7 | 11.4 | 2.1 | 2.8 | 1.4 | 1.6 | 20.6 |
| 90-91 | 31.8 | 66.2 | 35.4 | 81.8 | 10.9 | 3.0 | 2.2 | 1.0 | 2.1 | 22.7 |
| TOTALS | 31.6 | 64.3 | 34.9 | 78.9 | 11.2 | 2.5 | 2.5 | 1.2 | 1.9 | 21.6 |

**DUKE:**

PLAYER NUMBER

# Jason Williams

6' 2"

195 pounds

Guard

1999-2002

*Profile:* Jason Williams was one of Duke's most decorated players. He split national player of the year honors with teammate Shane Battier as a sophomore and swept them all as a junior.

But the 6' 2" guard also changed the way Mike Krzyzewski dealt with the growing number of early defections in his program. After Williams averaged 25.7 points in the 2001 NCAA Tournament and helped lead the Blue Devils to a third national championship, he seriously considered leaving for the NBA after hearing whispers he might be the number one pick in the draft.

Krzyzewski solved the problem by meeting with Williams' parents and setting up a plan whereby Williams could accelerate his class work with summer courses and graduate in three years, which he did, earning a degree in sociology.

It allowed Coach K to keep college basketball's premier player in his program – long enough to haunt neighborhood rival North Carolina for one more season.

When Williams was growing up in South Plainfield, N.J., he was a huge Carolina fan. He even had a Michael Jordan poster in his room. But Carolina coach Bill Guthridge told Williams that he already had his future point guard in Ronald Curry, opening the door for Krzyzewski to sign the next Johnny Dawkins.

Williams, a McDonald's All-American at St. Joseph's of Metuchen, N.J., was a three-year starter. He was forced to play a major role immediately after Trajan Langdon, Elton Brand, William Avery and Corey Maggette left early for the NBA and responded by being selected MVP of the ACC Tournament his freshman year.

That was only the beginning. Williams was a consensus first-team All-American the next two years. Williams averaged 19.3 points, 3.7 rebounds and 6.0 assists during his career and he helped Duke to a 95-13 record and three ACC championships. Similar to many of his fellow Dukies, he thrived in big games.

As a sophomore, he highlighted Duke's championship run by scoring eight points in just 14 seconds as the Blue Devils rallied from a 10-point deficit in the final 54 seconds of regulation to beat Maryland, 98-96, in overtime at Cole Field House. He scored 34 points – including 19 straight – as Duke defeated UCLA in the 2001 regional finals and 23 when the Devils rallied from 22 down to beat Maryland, 95-84, in the national semifinals.

Duke looked like it had a shot to repeat during Williams' junior year but was upset by Indiana, 74-73, in the Sweet 16. Williams drained a three to close the gap to one in the final seconds and was fouled on the play, but he uncharacteristically missed a free throw, and teammate Carlos Boozer missed a potential game-winning put back at the buzzer.

Williams was selected by the Chicago Bulls with the second pick overall later that spring.

*Dickie V's View:* Jason Williams came out of St. Joseph's in New Jersey with a great reputation. I first heard about him from Howard Garfinkel after he attended Five-Star camp the summer before his senior year. The Super Garf couldn't wait to tell me about him. He called, and he was screaming into the phone, "Dickie V, wait 'til you see this kid who's going to Duke."

I remember I did Jason's first game in college. Duke and UConn – who had played in the 1999 national championship game – were playing on opposite sides of a semifinal doubleheader in a preseason tournament at the Garden.

I'm salivating at the thought of doing a rematch for the title. But what happens? Duke loses to Stanford, and UConn loses to Iowa. And Jason got off to a slow start. He scored 13 points, grabbed 10 rebounds and had three assists. But he also shot just three for 15 and had six turnovers, and he was really pressing in an overtime loss. So then we had Duke and Connecticut in the consolation game.

It's the first time I can remember ESPN getting ready to do a third-place game. I was in the building at 4:30 p.m., standing with two Hall of Famers – Mike Krzyzewski of Duke and Jim Calhoun of UConn – while they were preparing, getting ready for tipoff, looking at an empty Garden.

I also remember Jason Williams coming by. I told him that it was going to be a pleasure covering him over the next four years and said, "Don't let that one game affect you." That kid was trying so hard to play well for his family and friends. But you could see greatness when he stepped on the court.

Eventually, things got better and Williams started playing before full houses, becoming a dominant player. I'll never forget his performance against Kentucky in the 2001 Jimmy V Classic at the Meadowlands. Duke was on the verge of getting blown out at the start of the second half when Mike Krzyzewski pulled his entire starting five, just to send a message. When he put them back in, Williams went crazy, carrying his team. He scored 23 of Duke's final 31 points in regulation and helped them wipe out a 22-point deficit. Williams finished with 38 and Duke won, 95-92, in overtime.

**J**ason Williams was a special player at Duke. I will never forget the show he put on in the second half against Kentucky at the Jimmy V Classic at the Meadowlands.

## #21. JASON WILLIAMS, DUKE

|  | MIN | FG% | 3P% | FT% | RPG | APG | TPG | BPG | SPG | PPG |
|---|---|---|---|---|---|---|---|---|---|---|
| 99-00 | 34.0 | 41.9 | 35.4 | 68.5 | 4.2 | 6.5 | 4.1 | 0.2 | 2.4 | 14.5 |
| 00-01 | 31.8 | 47.3 | 42.7 | 65.9 | 3.3 | 6.1 | 3.9 | 0.1 | 2.0 | 21.6 |
| 01-02 | 33.6 | 45.7 | 38.3 | 67.6 | 3.5 | 5.3 | 3.7 | 0.1 | 2.2 | 21.3 |
| **TOTALS** | 33.1 | 45.3 | 39.3 | 67.1 | 3.7 | 6.0 | 3.9 | 0.1 | 2.2 | 19.3 |

Williams was supposed to be one of the next great ones to play for the Chicago Bulls. I would have liked to see what he could have done, but he was involved in a bad motorcycle accident after his rookie year that resulted in a fractured pelvis, a broken leg and severe ligament damage to his left knee.

After that kind of accident, some athletes would have a chip on their shoulder and be bitter. This kid rolled with the punches and moved on, making the transition to the real world. He is now an executive with 24 Hour Fitness and works as an analyst with ESPN.

Wow, I'd better watch out. He's going to want my job, baby.

# DEPAUL:

PLAYER NUMBER 22

# Mark Aguirre

6' 6"

232 pounds

Forward

1978-1981

*Profile:* Before the Michael Jordan era began and before the 1986 Chicago Bears won the Super Bowl, the city of Chicago had compiled a sad history of sports futility.

But DePaul's powerful 6' 6" forward Mark Aguirre, a hometown hero from Westinghouse High, temporarily lifted the city out of the doldrums on his big shoulders when he led the late Hall of Famer Ray Meyer's Blue Demons to an NCAA Final Four appearance as a freshman in 1979 and back-to-back No. 1 rankings during his final two years in college.

Aguirre – who was famous for playing on his neighborhood courts on the west side from two in the afternoon until three in the morning when he was younger – was recruited by Meyer's son and first full-time assistant coach, Joey. When Aguirre was in the 11th grade, he was hoping to go to Marquette but that all changed when the late Al McGuire announced his retirement, effective at the end of the 1977 season.

Aguirre's decision to attend DePaul gave the Meyers instant street credibility in the rugged Chicago Public League and allowed them to recruit prep stars like Teddy Grubbs from King, Terry Cummings from Carver and Aguirre's high school teammate, Skip Dillard.

Aguirre could be moody and often fought the battle of the bulge, once acquiring the nickname of "The Muffin Man" when he ballooned up to 260 pounds. But he could score on anyone. Anyone. Aguirre averaged 24.0, 26.8 and 23.0 points in his three years as a starter.

He scored a school record 2,182 points, averaging 24.5 points and 7.9 rebounds while shooting 54.6

percent during his career for a rejuvenated independent that went 79-10. Aguirre was a unanimous first-team All-American in 1980 and 1981 and was selected National Player of the Year in both seasons. He also was named to the 1980 Olympic team that did not get to play when the United States boycotted the Moscow games because of the Soviet war in Afghanistan.

As towering as his individual performances were, his career at DePaul played out like a Greek tragedy, according to some. The Demons looked like they were on the verge of breaking Indiana State's 33-game winning streak in the NCAA semifinals. They were down, 75-74, with the ball. But Aguirre missed a potential 18-foot game winner and the Sycamores made a free throw to wrap up a 76-74 victory.

The next year, the Blue Demons were upset by UCLA, 77-71, in the second round. A svelte Aguirre, motivated by his experiences on the U.S. national team, spurned big NBA dollars to come back for his junior year and dominated the regular season again. But history repeated itself in March when DePaul suffered another second-round upset, losing to St. Joseph's, 49-48, when the Demons did not score a point or take a shot in the final six-and-a-half minutes. It was Aguirre's final game. He was so upset, he grabbed the game ball, ran out the door of the Dayton Arena and heaved it into the Great Miami River.

Aguirre may have been high maintenance, but there was no doubting his enormous talent.

Dallas selected Aguirre with the number one pick in the 1981 draft, taking him ahead of his childhood friend, Isiah Thomas, of Indiana.

**Dickie V's View:** I'll always remember Mark Aguirre because he was a star in the first game I ever did for ESPN – DePaul vs. Wisconsin in Chicago.

Aguirre was already a PTPer by then. He had taken DePaul to a third-place finish in the 1979 NCAA Tournament as a freshman and given the late Ray Meyer, who was a Hall of Fame coach, a new lease on life.

Here comes this kid from Chicago, who stays home, remains in his backyard. DePaul almost got Aguirre by accident. Joey Meyer was actually recruiting Aguirre's high school teammate, Eddie Johnson. Johnson went to Illinois, but Aguirre liked what Meyer was telling Johnson and decided he wanted to stay home and attend DePaul.

That was a great moment for DePaul basketball. Aguirre was like a pied piper, man. He opened the door for the Blue Demons to get blue chippers out of the Chicago Public League. Aguirre was the biggest reason why DePaul, which almost dropped the sport in 1971, was suddenly a national power, the No. 1 team in the country.

Body-wise, he was a lot like Larry Johnson and Adrian Dantley. What always impressed me about Aguirre were his hands. He was a great scorer. He had a scorer's mentality and knew how to create space as a big, wide body. Plus, he had that unique cockiness and arrogance that he utilized in a positive manner. When he stepped onto the floor, he thought he was the baddest dude ever to lace up a pair of sneakers. I ask you, who was going to argue with him?

DePaul's Mark Aguirre, known for his offensive prowess, showed he could play defense against Louisville's Jerry Eaves.

### #22. MARK AGUIRRE, DEPAUL

|  | MIN | FG% | 3P% | FT% | RPG | APG | TPG | BPG | SPG | PPG |
|---|---|---|---|---|---|---|---|---|---|---|
| 78-79 | 37.7 | 52.0 |  | 76.5 | 7.6 | 2.7 |  |  |  | 24.0 |
| 79-80 | 37.5 | 54.0 |  | 76.6 | 7.6 | 2.8 | 3.5 | 0.4 | 1.7 | 26.8 |
| 80-81 | 36.9 | 58.2 |  | 77.4 | 8.6 | 4.5 | 3.3 | 0.9 | 1.6 | 23.0 |
| **TOTALS** | 37.3 | 54.6 |  | 76.8 | 7.9 | 3.3 | 3.4 | 0.7 | 1.7 | 24.5 |

# NORTH CAROLINA:

## Antawn Jamison

6' 9"

223 pounds

Forward

1995-1998

*Profile:* Antawn Jamison thought he would ease his way into college basketball when he signed with North Carolina. The 6' 9" recruit had no idea that Rasheed Wallace and Jerry Stackhouse would both leave for the pros following their sophomore seasons after the Tar Heels advanced to the 1995 NCAA Final Four.

Jamison was thrust into the spotlight as a freshman. He surpassed Michael Jordan's statistical accomplishments his first year. Then he combined with Vince Carter to lead the Tar Heels to the 1997 NCAA Final Four as a sophomore in Dean Smith's final season. The next season, he gave new coach Bill Guthridge – a Smith assistant for 30 years – instant credibility by winning the AP, Wooden and Naismith awards, given to the National Player of the Year.

Jamison, a two-time first-team All-American who averaged 19 points and 9.9 rebounds during his three-year career, was a local high school star from Charlotte's Provence High who made good.

But he was born far away from Tobacco Road, in Shreveport, La. Jamison's father, Albert, built houses for the federal government, and his occupation took him to Charlotte, N.C., in 1990, months after Hurricane Hugo had ravaged South Carolina. He brought the family along because he believed that the Carolinas offered a better opportunity for his wife and three children.

Jamison, who was close to his family and attended church services regularly, wanted to stay close to home for college and chose North Carolina over South Carolina.

Carolina fans viewed Jamison as a combination of Bobby Jones and James Worthy, with his quickness and strength inside. He was the first player to be named All-ACC his first three seasons. In 1998, as a junior, he became only the third player in league history to be named ACC Player of the Year, ACC Tournament MVP and NCAA East Regional Most Outstanding Player.

The hallmark of his game was consistency. During his career, he had 51 double doubles, including five straight while leading the Heels to the 1998 Final Four. Jamison had a sensational junior year, averaging 22.2 points and 10.5 rebounds, leading the ACC in both categories.

Jamison went off for 20 points and 11 rebounds as UNC defeated UConn, 75-64, in an Elite Eight game that March. He never won a national championship but he will always be remembered for kissing the floor after a semifinal loss to Utah, the final game of his college career.

Jamison turned pro after the season and was selected by Golden State with the fourth pick overall in the draft. He returned to school to complete his degree work in 1999.

*Dickie V's View:* Antawn Jamison was the first big star of the post-Dean Smith era. Just before his junior year at North Carolina, Smith retired. He turned the team over to his long-time assistant Bill Guthridge.

Jamison and his teammate Vince Carter formed a dynamic duo and that certainly helped Guthridge make the transition from a second lieutenant to becoming the captain of one of the most prestigious programs in the nation.

Jamison was voted National Player of the Year for a 34-4 team that won the ACC Tournament and the made it to the Final Four. This guy was a machine. He was as intense a player as I've seen over 40 minutes. He was an automatic double double guy. He was almost a mini version of Moses Malone in terms of going after every rebound like it was his last meal.

It was a successful end to a long journey for Jamison, who was born in Shreveport, La., just a mile away from where Robert Parish, the great Boston Celtics' center, had grown up. His father, Albert, who worked in construction, built him his first hoop and attached it to a telephone pole behind his house.

His mother once claimed that the rim was 12 feet tall, which is two feet higher than a normal goal. That explains why Jamison developed that high-arching shot and why he became such a high riser. Jamison was finally able to touch the rim in eighth grade and tried to tear it down.

So dunking was no problem.

But his old neighborhood was. His mother was convinced it would be best to move to a different area where Antawn would have a chance to succeed. So the close-knit family moved to a safer place. His father took a job in construction in Charlotte after Hurricane Hugo and took his wife and three children with him.

Jamison became a star on the AAU circuit in Charlotte. He chose North Carolina after Dean Smith visited his home and told him he couldn't promise him an NBA contract, but he would guarantee that he would receive a quality education.

That thought, coming from one of the best coaches of all time, really sank in. Jamison said later showed him, "this life and this world are more than just basketball."

Antawn Jamison was North Carolina's first big star of the post-Dean Smith era. He was a consistent player, averaging just under a double-double per game.

## #23. ANTAWN JAMISON, NORTH CAROLINA

|  | MIN | FG% | 3P% | FT% | RPG | APG | TPG | BPG | SPG | PPG |
|---|---|---|---|---|---|---|---|---|---|---|
| 95-96 | 32.9 | 62.4 | 0.0 | 52.6 | 9.7 | 1.0 | 1.8 | 1.0 | 0.8 | 15.1 |
| 96-97 | 34.3 | 54.4 | 18.2 | 62.1 | 9.4 | 0.9 | 1.8 | 0.6 | 1.1 | 19.1 |
| 97-98 | 33.2 | 57.9 | 40.0 | 66.7 | 10.5 | 0.8 | 1.6 | 0.8 | 0.8 | 22.2 |
| **TOTALS** | 33.4 | 57.7 | 29.6 | 61.7 | 9.9 | 0.9 | 1.8 | 0.8 | 0.9 | 19.0 |

# INDIANA:

PLAYER NUMBER

## Steve Alford

6' 2"

183 pounds

Guard

1983-1987

*Profile:* Steve Alford was a Hoosier high school legend long before he became a star at Indiana. Playing for his father, Sam, in New Castle High School's 9,500-seat Chrysler field house, he averaged 37.2 points as a senior – going off for 57 in the state tournament semifinals – and won the state's coveted Mr. Basketball award in 1983.

There was never any suspense about where he would attend college. He actually committed to Bob Knight after his junior year, then proceeded to prove wrong the critics who felt he was too slow and too small to play in the Big Ten.

Alford was a gym rat and self-made player. He was a classic jump shooter who turned into a lethal weapon in Knight's motion offense, coming off screens to swish 20-footers effortlessly. He led IU in scoring for four years, averaging 19.5 points in 125 games. Alford was a three-time All-Big Ten selection and a two-time All-American as a junior and senior. He shot 53.3 percent from the field for his career and finished with 2,438 points, second on the school's all-time list behind Calbert Cheaney.

Alford's numbers would have been even higher had the NCAA instituted the three-point shot earlier in his career. He shot an incredible 53 percent from beyond the arc in 1987 – the first season the three-point rule was instituted – making seven of 10 three-point attempts and scoring 23 points as the 30-4 Hoosiers defeated Syracuse, 74-73, to win the school's fifth NCAA championship.

Alford made an immediate impact at IU, averaging 15.5 points, shooting 59.2 percent from the field and 91.3 from the line. He made six straight free throws down the stretch as the Hoosiers stunned the Michael Jordan-led North Carolina Tar Heels in the NCAA regional semifinals that spring, then capped off his freshman year by being selected for the 1984 Olympic team, which was coached by Knight. He was the youngest player on the team, but he averaged 10.3 points and shot 64.4 percent for a Jordan-led team that won a gold medal in the Los Angeles games.

Alford was the first IU player to be named the team MVP four times. He averaged 22.5 points as a junior and 22 points as a senior. His career free throw percentage of 89.8 percent is eighth on the NCAA all-time list.

Alford hoped to be drafted by the in-state Indiana Pacers in the 1987 draft. So did the rest of the state. When the Pacers selected Reggie Miller with the 11th pick in the first round, the large crowd at the Pacers' draft party booed. Alford slipped to the second round, where the Dallas Mavericks selected him.

He spent four years in the NBA, but the coach's son seemed destined for a career in coaching. He eventually became a Division I head coach at Southwest Missouri, Iowa and New Mexico.

*Dickie V's View:* Steve Alford was a local kid from New Castle, Ind., who attended Bob Knight's camp since he'd been in the sixth grade, then committed early to play for the General. He became an All-American at Indiana and one of the great shooters in the history of college basketball. He loved the Newcastle arena so much that he even proposed to his wife, Tanya, there the summer before his senior campaign at Indiana.

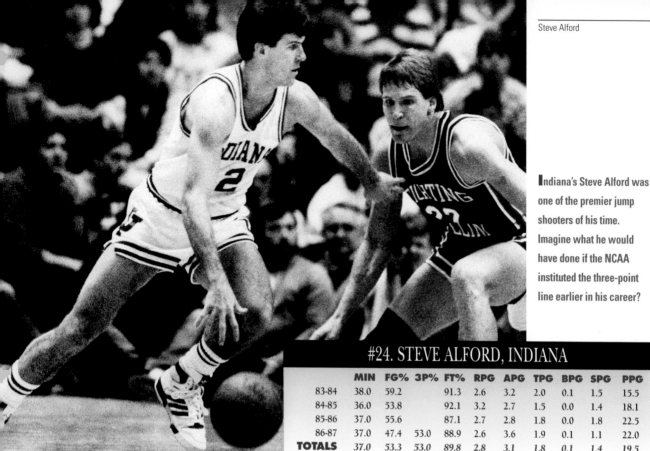

**I**ndiana's Steve Alford was one of the premier jump shooters of his time. Imagine what he would have done if the NCAA instituted the three-point line earlier in his career?

### #24. STEVE ALFORD, INDIANA

|        | MIN  | FG%  | 3P%  | FT%  | RPG | APG | TPG | BPG | SPG | PPG  |
|--------|------|------|------|------|-----|-----|-----|-----|-----|------|
| 83-84  | 38.0 | 59.2 |      | 91.3 | 2.6 | 3.2 | 2.0 | 0.1 | 1.5 | 15.5 |
| 84-85  | 36.0 | 53.8 |      | 92.1 | 3.2 | 2.7 | 1.5 | 0.0 | 1.4 | 18.1 |
| 85-86  | 37.0 | 55.6 |      | 87.1 | 2.7 | 2.8 | 1.8 | 0.0 | 1.8 | 22.5 |
| 86-87  | 37.0 | 47.4 | 53.0 | 88.9 | 2.6 | 3.6 | 1.9 | 0.1 | 1.1 | 22.0 |
| **TOTALS** | **37.0** | **53.3** | **53.0** | **89.8** | **2.8** | **3.1** | **1.8** | **0.1** | **1.4** | **19.5** |

Knight knew how valuable he was. When Alford d just completed his freshman year, he was asked try out for the 1984 Olympic team that won a gold edal in L.A. He made the squad because Knight eded somebody to knock down shots in case those ernational teams went zone. When Alford drove ck home with his parents after collecting his gold edal, there were billboards all over the state saluting n for his accomplishment. Trust me. They love eir basketball heroes in Hoosier Country.

Alford was the best I've seen in college at moving thout the basketball to get himself free for the shot. ice he got open, it was automatic. That motion me Knight ran at Indiana had Alford's name all over He was running guys into screens; then he would tch the ball and square up – you always felt the ball s going in.

And you were usually right. It did.

Playing for Bob Knight was not easy. Knight always demanded a lot from his players. During Alford's senior year, Michael Jordan ran into Knight at an airport and told him, according to a story in Alford's book, that he had bet Alford $100 he wouldn't last four years at IU.

"Tell him I owe him $100," Jordan said.

"The season's not over yet," Knight said, laughing.

Actually, Knight respected what Alford contributed to the program. After Indiana defeated Syracuse to win the 1987 national title, Knight was sitting on a chair next to his two sons and he motioned Alford to come over. Then he told Alford that he had gotten the most out of his eligibility.

Alford said Knight's comments meant so much to him that he was in tears.

# DUKE:  PLAYER NUMBER

## Shane Battier

6' 8"

220 pounds

Forward

1997-2001

*Profile:* Shane Battier had to be prodded into becoming the next Bill Bradley.

When the 6' 8" forward arrived at Duke from Detroit Country Day School in Birmingham, Mich., he brought along McDonald's All-American and Mr. Basketball pedigrees as well as an excellent academic reputation. But as a freshman and even as a sophomore, he deferred to upperclassmen and more assertive players, content to be that ultimate glue guy who played defense and made everyone else better with his fundamentally sound play – at times at his own expense.

After Duke lost to Connecticut in the 1999 NCAA Tournament championship game and four players – Elton Brand, Corey Maggette, William Avery and Trajan Langdon – left early for the NBA, Duke coach Mike Krzyzewski and assistant Quin Snyder knew it was time for a change. They told the unselfish Battier – a sophomore who had averaged just five shots as a freshman and scored in low double figures that year – it was time to step up his game.

Krzyzewski went one step farther, telling him to look in the mirror and visualize himself as the best player in the ACC.

Battier took that advice to heart.

He averaged 17.4 points, was a second-team All-American, a first team All-ACC selection and the NABC Defensive Player of the Year as a junior when Duke advanced to the Sweet 16 during a rebuilding year.

Then, as a senior, he took over college basketball. Battier averaged 19.9 points and 7.3 rebounds his final year, combining with fellow All-American Jason Williams to lead the top-ranked Blue Devils to an ACC regular-season and Tournament championship and the NCAA Tournament title. He swept all the major national player of the year awards, was the ACC Co-Player of the Year (along with Joseph Forte of North Carolina), the MVP of the ACC Tournament, the National Defensive Player of the Year for a third straight time and a first-team Academic All-American.

Battier played his best, most complete basketball during March Madness, averaging 22.5 points and 10.2 rebounds during the Blue Devils' six-game run. He scored 25 points in Duke's dramatic 22-point comeback victory over nemesis Maryland in the national semifinals at Minneapolis. Then he scored 18 points, grabbed 11 rebounds and contributed six assists as the Devils defeated Arizona in the finals. Battier, of course, was selected Most Outstanding Player of the Final Four. It was the perfect ending to a near-perfect career.

When Battier left Duke, he had scored 1,984 points, was first all-time in career steals, second in blocked shots and third in three-point field goals made. He also had a degree in religion.

Battier was selected by the Memphis Grizzlies with the sixth pick overall in the 2001 draft.

*Dickie V's View:* Belief is a powerful thing. Before Shane Battier entered his senior year at Duke, he wrote down a list of goals he wanted to accomplish:

"Making first-team All-American and Academic All-American. Winning a national championship. Becoming the national player of the year."

He did it all. And more.

Battier was so much more than just a great basketball player. He was a straight A student who conducted part of his interview with Duke's admissions director, Christopher Guttenburg, in German.

At Duke, Battier was a well-rounded student who had an interest in music, travel, religion and politics. He was one of my favorites of all time, one of the classiest kids I've ever been around.

There is no doubt that when Shane Battier takes the uniform off and goes to the real world, he's the kind of kid who might even do better than he did in the basketball world. There are no limits to where this kid can go. He could be the CEO of a Fortune 500 company. He could go into politics. Who knows? We could be looking at a future president of the United States. Mike Krzyzewski said he wanted to be head of the Senior Citizens for Battier if he runs in 2016. Battier said, if elected, he would appoint Coach K ambassador to Tahiti.

Hey, Digger worked for George Bush. Wonder if Shane has room for me in his cabinet?

Secretary of Hoops, baby.

I've always felt Shane Battier was a slam dunk for politics after his basketball career was over. He was one of the best defensive players I've seen in my 30 years calling basketball games.

## #25. SHANE BATTIER, DUKE

|  | MIN | FG% | 3P% | FT% | RPG | APG | TPG | BPG | SPG | PPG |
|---|---|---|---|---|---|---|---|---|---|---|
| 97-98 | 24.6 | 53.9 | 16.7 | 73.1 | 6.4 | 1.1 | 0.7 | 1.5 | 1.4 | 7.6 |
| 98-99 | 23.8 | 54.5 | 41.5 | 72.4 | 4.9 | 1.5 | 0.9 | 1.2 | 1.8 | 9.1 |
| 99-00 | 35.5 | 49.6 | 44.4 | 81.7 | 5.6 | 2.1 | 1.3 | 2.1 | 2.0 | 17.4 |
| 00-01 | 34.9 | 47.1 | 41.9 | 79.6 | 7.3 | 1.8 | 1.5 | 2.3 | 2.1 | 19.9 |
| **TOTALS** | 29.7 | 50.0 | 41.6 | 77.7 | 6.1 | 1.6 | 1.1 | 1.7 | 1.8 | 13.6 |

# ARIZONA:

**26**
PLAYER NUMBER

# Sean Elliott

6' 8"

220 pounds

Forward

1985-1989

**I** remember when Garf (Howard Garfinkel) told me about Sean Elliott. Garf was right on the money as Elliott led the Wildcats in scoring all four years.

*Profile:* Sean Elliott will always be known as Tucson's All-American.

The wiry 6' 8" forward grew up there and attended Cholla High Magnet School, where he averaged 31.3 points for a 24-3 team and was selected to play in the McDonald's All-American game.

As a sophomore in high school, he participated in Lute Olson's first summer camp at Arizona. Initially, he had no interest in signing with that Pac-10 program, which had been stuck at the bottom of the conference, even though his mother, Odiemae, went to college there.

Olson knew how good the young star could be after watching him work out against his players in summer pickup games at the Bear Down gym on campus.

Eventually he convinced Elliott that he could be a hometown hero and the linchpin for a dynasty in the desert. Elliott put his arm through a window and came within a fraction of an inch of cutting some ligaments just before the McDonald's game, preventing many big-name programs from seeing him in person, which turned out to be a benefit for Olson.

Elliott had a Magic Johnson-like influence on the program from the start. Elliott was arguably the best player in school history – a popular, accessible star who put the Wildcats on the national map. He was a two-time All-American and two-time Pac-10 Player of the Year who broke Kareem Abdul-Jabbar's old conference scoring record and was selected as the winner of the Wooden Award after his senior year in 1989.

Elliott led the Wildcats in scoring for all of his four years. He is still the school's all-time leading scorer with 2,555 points. He averaged 19.2 points, 6.1 rebounds and 3.4 assists in 133 games for a team that went to four straight NCAA Tournaments. He and teammate Steve Kerr led the Wildcats to a 35-3 record and their first Final Four in 1988.

After his junior year, Elliott thought seriously about turning pro. He changed his mind because he had played for the U.S. national team in the 1986 World Championships and wanted to play for the U.S. Olympic team. But John Thompson, the coach, cut him because he didn't think Elliott was aggressive enough on defense.

Elliott used that snub as motivation for a special senior year. He averaged 22.3 points for a Sweet 16 team and won six national player of the year awards.

*Dickie V's View:* Sean Elliott was a major coup for Lute Olson when he was building his program out in Arizona. He was a local, a big-time player out of the city of Tucson, and he chose to attend college right here in the desert.

One night, I remember the phone ringing. It was Howard Garfinkel, who had attended the McDonald's All-American game. "Dickie V," he said, "Get ready for your Diaper Dandies. And I'm going to give you one who's not getting a lot of PR because he was injured before the game.

"But you get ready, my friend, to talk about Sean Elliott."

Oh baby, was Garf on the money.

Elliott lived up to every single billing when he got to Arizona, setting the Pac-10's all-time scoring record when he was in school. He was a fantastic multi-talented guy who could break you down off the dribble. He had a great first step, but he also had a good touch and range on his jumper. He was like a point/forward. He had the mentality of a point guard, but the skill and mobility of a baseline player. And he helped lead the Wildcats to the first of Lute Olson's four Final Fours in 1988.

Elliott was selected by the San Antonio Spurs with the third pick overall in the 1989 draft and played in the league for 11 years. He played a big role in the Spurs' 1999 championship run, making a game-winning, 21-foot shot off his tiptoes to avoid going out of bounds against Portland in Game 2 of the Western Conference finals that became known as the "Memorial Day Miracle."

Shortly after the season, Elliott announced he had been playing despite having a kidney disease and he would require a transplant. He underwent surgery August 16 of that year, receiving a kidney from his brother. In March 2000, Elliott became the first player to return to the NBA after a kidney transplant. He retired the following year.

## #26. SEAN ELLIOTT, ARIZONA

|        | MIN  | FG%  | 3P%  | FT%  | RPG | APG | TPG | BPG | SPG | PPG  |
|--------|------|------|------|------|-----|-----|-----|-----|-----|------|
| 85-86  | 33.7 | 48.6 |      | 76.0 | 5.3 | 2.2 | 2.1 | 0.3 | 0.7 | 15.7 |
| 86-87  | 34.9 | 51.0 | 37.1 | 77.0 | 6.0 | 3.7 | 3.4 | 0.2 | 0.7 | 19.3 |
| 87-88  | 32.9 | 57.0 | 47.1 | 79.3 | 5.8 | 3.6 | 2.7 | 0.4 | 0.7 | 19.6 |
| 88-89  | 34.1 | 48.0 | 43.7 | 84.1 | 7.2 | 4.1 | 3.1 | 0.3 | 1.0 | 22.3 |
| TOTALS | 33.8 | 51.2 | 42.8 | 79.5 | 6.1 | 3.4 | 2.8 | 0.3 | 0.8 | 19.2 |

# NORTH CAROLINA:

**PLAYER NUMBER 27**

# Sam Perkins

6' 9"

235 pounds

Center

1980-1984

*Profile:* Sam Perkins may not have had the profile of teammates Michael Jordan and James Worthy when he played for the University of North Carolina, but the Tar Heels never could have won the 1982 national championship if he hadn't been on the court with them.

The long-armed 6' 9" Perkins – whose nickname was "Big Smooth" – was arguably the most consistent player ever to play for that perennial ACC power. He was a three-time All-American who averaged 15.9 points and 8.6 rebounds while never shooting less than 52 percent during his four-year career. Perkins helped lead the Tar Heels to three first-place finishes in the ACC, two Final Fours, an Elite Eight and a Sweet 16.

UNC coach Dean Smith knew he needed an established low post presence if he wanted to compete with Virginia and 7' 4" Ralph Sampson in the ACC. He found exactly what he was looking for when he signed Perkins out of Shaker High in Latham, N.Y., beating out Syracuse, UCLA, Houston and Notre Dame.

At the time, Perkins had played just two years of organized basketball. Perkins grew up in Brooklyn where he lived with his grandmother, Martha, a devout Jehovah's Witness, and his two sisters. As a child, he was a loner who didn't have enough confidence to play in the park, so he put up a makeshift hoop in his backyard – a milk crate tied to the bars covering the windows outside his boyhood home. The experiment did not last long. When the ball bounced off the bars, it made a terrible noise inside the house.

Perkins attended Tilden High but never went out for the team. He was discovered playing in a neighborhood tournament by Herb Crossman, a social worker who took him under his wing and taught him the nuances of the game. When Crossman received a job offer in Albany, he persuaded Perkins' grandmother to make him Perkins' legal guardian.

Perkins developed into a star in his new surroundings, making the McDonald's All-American game.

At Carolina, he had an instant impact as a freshman, when he was the MVP of the ACC Tournament. As a sophomore, he scored 25 points and grabbed 10 rebounds as the Tar Heels defeated Houston and Akeem Olajuwon in the national semifinals. He went on to become the co-captain of the 1984 Olympic gold medal team.

He was selected by the Dallas Mavericks with the fourth pick overall in the 1984 NBA draft.

*Dickie V's View:* Smooth. Smooth. Smooth. That's the way I'd describe North Carolina center Sam Perkins. On the surface, he must have appeared to be the third wheel on that 1982 team with Michael Jordan and James Worthy.

But the guy was fantastic.

When he was a senior in high school in upstate New York, they all wanted him, especially Syracuse. Oh, you have to believe Perkins had to break the heart of Jim Boeheim, who was salivating over the idea of having him in an Orange uniform. But when the Heels and Dean Smith come calling, that's a tough combo to beat.

Sam Perkins may not have received as much attention as Michael Jordan and James Worthy, but he was an important member of the North Carolina 1982 national championship team. Here he goes to the basket against Hall of Famer Akeem Olajuwon.

## #27. SAM PERKINS, NORTH CAROLINA

|  | MIN | FG% | 3P% | FT% | RPG | APG | TPG | BPG | SPG | PPG |
|---|---|---|---|---|---|---|---|---|---|---|
| 80-81 | 30.1 | 62.6 |  | 74.1 | 7.8 | 0.7 |  | 1.8 | 0.6 | 14.9 |
| 81-82 | 35.7 | 57.8 |  | 76.8 | 7.8 | 1.1 | 1.7 | 1.7 | 1.0 | 14.3 |
| 82-83 | 33.5 | 52.7 | 42.9 | 81.9 | 9.4 | 1.3 | 2.0 | 1.9 | 1.2 | 16.9 |
| 83-84 | 33.2 | 58.9 |  | 85.6 | 9.6 | 1.6 | 2.0 | 1.9 | 0.9 | 17.6 |
| **TOTALS** | **33.0** | **57.6** | ***42.9** | **79.6** | **8.6** | **1.2** | **1.4** | **1.8** | **0.9** | **15.9** |

*ACC used the three-point shot on an experimental basis starting in the 1982-83 season.

Perkins was 6' 9", had long arms and a wingspan that made him look bigger than seven feet. He blocked shots and was a good shooter who was perfect for Carolina's transition game in the secondary phase of Smith's fast break.

Perkins never cared about getting all the publicity, all he wanted to do was win. Therefore, playing with Michael Jordan and James Worthy, to Perkins, was a blessing. Remember, he went on to become a three-time All-American, a career double-figure scorer and a first round NBA draft pick.

This was simply another classic by the Michelangelo of college hoops, Dean Smith.

# PURDUE:

PLAYER NUMBER

## Glenn Robinson

6' 7"

225 pounds

Forward

1992-1994

*Profile:* Glenn Robinson picked up his nickname of "Big Dog" from the custodian at Roosevelt High School in Gary, Ind. The 6' 7" McDonald's All-American – who averaged 25.7 points, 14.6 rebounds and 3.8 blocked shots while leading his team to a state championship as a senior in 1991 – liked it so much, he had a picture of a scowling bulldog with a spiked collar tattooed on his chest.

The powerful Robinson was the pride of Gary, Ind., a downtrodden factory and refinery town outside Chicago with massive unemployment and crime rates. He never forgot where he came from while he lifted Purdue toward the top of the Big Ten standings.

Robinson sat out his freshman year because of academic issues. But once he became eligible, he made as big an impact as anyone in the history of the school. Robinson averaged 24.1 points as a sophomore – scoring 30 or more points seven times – and 9.2 rebounds for a less-than-balanced team that made it to the NCAA Tournament. He might have left for the NBA after that season, but he was upset when he made only second-team All-American.

When he was a junior, Robinson left no doubt who was the most dominant player in the country. He averaged 30.3 points and 10.1 rebounds, leading the country in scoring and becoming the first Big Ten player to lead the conference in both categories since 1978. He was a unanimous first-team All-American, Big Ten Player of the Year, and swept all the national player of the year awards, becoming the first Purdue player since John Wooden in 1932 to be named the best player in the country.

But just as importantly, he led Gene Keady's Boilermakers to their 19th Big Ten title, raising his level of play down the stretch.

With Purdue trailing Michigan by one point and just six seconds left in a road game at Ann Arbor, Robinson hit a running jumper at the buzzer to give the Boilermakers a 95-94 victory and a half-game lead in the Big Ten. Then he went off for 49 points against Illinois in the final game of the conference season to lock up the title.

Robinson also came up huge in the NCAA Tournament, scoring 44 points against Kansas in the Sweet 16 as the Boilermakers advanced to the Elite Eight.

When Robinson declared for the NBA after the season, he was a lock for the No. 1 pick. After being selected by the Milwaukee Bucks, his agent, Charles Tucker, asked for $100 million over 13 years. Bucks' owner Herb Kohl wound up giving him $68.15 million over 10.

*Dickie V's View:* I've always loved Gene Keady as a coach. He rarely had the best talent during his 25 years at Purdue. But when he retired in 2005, he had won six Big Ten championships and was awarded National Coach of the Year honors six times.

Despite that, sadly, none of his Boilermaker teams made it to the Final Four. That looked like it might change when he signed Glenn Robinson, a 6' 7" forward from Gary, who was the best prospect in the country.

Robinson came to Purdue with a big reputation – and he backed it up once he became

ademically eligible as a sophomore. He did a
umber on Connecticut in his college debut when he
ored 30 points and grabbed nine rebounds as the
ilermakers defeated the Huskies, 73-69, in the Hall
Fame Tip-Off Classic in Springfield, Mass.

Then he really really turned it on as a junior when
averaged more than 30 points and 10 rebounds.
led Purdue to the 1994 Big Ten title and carried
em all the way to the NCAA Elite Eight – scoring
points during an 83-78 victory over Kansas in the
utheast Regional semifinals in Knoxville.

Robinson went off for 30 points in the first half
one against the Jayhawks, who found out it was
arly impossible to guard him, especially when
8" teammate Cuonzo Martin was making a
hool-record eight three-pointers.

Robinson went on to be the first pick in the draft
at June. Once he got into the league, you heard
ople questioning his work ethic. I don't know
out the NBA; but in college, he was simply
nsational.

The Big Dog, Glenn Robinson,
was a scoring machine.
He led the nation with a 30.3
points per game average during
the 1993-94 campaign.

## #28. GLENN ROBINSON, PURDUE

| | MIN | FG% | 3P% | FT% | RPG | APG | TPG | BPG | SPG | PPG |
|---|---|---|---|---|---|---|---|---|---|---|
| 91-92 | | | | *Did Not Play* | | | | | | |
| 92-93 | 36.1 | 47.4 | 40.0 | 74.1 | 9.2 | 1.8 | 3.7 | 1.2 | 2.0 | 24.1 |
| 93-94 | 34.0 | 48.3 | 38.0 | 79.6 | 10.1 | 1.9 | 4.1 | 0.9 | 1.6 | 30.3 |
| **TOTALS** | *35.0* | *47.9* | *38.5* | *77.3* | *9.7* | *1.9* | *3.9* | *1.0* | *1.8* | *27.5* |

# HOUSTON:

PLAYER NUMBER

# Clyde Drexler

6' 7"

222 pounds

Forward

1980-1983

*Profile:* When Clyde Drexler was younger, nobody thought he could fly.

The 6' 7" Drexler was a self-described chubby pre-teen from the South Park neighborhood of Houston. He was too slow, couldn't jump and was constantly picked last in pickup games. But he reinvented himself, adopting a regimen of self-discipline and weight training that turned him into a sky walker with a 43-inch vertical leap.

As a senior, Drexler was an all-state selection at Sterling High who experienced success playing against older pro stars like Moses Malone and Robert Reid at Fonde Recreation Center, but he might have gone unnoticed on the recruiting scene. However, guard Michael Young, a teammate at Sterling, told a University of Houston assistant that Drexler was the best player he had faced that year.

Drexler signed with the Cougars. He went on to become "Clyde the Glide," the president of Phi Slamma Jamma, Houston's fabled, make-believe fraternity of high fliers.. He helped lead the Cougars to two consecutive Final Four appearances, losing to heavy underdog North Carolina State in the 1983 championship game.

Drexler – who, when he was with the Portland Trail Blazers, once dunked on an 11' 1" rim – was known as a great finisher and an acrobatic dunker. He was the most versatile player ever to wear a U of H uniform and the only Cougar to accumulate more than 1,000 points, 900 rebounds, 300 assists and 250 steals in his career.

Drexler averaged 15.2 points and 10.5 rebounds as a sophomore when Houston advanced to the Final Four for the first time since 1968. He was a first-team All-American and the MVP of the old Southwest Conference, averaging 15.9 points, 8.8 rebounds and 3.8 assists while shooting 53.6 percent and 73.7 percent from the line for a balanced 31-3 team that advanced to the NCAA championship game.

Drexler scored 22 points as Phi Slamma Jamma defeated a descendent of Louisville's Doctors of Dunk in a wild national semifinal dunkfest at The Pit in Albuquerque.

Houston might have won the title if Drexler hadn't picked up a fourth personal foul late in the first half against NC State and was of limited use during the second half of a 54-52 loss.

Drexler declared for the NBA draft after the season. He always wanted to play for the hometown Rockets, which had the first and third picks in the draft. He wound up being selected by Portland in the first round with the 14th pick overall. Eventually, he did return to Houston and won an NBA title there.

*Dickie V's View:* Clyde Drexler was one of the original high risers. He had that David Thompsonesque jumping ability. He was so explosive. He could change the complexion of the game with a momentous dunk.

When Drexler was at Houston, he was part of the Phi Slamma Jamma fraternity with Akeem Olajuwon and Michael Young. He was involved in that wild dunkathon against Louisville in the 1983 national semifinals at "The Pit" in Albuquerque. The Houston Cougars of Guy V. Lewis were a joy to watch. Their running and dunking styles were reminiscent of Louisville's Doctors of Dunk.

How ironic was it that they displayed a dunking show against the Cardinals in the 1983 semifinal game?

College basketball had entered the 21st century.

The negative, of course, is that Houston lost to NC State in the championship game and never had a chance to put on the gold ring.

But Drexler took Houston fans on some flights no one will ever forget.

Clyde Drexler was a high flier for the Houston Cougars. Here he tries to score on a Seton Hall opponent. Phi Slamma Jamma was an impressive group in the '80s.

## #29. CLYDE DREXLER, HOUSTON

|  | MIN | FG% | 3P% | FT% | RPG | APG | TPG | BPG | SPG | PPG |
|---|---|---|---|---|---|---|---|---|---|---|
| 80-81 | 33.1 | 50.5 |  | 58.8 | 10.5 | 2.6 | 1.9 | 0.9 | 1.9 | 11.9 |
| 81-82 | 33.7 | 56.9 |  | 60.8 | 10.5 | 3.0 | 2.9 | 1.1 | 3.0 | 15.2 |
| 82-83 | 34.9 | 53.6 |  | 73.7 | 8.8 | 3.8 | 2.7 | 0.5 | 3.3 | 15.9 |
| TOTALS | 33.9 | 53.8 |  | 64.3 | 9.9 | 3.2 | 2.5 | 0.9 | 2.8 | 14.4 |

# OHIO STATE:

## Jimmy Jackson

6' 6"

220 pounds

Guard/Forward

1989-1992

*Profile:* In many ways, Jimmy Jackson will always be considered the savior of Ohio State basketball in the post-Jerry Lucas era – a big-name, in-state recruit from Toledo who made the Buckeyes relevant again on the national stage after almost two decades of silence.

Jackson was a man-child. He was already 6' 2" and could dunk in the seventh grade. He was 6' 5" and 200 pounds when he was a high school freshman at Macomber-Whitney High School. Jackson became a four-year starter, a McDonald's All-American who averaged 27 points as a senior, and was named Mr. Basketball after leading Macomber to the Ohio state championship.

Ohio State assistant Randy Ayers, understanding the importance of keeping Jackson home, had recruited him hard for three years. Jackson narrowed his choices to two schools – Ohio State and Syracuse. On the day of his announcement, he couldn't resist tweaking Ayers. "Coach," he said during a phone call, "I've made my decision. I'm going to Syracuse."

Before Ayers could slam down the phone, Jackson told him he was only kidding.

The joke was on the rest of the Big Ten once Jackson arrived and Ayers took over for Gary Williams, who left for Maryland. Jackson could play three positions. He was strong enough to lead his team in rebounding as a junior and skilled enough to be a three-point threat.

The combination was lethal.

Jackson was the Big Ten Freshman of the Year, a two-time Big Ten Player of the Year, a two-time first-team All-American and the UPI National Player of the Year in 1992. He averaged 19.2 points and 5.9 rebounds, scoring 1,785 points during an abbreviated three-year career. He led the Buckeyes to Big Ten championships his sophomore and junior years in 1991 and 1992 and three consecutive NCAA Tournament appearances.

Jackson averaged 22.4 points and 6.8 rebounds as a junior when the Buckeyes made their strongest run in the NCAA Tournament since Ohio State made a Final Four appearance in 1968. Ohio State, which had beaten Michigan twice during the regular season, had to face the Fab Five again in the Southeast Regional final. Jackson scored 20 points, but the Wolverines bothered him with pressure, forcing him into nine turnovers during a 75-71 overtime loss.

Jackson declared for the draft after the season and was selected by Dallas with the fourth pick overall.

*Dickie V's View:* When Gary Williams was coaching Ohio State, he once said the Big Ten is state vs. state competition. You had to control your state in recruiting to have a shot to win that league.

When Fred Taylor was coaching Ohio State, he locked up Jerry Lucas and John Havlicek, and the Buckeyes won a national championship in 1960 and went to two more Final Fours. Ohio State got back to the Final Four in 1968 with Bill Hoskett and then made more waves nationally when they signed Clark Kellogg.

All of them were high school legends.

Jimmy Jackson fell into that same category when

he played for Macomber-Whitney High in Toledo. He was the best prospect to come out of the state in more than a decade. He had the body of a hard-nosed linebacker but he had soft hands and a great feel for the game.

Ohio State had fallen out of the conference picture, behind Indiana, Purdue, Iowa and Illinois. The school was desperate for a player who could turn it around. Maybe that's why they spent four years recruiting Jackson.

When Jackson signed with Ohio State, everything changed. He led them to a pair of Big Ten titles and took the Buckeyes to the Elite Eight in 1992 against Michigan's Fab Five.

I used to love doing Jackson's games at St. John Arena in Columbus. He always loved the big stage and the spotlight on him. It was almost like watching a star in concert, á la Bon Jovi, Bruce Springsteen or Beyoncé. I guess you get the picture my friends. Jimmy Jackson was a flat-out college superstar.

## #30. JIMMY JACKSON, OHIO STATE

|  | MIN | FG% | 3P% | FT% | RPG | APG | TPG | BPG | SPG | PPG |
|---|---|---|---|---|---|---|---|---|---|---|
| 89-90 | 34.5 | 49.9 | 35.6 | 78.5 | 5.5 | 3.7 | 3.2 | 0.5 | 1.3 | 16.1 |
| 90-91 | 32.0 | 51.7 | 33.3 | 75.2 | 5.5 | 4.3 | 3.2 | 0.8 | 1.8 | 18.9 |
| 91-92 | 35.4 | 49.3 | 40.7 | 81.1 | 6.8 | 4.0 | 3.4 | 0.3 | 1.7 | 22.4 |
| TOTALS | 34.0 | 50.3 | 37.6 | 78.4 | 5.9 | 4.0 | 3.3 | 0.5 | 1.6 | 19.2 |

Jimmy Jackson put Ohio State basketball back on the Big Ten map. Here he goes to the basket against rival Michigan. Jackson averaged 22.4 points per game during his final season as a Buckeye.

DUKE: PLAYER NUMBER

# Bobby Hurley

6' 0"

165 pounds

Guard

1989-1993

*Profile:* Bobby Hurley was the classic gym rat, a gritty point guard who tested his skills on the inner city playgrounds of beaten down Jersey City. He got to learn from and play for his father, Bob Sr., who transformed St. Anthony's High – which did not even have a home gymnasium and had to practice in the Bingo Hall down the street – into one of the great high school programs in history.

The 6' 0" Hurley, who played on four consecutive state championships in high school and was a McDonald's All-American, always wanted to play for North Carolina. But Dean Smith was more interested in Kenny Anderson of Archbishop Molloy at the time and Hurley didn't want to wait, jumping at the chance to sign with rival Duke when Mike Krzyzewski visited his home.

He rapidly became Krzyzewski's coach on the floor, a four-year starter who averaged 12.4 points and 7.7 assists for his career. He played a major role on national championship teams in 1991 and 1992 and helped his team make three trips to the Final Four. At the time, he set NCAA records for career assists (1,076) and total assists in the NCAA Tournament (145).

Hurley's first trip to the Final Four was a medical disaster. Duke advanced to the finals against powerful UNLV; but Hurley, then just a freshman, fell victim to a stomach flu the night before the title game and was all but useless against Rebel pressure, shooting zero for three with five turnovers in 32 minutes during an embarrassing 103-73 beat down.

Hurley used that loss as motivation when the

Blue Devils played top-ranked 34-0 Vegas again the next year in the national semifinals. He played a near-perfect game, draining a three-point jumper – that Duke historian Bill Brill claimed was "the bigge[st] shot" in school history – to cut a 76-71 Vegas lead t[o] two and ignite a rally that gave the Blue Devils a 79-77 victory. Duke won its first national title two days later, defeating Kansas, 72-65, in the finals.

Hurley came up even bigger in the 1992 NCAA Tournament when he was selected Most Outstanding Player of the Final Four as Duke completed the double. He scored 26 points in an 81-78 victory over Indiana in the national semifina[l] and then helped fuel a 71-51 victory over another Big Ten team, Michigan, in the finals.

His senior year didn't quite have the fairy tale ending he hoped for with Duke losing to Cal in the second round, but he had his number retired and w[as] selected by Sacramento with the seventh pick overa[ll] in the 1993 NBA draft.

*Dickie V's View:* I don't know about you, but I just love gym rats, man. And Bobby Hurley was on[e] of the best.

He was the ultimate point guard, the guy who made it happen. He probably got that way from playing for his dad, Bob Sr., at St. Anthony's, and Mike Krzyzewski at Duke – two of the most intense competitors you could ever meet.

He brought that street toughness with him to Duke where he teamed with Christian Laettner and Grant Hill to lead the Blue Devils to two straight

national championships in 1991 and 1992. He was the perfect Mike Krzyzewski point guard. He was all about winning.

The big rap on him when he arrived in the ACC was that he couldn't make perimeter shots. Hurley made himself one of the leading three-point shooters in the history of Duke basketball. He made one of the most important trifectas in Blue Devil basketball when he drilled a three against Vegas that cut a 76-71 UNLV lead to two. Duke gained momentum at that moment and pulled off the big upset in the 1991 tournament semifinal game.

There's one thing I'll always remember about Bobby Hurley: Duke was getting ready to play North Carolina during the regular season his senior year. The day before the game, in practice, there's a loose ball and he's diving on the floor for it. I said to him, "Bobby, has anybody told you that you made the team?"

And he simply said, "That's just the way I play." I guess playing for his dad, who, to me, should be a member of the Naismith Basketball Hall of Fame for his scholastic achievements at St. Anthony's, and playing for Mike Krzyzewski will teach you how to be tenacious.

**Bobby Hurley was like a coach on the floor for Mike Krzyzewski. Here he drives past Indiana's Greg Graham during the 1992 Final Four. Duke ended up winning consecutive national championships in 1991 and '92.**

## #31. BOBBY HURLEY, DUKE

|  | MIN | FG% | 3P% | FT% | RPG | APG | TPG | BPG | SPG | PPG |
|---|---|---|---|---|---|---|---|---|---|---|
| 89-90 | 33.4 | 35.1 | 35.7 | 76.9 | 1.8 | 7.6 | 4.4 | 0.0 | 1.8 | 8.8 |
| 90-91 | 34.7 | 42.3 | 40.4 | 72.8 | 2.4 | 7.4 | 3.9 | 0.1 | 1.3 | 11.3 |
| 91-92 | 33.6 | 43.3 | 42.1 | 78.9 | 2.0 | 7.6 | 3.5 | 0.0 | 1.1 | 13.2 |
| 92-93 | 35.6 | 42.1 | 42.1 | 80.3 | 2.6 | 8.2 | 3.4 | 0.0 | 1.5 | 17.0 |
| **TOTALS** | 34.3 | 41.0 | 40.5 | 77.6 | 2.2 | 7.7 | 3.8 | 0.0 | 1.5 | 12.4 |

# CALIFORNIA:

## Jason Kidd

6' 4"

212 pounds

Guard

1992-1994

*Profile:* Jason Kidd is generally considered the best point guard ever to come out of the Bay area and the player who put Cal basketball back on the map.

He was a middle school prodigy who was fixated on Magic Johnson and learned how to play the position from Gary Payton, a future NBA All-Star from the neighborhood who was four years older than Kidd and took him under his wing. Kidd would take the bus from upper-middle-class Oakland Hills downtown and accompany Payton to play in pickup games in the rough and tumble Oakland city playgrounds.

He learned how to survive and thrive, discovering that passing the ball was the best way to get into the games against older players.

A two-time California player of the year, Kidd led St. Joseph's in Alameda to a pair of California state championships. He was selected national prep player of the year after averaging 25 points, 10 assists and 4.9 rebounds as a senior. He was so big, St. Joseph's wound up moving some of its most important games out of its 1,800-seat high school gym and into Oakland Arena, playing before crowds of 15,000.

The 6' 4" physically mature Kidd could have gone anywhere. But he pulled a major surprise when he chose Cal – which was coming off a 10-18 season and had not won a Pac-10 title since 1959 – over Kentucky, Ohio State, Arizona and Kansas.

Kidd immediately injected renewed excitement into the Cal program. Despite a potentially turbulent freshman year that was marked by a coaching change midway through the year, Kidd led the Bears to two wins over bitter Pac-10 rival Stanford. He was

ected first-team All-Pac-10 and National eshman of the Year after averaging 13 points, 7.7 ists and 4.9 rebounds and leading the Bears to the 93 NCAA Tournament. Kidd has two highlight oments there, making game-winning shots against U and defending national champion Duke as Cal vanced to the Sweet 16.

He was even better the next season, averaging .7 points, 6.9 rebounds and an eye-popping assists, breaking his own school record while ding the Bears back to a second consecutive NCAA urnament appearance. He was the first sophomore win the Pac-10 Player of the Year and the first l player to be named a consensus first-team -American since Darrell Imhoff in 1960.

Kidd declared for the draft after the season and s selected by Dallas with the second pick overall.

*ckie V's View:* I had heard about Jason Kidd en he played for St. Joseph's High School in meda, Calif., which is located outside the city Oakland. He had a pro body coming out of high ool. In fact, when I see LeBron James and how ong and thick his body is, it brings back memories Jason Kidd when he made the transition to college.

And he played with such an air of confidence.

With Jason, from the moment I met him, I felt he s The Man when he had the ball in his hands. He s in total control because of his ability to handle e rock and make other players better. He had great ion, an incredible flair for the game and was very ong with the basketball. He was great in the open or, willing to attack the basket and was incredible at breaking people down and creating opportunities for others in terms of three-on-two or two-on-one situations.

Did you check out his assist totals at Cal? He averaged 7.7 assists as a freshman and 9.1 as a sophomore. I can see why he was selected to be the point guard on the U.S. gold-medal winning team in Beijing. What makes Kidd a special point guard is he always thinks pass first, shoot second and always strives to get his teammates an open, easy look.

Back then, I remember being really excited to see him play in person. ESPN actually did a Cal game when he was there. Normally, we're not doing Cal games, but everything changed after he arrived. He brought so much excitement to the Bay area.

## #32. JASON KIDD, CALIFORNIA

|         | MIN  | FG%  | 3P%  | FT%  | RPG | APG | TPG | BPG | SPG | PPG  |
|---------|------|------|------|------|-----|-----|-----|-----|-----|------|
| 92-93   | 31.8 | 46.3 | 28.6 | 65.7 | 4.9 | 7.7 | 3.9 | 0.3 | 3.8 | 13.0 |
| 93-94   | 35.1 | 47.2 | 36.2 | 69.2 | 6.9 | 9.1 | 4.3 | 0.3 | 3.1 | 16.7 |
| **TOTALS** | 33.5 | 46.8 | 33.3 | 67.7 | 5.9 | 8.4 | 4.1 | 0.3 | 3.5 | 14.9 |

Jason Kidd was a special player coming out of high school. He lived up to his billing, helping revitalize the California Golden Bears basketball program.

# INDIANA: 33

PLAYER NUMBER

## Calbert Cheaney

6' 7"

209 pounds

Small

Forward/

Big Guard

1989-1993

*Profile:* Calbert Cheaney is the classic example of a player who maximized his skills under the demanding Hall of Fame coach Bob Knight. He was a good high school player at William Henry Harrison High in Evansville, Ind. But because he broke his foot midway through his senior year, he was the least acclaimed player in IU's top-ranked recruiting class of 1989, which included Lawrence Funderburke, Chris Lawson, Pat Graham, Greg Graham and Chris Reynolds.

Knight, who scouted Cheaney in a high school game against Jasper where he shot just six for 32 and his team lost badly, initially didn't think Cheaney was good enough to play in the Big Ten. He had to be convinced by some of his assistants, who watched Cheaney play that summer, to become involved in recruiting Cheaney again.

It was a wise decision.

Four years later, in 1993, the smooth lefthander with the near-perfect stroke, insatiable work ethic and a nearly unstoppable mid-range game that was perfect for Knight's motion offense, swept all 12 national player of the year awards. He led his team to Big Ten championships, in 1991 and 1993, 105 career victories – the most of any Hoosier – and a trip to the 1992 Final Four.

Cheaney, a three-time All-American and four-time IU MVP, led IU in scoring for four straight years. He scored 30 or more points 13 times and averaged 19.8 points for his career. He finished with 2,613 points, leaving Bloomington as the all-time leading scorer in school and Big Ten history – a record that still stands. IU was ranked in the top 10 in 51 of his final 53 weeks and might have won a national championship in 1993 if 6' 10" sophomore forward Alan Henderson

hadn't torn his ACL in practice. Henderson attem to make a comeback in the post-season, but he w never the same player.

As it was, Cheaney, the Big Ten MVP, averaged 22.4 points as a senior and led the 31-4 Hoosiers victory in the preseason NIT, a sweep of Michiga and a 17-1 first-place finish in the Big Ten. IU wa ranked No. 1 in the AP poll most of the year and reached the regional final before Kansas took advantage of the lack of Henderson's inside scori and defense to eliminate the Hoosiers, 83-77.

Cheaney eventually was selected by the NBA Washington Bullets with the sixth pick overall in 1993 draft.

*Dickie V's View:* Calbert Cheaney got less hyp than the rest of Bob Knight's number one-ranked 1989 recruiting class at Indiana. He had missed half of his senior season in high school because o broken foot and he came in with all those McDor All-Americans.

But after four years, he turned out to be one o best players in school history. He was a great shoo a pure scorer who became a three-time All-Ameri National Player of the Year in 1993 and the schoo all-time leading scorer. He played on a couple of Big Ten championship teams and one that went t Final Four in 1992.

What made him special? Consistency. Consistency. Consistency.

Every game, man, you knew you were going t get a solid yeoman's job out of him, and he was g to put points on the board. When the game starte you knew you were going to get 20 from Calbert Cheaney.

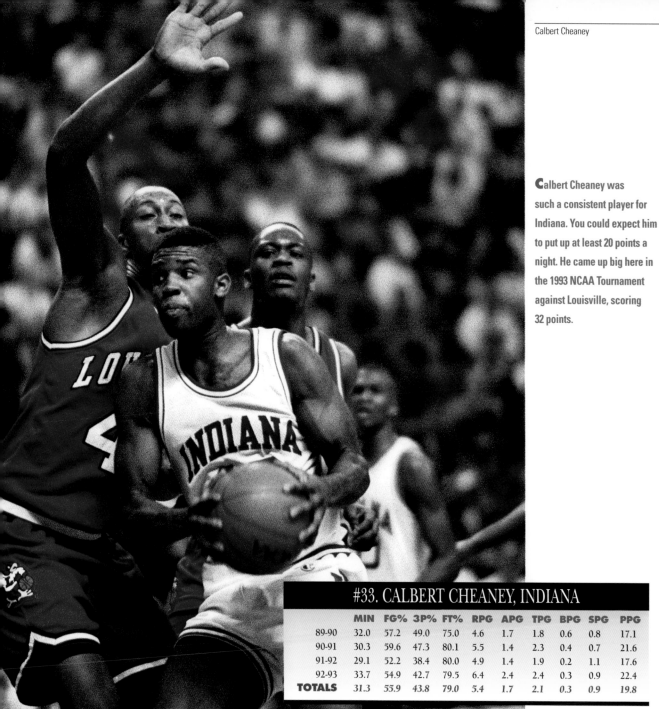

Calbert Cheaney was such a consistent player for Indiana. You could expect him to put up at least 20 points a night. He came up big here in the 1993 NCAA Tournament against Louisville, scoring 32 points.

### #33. CALBERT CHEANEY, INDIANA

|         | MIN  | FG%  | 3P%  | FT%  | RPG | APG | TPG | BPG | SPG | PPG  |
|---------|------|------|------|------|-----|-----|-----|-----|-----|------|
| 89-90   | 32.0 | 57.2 | 49.0 | 75.0 | 4.6 | 1.7 | 1.8 | 0.6 | 0.8 | 17.1 |
| 90-91   | 30.3 | 59.6 | 47.3 | 80.1 | 5.5 | 1.4 | 2.3 | 0.4 | 0.7 | 21.6 |
| 91-92   | 29.1 | 52.2 | 38.4 | 80.0 | 4.9 | 1.4 | 1.9 | 0.2 | 1.1 | 17.6 |
| 92-93   | 33.7 | 54.9 | 42.7 | 79.5 | 6.4 | 2.4 | 2.4 | 0.3 | 0.9 | 22.4 |
| TOTALS  | 31.3 | 55.9 | 43.8 | 79.0 | 5.4 | 1.7 | 2.1 | 0.3 | 0.9 | 19.8 |

I sing his praises because of his work ethic. He [w]as a lot like Steve Alford in that respect. He really, [re]ally made the most out of the system – learning [h]ow to utilize screens to free himself up, a lost art [n]owadays.

When Cheaney broke the Big Ten career scoring record against Northwestern his senior year at Assembly Hall, the General actually broke with tradition and stopped the game so the fans could recognize it. Knight felt a great kid had achieved a great honor.

# GEORGETOWN:

**PLAYER NUMBER**

## Allen Iverson

6' 0"

165 pounds

Guard

1994-1996

*Profile:* Allen Iverson has been known as "The Answer" ever since he was a dual-sport star on two state championship teams in football and basketball at Bethel High in Hampton, Va. But Iverson was a child of poverty, and his life temporarily spun out of control, leaving questions about his future before Georgetown coach John Thompson stepped in to offer assistance and a measure of stability.

Iverson was involved in a huge 1993 bowling alley fight between two groups of teenagers that escalated out of control. He was only 17 at the time, but was convicted as an adult on a felony charge of "maiming by mob" and spent four months in jail before then-Virginia Governor Douglas Wilder granted him clemency, releasing him from his sentence. The conviction was later overturned on appeal, but the damage was done. Iverson's mother, Ann, called Thompson and asked him to find a refuge for her son. Thompson offered Iverson a scholarship but told him he would send him home if he did not comply with the strict coach or the school's honor code.

The compact Iverson was an art major who painted beautiful pictures on the court, quickly emerging as the most exciting and fearless guard ever to play for the Hoyas.

He was a prolific scorer who was blessed with super quickness and a killer crossover dribble. He was selected Big East Rookie of the Year as a freshman, when he averaged 20.4 points, and led Georgetown to the Sweet 16 in 1995.

Then he shifted his game into another gear, averaging 25 points, 4.7 assists and 3.4 steals as a sophomore when he became a consensus first-team All-American on a team that terrorized the Big East and advanced to the NCAA East Regional final before losing to UMass.

Iverson's game could be wild and reckless at times, but he set school single-season records for points, steals and three-pointers. He was also a two-time Big East Defensive Player of the Year.

When he declared for the NBA draft at the end of the season to help his family financially, he left as the Hoyas' all-time leader in career scoring percentage, averaging 23 points per game.

The Philadelphia 76ers, who won the lottery, thought enough of his immense talent to select him first overall.

*Dickie V's View:* John Thompson was always a great father figure for kids, especially ones like Allen Iverson, who needed some guidance, some direction after he got into that bowling alley fight in Virginia and spent time in jail.

Thompson was an authority figure Iverson could look up to once he came to Georgetown. I have great respect for people who want to give others second chances. Come on. Life is complicated at times. Everyone makes mistakes – some bigger than others. If people get another chance, you have to hope they take advantage of it.

Iverson did.

He became a star at Georgetown, went on to the NBA after two years and became a multi-multi-millionaire.

I went to see him play early in his career with the Hoyas. Jerry West and all the scouts were there, scouting him. I remember thinking this kid must be special. Five minutes into the game, I understood why they were in the building.

Iverson was so quick and such a great athlete. Did you know he was a superb high school quarterback from the Tidewater, a big-time football hotbed in southern Virginia?

They tell me when he rolled out with a football you may as well forget about it. It was Touchdown City, baby.

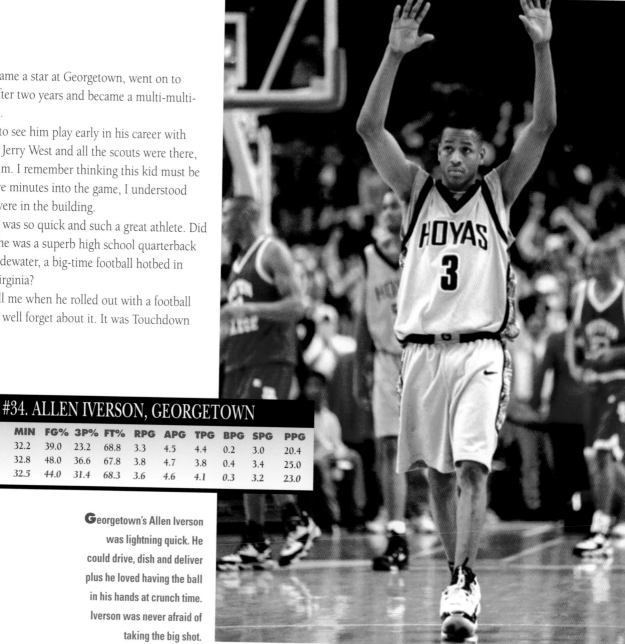

## #34. ALLEN IVERSON, GEORGETOWN

|        | MIN  | FG%  | 3P%  | FT%  | RPG | APG | TPG | BPG | SPG | PPG  |
|--------|------|------|------|------|-----|-----|-----|-----|-----|------|
| 94-95  | 32.2 | 39.0 | 23.2 | 68.8 | 3.3 | 4.5 | 4.4 | 0.2 | 3.0 | 20.4 |
| 95-96  | 32.8 | 48.0 | 36.6 | 67.8 | 3.8 | 4.7 | 3.8 | 0.4 | 3.4 | 25.0 |
| TOTALS | 32.5 | 44.0 | 31.4 | 68.3 | 3.6 | 4.6 | 4.1 | 0.3 | 3.2 | 23.0 |

Georgetown's Allen Iverson was lightning quick. He could drive, dish and deliver plus he loved having the ball in his hands at crunch time. Iverson was never afraid of taking the big shot.

# MICHIGAN:

**PLAYER NUMBER 35**

# Chris Webber

6' 9"

245 pounds

Forward

1991-1993

*Profile:* Chris Webber was the most highly re-cruited prospect in the state of Michigan since Earvin "Magic" Johnson. The powerful 6' 9", 245-pound forward from Detroit Country Day School in Birmingham, led his team to three consecutive state championships. He was a McDonald's All-American who was selected the national high school player of the year.

When he chose Michigan over Kentucky, Duke, Minnesota and in-state rivals Detroit and Michigan State, he changed the culture of sport forever at that Big Ten school.

Webber entered Michigan with the best class in school history – center Juwan Howard and guards Jalen Rose, Jimmy King and Ray Jackson. Together, they became known as the "Fab Five". They made history as the first team with five freshman starters to reach the NCAA Final Four, advancing to the championship game in 1992 and again as sophomores in 1993.

Webber was the self-appointed leader of this hip hop, trash-talking pack, a 1993 consensus first-team All-American who powered his way to 15.5 points and 10.0 rebounds, becoming the first freshman to lead the Big Ten in that category. He led the young Wolverines to an overtime 75-71 upset of Big Ten champion Ohio State in the Southeast Regional finals. Michigan lost to Duke in the championship game, but Webber made the Final Four all-tournament team.

Webber took his game to the next level as a sophomore when he averaged 19.2 points and 10.1 rebounds for a 31-5 team that advanced to another final, this time against North Carolina.

The game was close, but Webber made an infamous mistake that haunted him for the rest of his career. With Michigan trailing 73-71, Webber called a timeout with 11 seconds left when his team didn't have any remaining, resulting in a technical foul that clinched the title for the Tar Heels.

Webber declared for the NBA after the season and became the first sophomore since Magic Johnson in 1979 to be selected with the first pick overall when the Orlando Magic drafted him.

His legacy as one of Michigan's all-time greats seemed secure until an investigation into gambling activities involving a Michigan booster, the late Ed Martin, turned up evidence that Martin had supplied Webber and three other Michigan players – Robert Traylor, Maurice Taylor and Louis Bullock – with $616,000 in illicit loans.

Due to concerns that Webber's amateurism had been compromised, Michigan forfeited its 1992 national semifinal victory over Cincinnati as well as its national runner-up status in the 1992 tournament. It also forfeited the entire 1992-1993 season. The school deleted Webber's records from its record book. The NCAA also ordered Michigan to disassociate itself from Webber until 2012.

*Dickie V's View:* It's hard to know how history will judge Chris Webber. Was he the 19-year-old freshman who was the star of the 1992 Fab Five, the most exciting team in Michigan history? Or is he the guy who called that timeout he didn't have in the 1993 national championship game and later had all his records wiped out because of his association with the late Ed Martin?

I do know this: From a pure basketball standpoint, when Webber was on the floor, he was a dominating shot blocker and a physical presence on the interior.

Having recruited in the Motor City when I was the head coach of the University of Detroit, many of my old friends couldn't wait to call me about this future superstar when he arrived at Detroit Country Day.

I remember getting a phone call from an avid Michigan alum and a personal friend of mine, Rocky Ross. He was screaming over and over again how Webber would be a future college All-American.

Hey Garf, watch out. This guy's after your job as an evaluator of talent because he was right, baby.

Webber was the catalyst for the Fab Five, who created a brand name for themselves with the baggy pants, the black sneakers and their trash-talking, chest-bumping attitude. It's incredible – five freshmen playing as a unit in the Big Ten, going to the Final Four. They had such confidence and felt they could play with anybody from the moment they arrived in Ann Arbor. Based on the results, you would have to say that members of the Fab Five were right on target with their feelings.

Certainly, he was tainted by the scandal and I know he was hurt when the NCAA ordered Michigan to disassociate itself from him. He still loves Michigan and I'm sure deep down if he had a chance to do it over again, things might have turned out a little differently.

**C**hris Webber was the most highly recruited player from the state of Michigan since Magic Johnson. He was a force inside as part of the Fab Five, changing the culture in Ann Arbor.

### #35. CHRIS WEBBER, MICHIGAN

|  | MIN | FG% | 3P% | FT% | RPG | APG | TPG | BPG | SPG | PPG |
|---|---|---|---|---|---|---|---|---|---|---|
| 91-92 | 31.9 | 55.6 | 25.9 | 49.6 | 10.0 | 2.2 | 2.8 | 2.5 | 1.6 | 15.5 |
| 92-93 | 31.8 | 61.9 | 33.8 | 55.2 | 10.1 | 2.5 | 2.9 | 2.5 | 1.4 | 19.2 |
| **TOTALS** | 31.8 | 58.9 | 30.6 | 53.0 | 10.0 | 2.4 | 2.9 | 2.5 | 1.5 | 17.4 |

## WICHITA STATE:

# Xavier McDaniel

6' 7"

205 pounds

Forward

1981-1985

*Profile:* In his own way, Xavier McDaniel, a.k.a. "The X Man," made just as big an impact in the Missouri Valley Conference in the early 1980s as Michael Jordan did in the ACC.

McDaniel, who was a first-team All-American in 1985, averaged 18.4 points and 11.6 rebounds while shooting 56.4 percent during a brilliant four-year career with Wichita State. He was an aggressive physical presence, and was the first player in NCAA history to lead the nation in scoring and rebounding. He averaged 27.2 points and 14.8 rebounds during his senior year in 1985.

The bald-headed McDaniel was a fierce rebounding machine who also led the country with 14.4 rebounds as a sophomore in 1983 – even though Patrick Ewing, Akeem Olajuwon and Ralph Sampson were still playing college ball.

McDaniel was a two-time Valley Player of the Year as a junior and senior and a three-time All-MVC, upstaging two of the greatest players to wear Wichita State uniforms – Antoine Carr and Cliff Levingston.

McDaniel came to Wichita State from A.C. Flora High in Columbia, S.C., where he combined with future DePaul star Ty Corbin to lead his team to a state championship in 1980. As luck would have it, Wichita State's football coach at the time, Jeff Jeffries, had an assistant who lived across the street from McDaniel's family. McDaniel liked the idea of playing with Carr and Levingston.

But the euphoria didn't last long.

*Photo Courtesy of Wichita State Sports Information.*

When McDaniel was a freshman, he averaged just 8 points and considered transferring because he isn't getting enough playing time. Midway through that season, the NCAA hammered Wichita State ? 44 violations, ruling the Shockers ineligible for st-season play that year and the next. Levingston clared for the NBA at the end of the 1982 season, d center Greg Dreiling transferred to Kansas. But rr and McDaniel stayed and combined to lead the ockers to a 25-3 record in 1983. In 1985, Wichita ate returned to the NCAA Tournament after a o-year post-season ban.

McDaniel took over in 1984, averaging 20.6 ints and 13.1 rebounds as a junior, before leading e Shockers to a Missouri Valley Tournament ampionship and an automatic bid to the NCAA urnament his senior year.

He left with 2,152 career points and 1,359 career bounds and was selected by Seattle with the fourth ck overall in the 1985 draft.

*ickie V's View:* When Xavier McDaniel signed th Wichita State in 1981, he thought he would be rt of a budding Midwest dynasty.

The Shockers were returning five of their top ven players from a 26-7 team that had big-time lent – including bookend forwards Antoine Carr d Cliff Levingston. They had beaten Kansas and lvanced to the 1981 NCAA Midwest Regional finals. ley had added two more local stars – 7' 1' center

Greg Dreiling and guard Aubrey Sherrod. But the NCAA had put them on two years' probation, and McDaniel spent most of his career in limbo. Even though Wichita State went 23-6 and 25-3 his freshman and sophomore years, they couldn't play in the post-season tournament.

But that didn't stop McDaniel from making a reputation for himself. "The X Man" had super powers, baby. He led the country in scoring once and rebounding twice as a sophomore and senior and he led his team to an NCAA appearance in his final year in 1985.

## #36. XAVIER MCDANIEL, WICHITA STATE

| | MIN | FG% | 3P% | FT% | RPG | APG | TPG | BPG | SPG | PPG |
|---|---|---|---|---|---|---|---|---|---|---|
| 81-82 | 13.5 | 50.4 | | 62.8 | 3.7 | 0.5 | 0.9 | 0.2 | 0.4 | 5.8 |
| 82-83 | 35.3 | 59.3 | | 54.1 | 14.4 | 1.5 | 2.8 | 1.0 | 0.8 | 18.8 |
| 83-84 | 37.7 | 56.4 | | 68.0 | 13.1 | 2.4 | 3.3 | 1.3 | 1.2 | 20.6 |
| 84-85 | 36.9 | 55.9 | | 63.4 | 14.8 | 2.2 | 3.2 | 1.0 | 1.5 | 27.2 |
| **TOTALS** | *31.1* | *56.4* | | *62.4* | *11.6* | *1.7* | *2.6* | *0.9* | *1.0* | *18.4* |

The X Man, Xavier McDaniel, made Wichita State a power in the Missouri Valley Conference. McDaniel led the nation in both scoring and rebounding during the 1984-85 season.

# CONNECTICUT:

PLAYER NUMBER

# Ray Allen

6' 5"

205 pounds

Forward/
Guard

1993-1996

*Profile:* Ray Allen got a taste of Hollywood when he co-starred with Denzel Washington in Spike Lee's movie *He Got Game* – playing the role of Jesus Shuttlesworth, a heavily recruited blue chip prospect from Brooklyn who has to choose between doing the right thing or material gain when selecting a college.

In real life, the 6' 5" Allen took a different path to stardom at Connecticut. He was a military brat whose father was an Air Force mechanic. The family spent time living on bases in California, England, Germany, Oklahoma and South Carolina.

Allen has seen much of the world. He used to watch the space shuttle land at Edwards Air Force Base and saw the changing of the guard at Buckingham Palace. A friend once sent him a small piece of the Berlin Wall after it came down. He was the best player at Shawir Air Force Base in Dalzell, S.C., in ninth grade. By his junior year in high school, he was the best prospect in the state.

Allen, who led Hillcrest High to the state championship in 1993, was recruited heavily by Kentucky. But he chose Connecticut because he liked the coaches and they promised him it would be his program after two years.

Actually, it took only one.

After UConn's 6' 8" junior All-American forward Donyell Marshall declared for the pros after a Sweet 16 run in 1994, Allen became the first option offensively for this Big East team as a sophomore. He responded by making first-team All-American as a sophomore after scoring 21.1 points, grabbing 6.8 rebounds and contributing 2.3 assists for a team that won the 1995 Big East regular-season title and advanced to the NCAA West Regional finals, before

losing to eventual champion UCLA in a game where Allen scored 36 points.

Allen, the best pure shooter ever to play for Jim Calhoun, was even more productive the next year, when he made first-team All-American for a second straight season. He was also named Big East Player of the Year after averaging 23.4 points, 6.5 rebounds and 3.3 assists while shooting 46.6 percent from three-point range and making 81 percent from the line for a 31-3 team that won 23 straight at one point. Allen, who set a school single-season record with 115 threes that year, punctuated his season by making the game-winning shot as the Huskies rallied from 11 points down in the final four minutes to defeat Georgetown, 76-75, in a dramatic Big East Tournament final at the Garden.

UConn fell short of making the Final Four, losing to Mississippi State in the Sweet 16, but Allen's legacy was cemented with three Big East regular-season titles and 1,922 career points.

He was selected by Minnesota with the fifth pick overall in the 1996 draft.

*Dickie V's View:* Ray Allen was the best player ever at UConn.

I spoke at a big banquet when he was senior at Hillcrest High School in Dalzell, S.C., and everybody was raving about him. To be honest with you, I had some doubts because I had not seen him. My biggest question: Why is this kid – if he's that good – leaving South Carolina and the SEC, going all the way up to Connecticut and the Big East?

Not that Connecticut wasn't a national power, but many times, down South, a great player never gets

he chance to leave home. Later, I heard Rick Pitino
f Kentucky had shown interest in him.

When I first saw him play in college, I could
nderstand why Jim Calhoun was so excited when
e signed him. He had the great bounce off the floor
nd a quick release shooting the basketball. He just
emed to understand how to play. He had a positive
titude, which was reflected by his mental
ughness.

He played in the Big East at the same time as
erry Kittles of Villanova and Allen Iverson of
eorgetown. You just stood around and watched
ose three in awe. They all had that star charisma.
l of them were first-round draft picks.

Allen went on to get a shot at Hollywood,
pearing with Oscar winner Denzel Washington,
ho plays his father, in Spike Lee's 1998 movie
e Got Game. Washington played freshman ball for
. Carlesimo at Fordham and has become a mega,
ega movie star, while Allen became one of the best
ree-point shooters in the history of the NBA. Wash-
gton, one of my favorite actors of all time, loves
oops and has been an avid supporter of one of my
orite groups, the Boys and Girls Clubs of America.

Hey, baby, I wonder if they talked any hoops
ile they were on the set.

I can't believe it. I had a little cameo in the movie
Got Game and I wasn't even nominated for "Best
pporting Actor." Also, you can take it to the bank
at my check didn't match Raymond's.

**R**ay Allen came to Connecticut from the state of
South Carolina. Coach Jim Calhoun was happy that
he came north. Allen was arguably the best pure
shooter to play for the Hall of Fame coach.

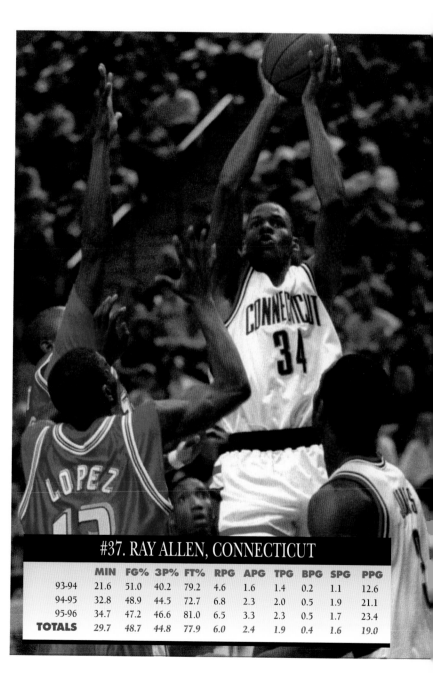

## #37. RAY ALLEN, CONNECTICUT

|       | MIN  | FG%  | 3P%  | FT%  | RPG | APG | TPG | BPG | SPG | PPG  |
|-------|------|------|------|------|-----|-----|-----|-----|-----|------|
| 93-94 | 21.6 | 51.0 | 40.2 | 79.2 | 4.6 | 1.6 | 1.4 | 0.2 | 1.1 | 12.6 |
| 94-95 | 32.8 | 48.9 | 44.5 | 72.7 | 6.8 | 2.3 | 2.0 | 0.5 | 1.9 | 21.1 |
| 95-96 | 34.7 | 47.2 | 46.6 | 81.0 | 6.5 | 3.3 | 2.3 | 0.5 | 1.7 | 23.4 |
| **TOTALS** | 29.7 | 48.7 | 44.8 | 77.9 | 6.0 | 2.4 | 1.9 | 0.4 | 1.6 | 19.0 |

# BRADLEY:

PLAYER NUMBER

# Hersey Hawkins

6′ 3″

190 pounds

Guard

1984-1988

*Profile:* Hersey Hawkins was the most prolific scorer in Bradley history, scoring 3,008 points in his four-year career, exploding for 30 or more points 37 times and setting the all-time Missouri Valley Conference individual game scoring record, with 63 points against Detroit in 1988.

He wasn't Oscar.

Who was?

But he left an indelible imprint as a two-time Valley Player of the Year, and a first-team All-American and National Player of the Year in the 1988 season when he led the country in scoring, averaging 36.3 points per game – surpassing Oscar Robertson's 35.1 point average in 1957-58.

Not bad for a high flying, undersized center from Westinghouse High in Chicago who played for the late coaching legend Frank Lollino Sr. Lollino – who coached four NBA players, including Mark Aguirre – had to convince Bradley coach Dick Versace that Hawkins had skills that would translate into the college game.

Versace, a long-time Chicago high school coach, arranged to go to the vocational school to watch Hawkins in a private practice. Other than the coaches and players, he was the only one in the gym. Versace watched Hawkins play guard for two hours, apologized for ever doubting him, and then signed him.

"The Hawk" soared as soon as he suited up in Peoria, leading the Braves to MVC regular- season and tournament titles – in 1986 under Versace and

in 1988 under coach Stan Albeck. Hawkins had his coming-out party as a sophomore, averaging 18.7 points as the Braves climbed into the top 10, finishe 16-0 during the Valley regular season, then advance to the second round before losing to eventual national champion Louisville.

Hawkins almost left after that season. Before the start of his junior year, Versace resigned after the NCAA hit the program with sanctions. Former Bradley player Albeck replaced him. Hawkins nearl transferred to Villanova. Albeck convinced him to stay, even though Bradley would be ineligible for post-season play, by promising him that he would play up tempo and utilize Hawkins' three-point ski Hawkins went off, averaging 27.2 points as a junior before staging his grand finale as a senior, when he scored more than 50 points twice and more than 4( nine times.

Hawkins was the best pure shooter on the 1988 Olympic team, which won a bronze medal in South Korea. He was selected by the Los Angeles Clippers with the sixth overall pick in the 1988 NBA draft, then traded to the Philadelphia 76ers.

*Dickie V's View:* Hersey Hawkins was a flat out, prolific big-time scorer. Dick Versace was a Nationa Coach of the Year when he was at Bradley during Hawkins' early years. Versace was always singing the praises of Hawkins, especially about his unique way of putting points on the board. I guess Dick should know. He used to coach on the high school level in

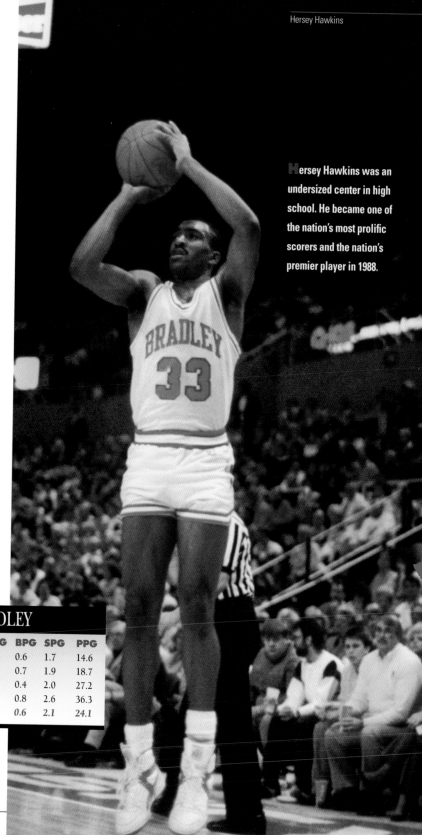

he city of Chicago, and he's seen all the superstars
that came through the Public League there.

Versace started a pipeline from that city with
Mitchell Anderson. He had to be convinced to take
Hawkins because he was a center in high school. But
Hawkins made the transition to big guard.

Versace was always talking about The Hawk's
ability to score in a variety of ways. He scored deep
and around the basket. He had more ways to score
than Baskin-Robbins has flavors. In his senior season,
e averaged more than 35 points a game and had 37
0-point games in his career. I ask you, my friends,
ould you label him a scoring machine?

Mr. Versace was right on the money in describ-
ing his PTPer. To put it very bluntly, you needed a
omputer to tally Hawkins' point totals.

Hawkins played in the Missouri Valley
onference, which had great tradition, especially
ack in the '50s when Bradley was ranked No. 1
nd Oscar Robertson – The Big O – played for
incinnati. Let me tell you, when you talk about
rsatility, nobody in the history of the game could
ore, rebound, pass and dominate a game like The
g O. But The Hawk flew almost as high.

**Hersey Hawkins was an undersized center in high school. He became one of the nation's most prolific scorers and the nation's premier player in 1988.**

## #38. HERSEY HAWKINS, BRADLEY

| | MIN | FG% | 3P% | FT% | RPG | APG | TPG | BPG | SPG | PPG |
|---|---|---|---|---|---|---|---|---|---|---|---|
| 84-85 | 37.4 | 58.1 | | 77.1 | 6.1 | 2.7 | 2.1 | 0.6 | 1.7 | 14.6 |
| 85-86 | 36.9 | 54.2 | | 76.8 | 5.7 | 3.0 | 2.0 | 0.7 | 1.9 | 18.7 |
| 86-87 | 38.0 | 53.3 | 28.7 | 79.3 | 6.7 | 3.6 | 3.4 | 0.4 | 2.0 | 27.2 |
| 87-88 | 39.1 | 52.4 | 39.4 | 84.8 | 7.8 | 3.6 | | 0.8 | 2.6 | 36.3 |
| **TOTALS** | 37.8 | 53.9 | 35.9 | 80.6 | 6.5 | 3.2 | 2.5 | 0.6 | 2.1 | 24.1 |

*Photo Courtesy of Bradley University.*

# LA SALLE:

PLAYER NUMBER

## Lionel Simmons

6' 7"

210 pounds

Forward

1986-1990

*Profile:* La Salle built its basketball tradition on the backs of great players like 1955 National Player of the Year and Naismith Hall of Famer Tom Gola, the late Kenny Durrett and the 1980 National Player of the Year, Michael Brooks.

No one expected Lionel Simmons to join that elite group.

When Simmons was a 6' 5" senior at Philadelphia's Southern High, he had an early interest in Villanova, but the coaching staff there wasn't sure that he could make the transition from center to small forward. Eventually, Simmons chose the Explorers over Boston College, Old Dominion and Big 5 rival, Temple.

He became a local hero as soon as he stepped onto the 20th and Olney campus. "The L Train" led La Salle, then a member of the Metro Atlantic Athletic Association, to the 1987 NIT championship game and three consecutive trips to the NCAA Tournament. He averaged 24.6 points and 10.9 rebounds during his four-year career, finishing with 3,217 points – third in NCAA history behind Pete Maravich of LSU (3,667) and Freeman Williams of Portland State (3,249).

Simmons, who recalls being the last player selected in pickup games on the local playground, escaped from a violent, drug-infested neighborhood to become a perfect role model in his own backyard. He had a chance to turn pro after his junior year when he averaged 28.4 points and 11.4 rebounds for a 26-6 NCAA team.

His coach, Speedy Morris, said he was contacted by one NBA team that promised to draft Simmons and guaranteed a four-year contract worth $2 million. When Morris told Simmons, it took him only a moment to respond. "That's an awful lot of money," Simmons told Morris. "But I told my mother I would graduate."

He did, with a degree in criminal justice, but not before he led the Explorers to their best season since 1969, when La Salle was ranked second in the country.

Simmons, who had expanded his skills to become a three-point threat who could lead his team on the break in Morris' up tempo offense, averaged 26.5 points, 11.1 rebounds, 3.6 assists and two blocks as a senior, shooting 51.3 percent from the field and 47.7 percent from three-point range for a 30-2 team that also included future NBA prospects Doug Overton and Randy Woods, and reached the second round of the NCAA Tournament. He was a first-team All-American and received both the Wooden and Naismith National Player of the Year awards.

He was selected by the Sacramento Kings with the seventh pick overall in the 1990 draft.

*Dickie V's View:* I can still remember when I was younger, reading all about the teams in Philly – La Salle, Villanova, St. Joseph's, Penn and Temple. Man, doubleheaders at the Palestra were special.

And I couldn't wait to make a visit to the Palestra. I went down there with a buddy of mine. We didn't have tickets, but somehow we managed to get in to

watch Penn vs. Princeton and the Senator, Mr. Bill Bradley.

I also remember going to Philly to see Calvin Murphy and his offensive talents hook up against the great ball zone of Jack Kraft and Villanova in the first round of the 1970 NCAA Tournament.

The Big 5 always had great coaches – Dr. Jack Ramsay, Harry Litwack, Jack Kraft, Chuck Daly, Rollie Massimino and John Chaney – and current stars like Phil Martelli of St. Joe's, Jay Wright of Villanova and Fran Dunphy of Temple.

Each of those teams took a turn going to the Final Four and they all had big stars before the birth of the Big East.

Lionel Simmons is a big part of that tradition – a local kid from the Philadelphia Public League who stayed in his backyard and became an All-American playing for Speedy Morris.

Simmons was such a prolific scorer at La Salle. He scored more than 3,000 points in his career. He was a big name, a special player – like past La Salle greats Tom Gola, Kenny Durrett and Michael Brooks – and he gave that school a lot of national publicity when he was named National Player of the Year in 1990.

**W**hen the L-Train was coming, you knew it was going to be a long night. La Salle's smooth forward could beat you in so many ways.

## #39. LIONEL SIMMONS, LA SALLE

|  | MIN | FG% | 3P% | FT% | RPG | APG | TPG | BPG | SPG | PPG |
|---|---|---|---|---|---|---|---|---|---|---|
| 86-87 | 38.0 | 52.6 | 33.3 | 76.3 | 9.8 | 1.8 | 2.8 | 1.4 | 1.6 | 20.3 |
| 87-88 | 39.0 | 48.5 | 25.0 | 75.7 | 11.4 | 2.5 | 2.9 | 2.3 | 2.1 | 23.3 |
| 88-89 | 38.9 | 48.7 | 37.5 | 71.1 | 11.4 | 3.0 | 2.9 | 1.9 | 1.7 | 28.4 |
| 89-90 | 38.1 | 51.3 | 47.7 | 66.1 | 11.1 | 3.6 | 2.8 | 2.0 | 1.9 | 26.5 |
| **TOTALS** | *38.5* | *50.1* | *41.5* | *72.2* | *10.9* | *2.7* | *2.9* | *1.9* | *1.8* | *24.6* |

# NORTH CAROLINA:

**40**

PLAYER NUMBER

## Brad Daugherty

6' 11"

254 pounds

Center

1982-1986

*Profile:* When Brad Daugherty entered North Carolina in 1982, he was such a huge NASCAR fan, he wanted to wear No. 43 on his uniform because it was his high school number and the same number his idol, Richard Petty, wore.

Daugherty lost a coin flip with freshman teammate Curtis Hunter for that opportunity and ended up wearing No. 42. But he soon got over that disappointment.

The 6' 11" center from Charles D. Owen High in Black Mountain, N.C., methodically developed under Dean Smith into one of the best big men in North Carolina's rich history. Daugherty averaged 14.2 points, 7.4 rebounds while shooting 62 percent – a school record. He was a two-time first-team All-ACC selection and a consensus first-team All-American.

Daugherty took an unusual path to stardom. He grew up on a 50-acre farm with his family – which also included his cousins and his grandmother – in a mountain town near Asheville. There were cattle and horses; his father also raised pigs.

Daugherty also grew up with a love of racing. His father and uncle built hot rods, which they raced every Sunday night on an old half-mile stretch on the side of the mountain near where he lived. One of the biggest thrills of his youth was traveling to Daytona with his father and meeting Richard Petty.

Daugherty was a manager on the student basketball team as a 10th grader before he was convinced to try out. Carolina recruited him for his potential. When he arrived on campus, he was only 16 years old and weighed a hefty 254 pounds. Smith originally planned to redshirt him. But after forward James Worthy declared early for the draft, Daugherty was plugged into the starting lineup.

It took Daugherty time to adjust; but once assistant coach Roy Williams got him in shape, he started to blossom in the post-Michael Jordan era, averaging 17.3 points and 9.7 rebounds as a junior in 1985 and 20.2 points and nine rebounds while shooting 64.8 percent his senior year. Carolina won 111 games and three ACC regular-season championships during Daugherty's career. Unfortunately, he had the dubious distinction of being part of the first class since 1966 not to make an appearance at the Final Four.

The Philadelphia 76ers thought enough of him to make him the first pick overall, ahead of Len Bias, in the 1986 draft.

*Dickie V's View:* Brad Daugherty was a great team player at Carolina who went on to become the first pick in the draft.

That's why I think so many players who come out of the Dean Smith system go on to put up big numbers in the NBA. Jordan, Worthy, Perkins, Daugherty – they all learned so much about the fundamentals of the game and how to play within the team concept. Daugherty really knew how to play the low post.

Everything just seemed to come so easily for him. When the night ended, you never realized how many points and rebounds he had until you peeked at the score sheet and saw those 20 points and 10 rebounds staring back at you.

He was a country kid who grew up on a farm in the mountains of North Carolina and was really into NASCAR. Daugherty used to do college basketball for ESPN, but he left us for one of his real loves and now is a star analyst for ABC and ESPN in breaking down

Brad Daugherty was tough to stop inside. He later went on to be the No. 1 overall pick in the NBA draft and a future owner in NASCAR.

## #40. BRAD DAUGHERTY, NORTH CAROLINA

|  | MIN | FG% | 3P% | FT% | RPG | APG | TPG | BPG | SPG | PPG |
|---|---|---|---|---|---|---|---|---|---|---|
| 82-83 | 23.3 | 55.8 | 0.0 | 66.3 | 5.2 | 0.9 | 1.5 | 1.0 | 0.3 | 8.2 |
| 83-84 | 27.4 | 61.0 |  | 67.8 | 5.6 | 1.4 | 1.9 | 1.0 | 0.6 | 10.5 |
| 84-85 | 34.7 | 62.5 |  | 74.2 | 9.7 | 2.1 | 2.9 | 1.3 | 0.8 | 17.3 |
| 85-86 | 32.0 | 64.8 |  | 68.4 | 9.0 | 1.8 | 2.3 | 1.1 | 1.0 | 20.2 |
| **TOTALS** | **29.4** | **62.0** | ***0.0** | **70.0** | **7.4** | **1.6** | **2.1** | **1.1** | **0.7** | **14.2** |

*ACC used the three-point shot on an experimental basis starting in the 1982-83 season.*

...ties of all the drivers on the NASCAR circuit. ...'m not a pedal-to-the-metal guy, but I did get the ... of him once on the basketball court. We were ...g a game together for ESPN at Georgia Tech and ...s on the court with him, getting the crowd really ...ted. So I started backing him down one-on-one

and I said, "I want to you to block this." So I flipped up this crazy underhand shot and it went in, and the crowd went absolutely bananas.

He said to me, "Let's try this again."

And I said, "Uh, uh. One time is enough for me, baby."

# MICHIGAN:

PLAYER NUMBER

# Glen Rice

6' 7"

215 pounds

Forward

1985-1989

*Profile:* When Glen Rice returned to the University of Michigan's Crisler Arena to have his No. 41 retired at halftime of a game against Indiana in 2005, he gave the crowd a quick history lesson.

"This is the house that Cazzie Russell built," the Wolverines' 6' 7" former star forward said. "I appreciate being able to occupy a room in it."

He deserved a wing of his own after capping off his senior year by leading a talented Wolverines' team – with four future NBA first-round picks – to the 1989 national championship.

Rice came to Michigan from Northwestern High in Flint, Mich., where he had been voted the first Mr. Basketball in that city's history after averaging 28.6 points as a senior for a team that won its second consecutive state Class A championship.

Rice went from a slender outside shooter to a lethal offensive scoring machine who averaged 18.2 points and 6.4 rebounds during his career and led the Big Ten in scoring his junior and senior years, averaging 22.1 and 25.6 points. In his four years, Rice never shot less than 55 percent. He shot 57.7 percent from the field, 51.6 percent from the three and made 83.2 percent from the line as a senior when he was selected a unanimous first-team All-American.

But Rice will always be remembered for his run in the NCAA Tournament when he averaged 30.7 points and became the single-season scoring leader in tournament play with 184 points, breaking Bill Bradley's 24-year-old record at Princeton. Bradley scored 177 in five games.

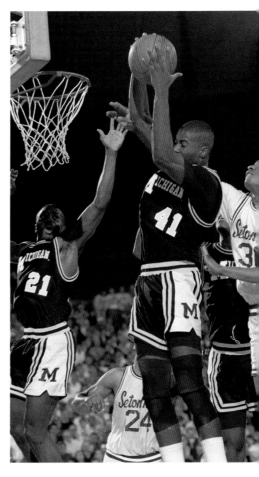

Rice created a security blanket for interim coach Steve Fisher, who replaced Bill Frieder just before the start of the tournament. He scored 23 points in first-round 92-87 scare against Xavier, then shot 10 for 22 during a 36-point explosion against South Alabama. Rice made eight threes and scored 34 points during a Sweet 16 victory over North Carolina

team that had eliminated the Wolverines from the
urnament two years running. He scored 32 points
an easy 102-65 victory over Virginia in the regional
als. He had 28 as Michigan – which had lost to Big
n rival Illinois twice during the regular season –
nned the Illini, 83-81, in the national semifinals.
en he finished up with 31 points and 11 rebounds
ring an 80-79 overtime victory over Seton Hall in
finals.

Overall, Rice made 27 of his 49 three-point
empts in March Madness. "That's as fine a six-
ne-under-pressure exhibition of big-time shooting
I've ever witnessed," Fisher said. "When he missed,
u kind of blinked and said, `Did he really miss?'"

To the surprise of none, Rice was voted the Most
utstanding Player in the Final Four.

Miami selected him with the fourth pick in the
89 draft.

*ickie V's View:* Most people think that most of
e prime-time players come from big cities like
w York, Chicago and Los Angeles. But what about
nt, Mich.? That city has had its problems in the
st with a depressed economy, but it's more than just
e backdrop for the movie *Roger and Me.* The city
s produced an assembly line for great basketball
ent.

Glen Rice of Michigan was one of the first
ime-time players to come out of Flint. I'm not
ocked that he arrived in Ann Arbor. Bill Frieder
s a superstar high school coach in Flint before
became the head coach of the Wolverines, and

therefore had many contacts in the Flint area. And
there is no one I have ever met who worked as
tenaciously as he did in the recruiting battles.

When he was after you, the race was usually over.

Rice, you just knew, was going to wind up
wearing the colors of the Maize and Blue.

He had a fantastic senior year in college and an
even more historic 1989 NCAA Tournament, when
the Wolverines cut the nets down.

I wasn't sure what would happen after athletic
director Bo Schembechler – Mr. Football in Ann
Arbor – changed coaches just before the start of
March Madness. Schembechler replaced Frieder with
Fisher when word got out that Frieder was accepting
the head coaching job at Arizona State.

Fisher made the most of his golden opportunity.
Rice was on fire as he averaged 30 points per game
during the tournament and also had 31 points in the
championship game when the Wolverines defeated
my alma mater, Seton Hall, for the national title.

Hail to the Victors, baby.

**G**len Rice put on a show
during the 1989 NCAA
Tournament. He was a
scoring machine as the
Wolverines edged Seton
Hall to win the national
championship. Rice had
31 points in the title game.

## #41. GLEN RICE, MICHIGAN

| | MIN | FG% | 3P% | FT% | RPG | APG | TPG | BPG | SPG | PPG |
|---|---|---|---|---|---|---|---|---|---|---|
| 85-86 | 16.3 | 55.0 | | 60.0 | 3.0 | 0.7 | 0.9 | 0.2 | 0.4 | 7.0 |
| 86-87 | 33.0 | 56.2 | 25.0 | 78.7 | 9.2 | 2.4 | 2.1 | 0.5 | 0.4 | 16.9 |
| 87-88 | 35.0 | 57.1 | 42.9 | 80.6 | 7.2 | 2.8 | 2.1 | 0.3 | 1.1 | 22.1 |
| 88-89 | 34.0 | 57.7 | 51.6 | 83.2 | 6.3 | 2.3 | 2.2 | 0.3 | 1.1 | 25.6 |
| **TOTALS** | 29.8 | 56.9 | 48.0 | 79.7 | 6.4 | 2.0 | 1.8 | 0.3 | 0.8 | 18.2 |

# GEORGIA TECH:

PLAYER NUMBER

## Kenny Anderson

6' 2"

168 pounds

Guard

1989-1991

*Profile:* When Marty Blake, the NBA's director of scouting, boldly predicted that Kenny Anderson would be the most exciting point guard to hit college basketball in 50 years, who could argue?

Anderson, who grew up on the playgrounds of LeFrak City in Queens and attended Archbishop Molloy, was a four-time All-New York City selection and the first player since Kareem Abdul-Jabbar to make the Parade All-American team three years running. He set a New York state record for career scoring with 2,621 points that stood for 18 years, even though he was held out of the first quarter of games his freshman year by his coach, Jack Curran.

Everyone knew Anderson would be a star in college.

The only question was where.

Most expected Anderson to follow in the footsteps of former Molloy star Kenny Smith and attend North Carolina or sign with Syracuse, which had made great inroads in recruiting this area.

But he surprised everyone when he chose Georgia Tech. Anderson, a McDonald's All-American, liked the idea of playing for Bobby Cremins, who promised to give him the freedom he wanted to run a team.

Over the next two years, the 6' 2" slightly built Anderson became known as "The Wizard of Ahhs" to Tech fans because of his flair for the game.

He was the starting point guard as a freshman on the Yellow Jackets' first Final Four team in 1990, combining with 6' 8" wing Dennis Scott and 6' 4" guard Brian Oliver to form "Lethal Weapon Three." All three players averaged more than 20 points per game.

Anderson, a first-team All-ACC pick as a freshman and the National Freshman of the Year, averaged 20.6 points, 5.5 rebounds and 8.1 assists in his first year. He made an historic jumper at the buzzer against Michigan State in the Sweet 16 to force the game into overtime – which Tech won to keep its hopes of a national title alive. Who knows? If Anderson had not picked up four fouls in the national semifinal matchup against UNLV, Tech mig[ht] have been the national champion.

Anderson's star shone even brighter the followin[g] year – out of necessity. Scott left for the pros and Oliver graduated, leaving Anderson, who was force[d] to generate offense by himself. He responded by averaging 25.9 points, 5.7 rebounds and 5.6 assists for the Jackets, going off for a school-record 50 poi[nts] during a 135-94 victory over Loyola Marymount in which he shot 18 for 27 and made eight threes. He made first-team All-American.

Anderson, who promised his mother he would stay in school for two years, declared for the draft after the season, which ended with a second-round NCAA loss.

He was selected by the Nets with the second pic[k] overall that June.

*Dickie V's View:* Bobby Cremins coached three great point guards at Georgia Tech – Mark Price, Stephon Marbury and Kenny Anderson. They all made All-American.

But only one – Anderson – led the Yellow Jackets to a Final Four. And he did it as a freshman. Anderson, no doubt about it, was the catalyst for

hat team. He came to Tech from Archbishop Molloy
Queens, where he played for the legendary high
chool coaching superstar Jack Curran. Curran also
oached Kenny "The Jet" Smith – who went on to
an All-American at North Carolina before an
ustrious NBA career. Now Smith sits with host
nie Johnson and sidekick Charles Barkley having
blast talking about the game he dearly loves.

Hey, let's get back on track, baby. Anderson
emed destined to become a star from the time he
as in ninth grade. The two years at Georgia Tech
ere just further proof.

I'll never forget doing a Tech game on ESPN when
nderson was show time. I mean, he was going
rough his legs, behind his back. It was incredible,
man. And I was running out of adjectives to describe
him.

I ran into Bill Cosby later that year at Madison
Square Garden and he said to me, "Wow. I love that
kid from New York City and Georgia Tech, Dick. I
was getting a big kick out of it. He was shaking and
baking big time."

Wow. You had to be pretty good to impress
The Cos.

**K**enny Anderson came out
of Archbishop Molloy High
School in New York City with
an incredible amount of hype.
He lived up to that billing as a
star guard for Bobby Cremins'
Yellow Jackets.

### #42. KENNY ANDERSON, GEORGIA TECH

|  | MIN | FG% | 3P% | FT% | RPG | APG | TPG | BPG | SPG | PPG |
|---|---|---|---|---|---|---|---|---|---|---|
| 89-90 | 37.7 | 51.5 | 41.0 | 73.3 | 5.5 | 8.1 | 4.0 | 0.1 | 2.3 | 20.6 |
| 90-91 | 38.9 | 43.7 | 35.1 | 82.9 | 5.7 | 5.6 | 3.8 | 0.1 | 3.0 | 25.9 |
| **TOTALS** | 38.3 | 47.3 | 37.4 | 78.7 | 5.6 | 7.0 | 3.9 | 0.1 | 2.6 | 23.0 |

# CONNECTICUT:

## Richard Hamilton

6' 6"

185 pounds

Guard

1996-1999

*Profile:* Richard "Rip" Hamilton never had to worry about watching himself in action. His father, "Big Rip," videotaped every one of his games beginning with the seventh grade and has a library of more than 400 tapes that are stored in his Coatesville, Pa., home.

The lean 6' 6" Hamilton, who drew comparisons to Reggie Miller in college, created his own highlight film at Connecticut where he became a master of the mid-range game, a two-time All-American, and won at least a piece of the Big East Player of the Year award twice. As a junior, he led the Huskies to their first national championship in 1999.

Hamilton had always been overshadowed by Kobe Bryant of neighboring Lower Merion when he played for Coatesville. But he joined Bryant in the McDonald's All-American game and then stepped into the limelight at UConn.

Hamilton became an immediate starter as a freshman, averaging 25 points during a six-game NIT run when the Huskies, going through a rare rebuilding cycle, reached the finals of that post-season tournament.

As a sophomore, he became a star, averaging 21.5 points for a team that won the Big East regular season and advanced to the 1998 NCAA East Regional finals. He made the game-winning 12-foot shot at the buzzer of a 75-74 victory over Washington in the Sweet 16. Carolina knocked the Huskies out of the tournament two nights later.

Hamilton got the inspiration to take his game to a higher level from his late grandfather, Edward, a former steel worker, who had become seriously ill with lung cancer. When Hamilton tried out for the U.S. World Championship team, he suffered a broken right foot. Hamilton spent the rest of the summer convalescing at home and visited his grandfather almost every day. He got to say goodbye before his grandfather died that fall.

Hamilton, who wears a tattoo of a cross with the inscription "Edward Hamilton, Oct. 9, 1922 – Sept. 25, 1998" on his upper right arm, re-dedicated himself to the sport. He got off to a slow start because of rehab but came on strong his junior year, averaging 21.5 points, 4.8 rebounds and 2.7 assists while shooting 34.7 percent from three and 83.3 percent from the line for a team that won both the Big East regular season and tournament.

Hamilton went on to be selected Most Outstanding Player in the NCAA Tournament after scoring 27 points and making a huge three-pointer that sent the Huskies up five midway through the second half of a 77-74 victory over Duke in the finals.

He declared for the NBA draft after the season and was selected by the Washington Wizards with the seventh pick overall.

*Dickie V's View:* Going to Rip Hamilton Sr.'s home in Coatesville, Pa., must be like visiting Blockbuster. He has all those tapes of his son's career, starting back in the seventh grade. It must be like watching a never-ending version of *SportsCenter* highlights.

I first heard about Richard Hamilton from my guy Sonny Vaccaro who invited Hamilton to his ABCD camp up at Fairleigh Dickinson University and gave me a buzz about Hamilton's ability to shoot the rock. Hamilton was underrated back then because he was always being compared to Kobe. They played on the same AAU team and Hamilton competed against Kobe in the Pennsylvania state playoffs.

Kobe was The Man. All those TV crews from up and down the East Coast showed up when he announced he was going pro out of Lower Merion High School.

Hamilton had one TV crew show up when he signed with Connecticut.

But once he got up to Storrs and started playing for Jim Calhoun, his game kept getting better and better. He became the star of the Huskies' first national championship team in 1999.

His greatest asset in college was his ability to make shots. Hamilton always had the ability to get free for the shot despite the fact defenses did everything possible to deny him the ball. When he came off the screen to shoot the J for the Huskies, you always felt it was NBN, Nothing But Nylon. Put it in the book and get back on defense.

He was as automatic as Peyton Manning in football. When Manning dropped back in the pocket to pass for the Tennessee Vols, you always felt it would be completed, baby.

**Richard Hamilton came from the state of Pennsylvania to help Connecticut capture the national championship in 1999. He later led the Detroit Pistons to the promised land, winning an NBA title in 2004.**

## #43. RICHARD HAMILTON, CONNECTICUT

|  | MIN | FG% | 3P% | FT% | RPG | APG | TPG | BPG | SPG | PPG |
|---|---|---|---|---|---|---|---|---|---|---|
| 96-97 | 30.6 | 38.6 | 37.6 | 78.4 | 4.3 | 2.8 | 3.0 | 0.3 | 1.3 | 15.9 |
| 97-98 | 32.5 | 44.0 | 40.4 | 84.3 | 4.4 | 2.4 | 2.2 | 0.2 | 1.5 | 21.5 |
| 98-99 | 32.1 | 44.3 | 34.7 | 83.3 | 4.8 | 2.7 | 2.4 | 0.3 | 1.2 | 21.5 |
| **TOTALS** | 31.8 | 42.6 | 37.8 | 82.6 | 4.5 | 2.6 | 2.5 | 0.3 | 1.3 | 19.8 |

# DUKE: 44

PLAYER NUMBER

# J.J. Redick

6' 4"

190 pounds

Guard

2002-2006

*Profile:* J.J. Redick developed that beautiful shooting touch of his by practicing for hours on a backyard hoop on an unpaved road made of dirt and gravel near his parents' house on a quiet mountaintop in Cave Springs, a suburb of Roanoke, Va.

The results of that work became obvious during the four years he played for Duke.

Redick, who won the Rupp Trophy as National Player of the Year as a junior in 2005 and swept all the major awards as a senior in 2006, was a two-time first-team All-American. He became the all-time leading scorer in the rich history of the ACC with 2,769 points – breaking the old record set by Dick Hemric of Wake Forest 51 years earlier.

The son of a talented stoneware potter, Redick loved to write poetry. He gave Duke fans a preview of coming attractions when he was named MVP of the McDonald's All-American game after scoring 26 points and winning the three-point shooting contest.

Redick quickly developed into the most dangerous shooter in the country. He set an NCAA record for career three-point goals with 457 and was

lethal from the line, making 91.2 percent of his free throw attempts, and 54 in a row at one point betwe his junior and senior years.

Redick was voted the ACC Player of the Year his final two seasons when he averaged 21.8 points and 26.8 points. He was selected MVP of the ACC Tournament as a freshman after scoring 30 points against North Carolina State in the championship game. He played on four NCAA Tournament teams and participated on a Final Four team as a sophomore and three Sweet 16s.

Redick was beloved by Duke fans, but he was constantly targeted for abuse by opposing fans and at one point was labeled the most hated athlete in America. After students at Maryland and North Carolina State discovered his cell phone number, Redick estimated he received between 50 and 75 calls a day from opposing fans.

His college career ended with a loss to LSU in the South Regional semifinals in Atlanta.

The Orlando Magic selected him with the 11th pick in the NBA draft.

*Dickie V's View:* As a freshman, Redick was a true Diaper Dandy, man. But who would have thought that we were watching the ACC's all-time leading scorer? Yes, we knew he was incredible on the foul line. But think about some of the people who have worn uniforms in the conference – Hall of Fame talents like Michael Jordan, David Thompson and on and on.

Yes, my friends, Redick is numero uno.

Redick was as good a shooter as I've seen during my tenure at ESPN. His stats didn't always tell the story of how good a shooter he was because, at times, he would force some impossible shots. I'd put him up there with Chris Mullin, Steve Alford, Reggie Miller, Stephen Curry, etc. He made himself even better his last two years once he trimmed down and developed mid-range game.

To me, he set a standard.

How big?

I remember getting a tape from Lute Olson of Arizona about his guard, Damon Stoudamire. Lute felt that Stoudamire was being overlooked. "All you guys are talking about Redick. Check out my guy's numbers," he said.

I can certainly respect the Hall of Fame coach's loyalty to his player. And if you look at pure shooting stats, Redick didn't always stand out because on many occasions teams zeroed in on him and forced him to take some lower-percentage shots. But the numbers don't lie.

Redick set an NCAA Division I record for the most three-pointers in a career, passing Curtis Staples of Virginia. Then he shattered Duke's career scoring mark previously held by Johnny Dawkins.

You get the message.

I still remember him battling Adam Morrison – who was having a great season out at Gonzaga – for National Player of the Year his senior year. The two guys were friends, and I actually thought they should have split the awards to make everyone happy. It happened before with Patrick Ewing and Chris Mullin in 1985.

But Redick swept them all.

I'm sure that made the rest of the ACC happy.

Only kidding, man. In all my years of doing games for ESPN, I never saw a player so despised by opposing crowds. The abuse he took on the road was incredible. He responded on the court. It almost seemed to bring out the best in him. He used it as an emotional lift.

**J. J. Redick always impressed me with his tenacity. He was hated and maligned everywhere he went in ACC country as opposing fans were vicious. Redick went on to become the ACC's all-time leading scorer.**

### #44. J.J. REDICK, DUKE

|  | MIN | FG% | 3P% | FT% | RPG | APG | TPG | BPG | SPG | PPG |
|---|---|---|---|---|---|---|---|---|---|---|
| 02-03 | 30.7 | 41.3 | 39.9 | 91.9 | 2.5 | 2.0 | 1.6 | 0.1 | 1.2 | 15.0 |
| 03-04 | 31.1 | 42.3 | 39.5 | 95.3 | 3.1 | 1.6 | 1.9 | 0.1 | 0.7 | 15.9 |
| 04-05 | 37.3 | 40.8 | 40.3 | 93.8 | 3.3 | 2.6 | 2.5 | 0.1 | 1.1 | 21.8 |
| 05-06 | 37.3 | 47.0 | 42.1 | 86.3 | 2.0 | 2.6 | 2.5 | 0.1 | 1.4 | 26.8 |
| **TOTALS** | 34.0 | 43.3 | 40.6 | 91.2 | 2.7 | 2.2 | 2.1 | 0.1 | 1.1 | 19.9 |

# NORTH CAROLINA:

**Tyler Hansbrough**

6' 9"

250 pounds

Forward

2005-2009

*Profile:* North Carolina's three-time All-American, first-team All-ACC center and 2008 consensus National Player of the Year, Tyler Hansbrough was easily the most competitive player in the Atlantic Coast Conference his first three years on campus.

But the Tar Heels' powerful 6' 9", 250-pound junior had some unfinished business before he left for the NBA, which is why he came back for his senior year. He wanted one last shot at winning a national championship.

Hansbrough, who averaged 22.6 points, 10.2 rebounds and had 27 20-point games and 19 double doubles, was the ACC Player of the Year and ACC Tournament MVP as a junior on the 2008 Carolina team that advanced to the Final Four.

He's always been driven to succeed.

Hansbrough spent countless hours redefining his body in the weight room. And that's where he picked up his nickname – "Psycho T" – from Carolina's strength and conditioning coach Jonas Sahratian. Hansbrough recalled, "I started screaming during lifts and he started calling me 'Psycho T.' I never thought it would get this big." The legend of "Psycho T" grew when Hansbrough started pushing Sahratian's SUV around the Smith Center parking lot to strengthen his legs. "He works as hard as any player I have ever coached," North Carolina coach Roy Williams said.

Hansbrough grew up in Poplar Bluff, Mo., a small town of 18,000 known as "The Gateway to the Ozarks," located a half-hour drive from the Arkansas border. He is an extra-large Opie who, when he's home during the summer, still loves fishing, driving his pickup truck and playing Texas-style ping pong

with his buddies. That's a blood sport whose rules are simple: Win two straight points and your opponent has to lift his shirt so you get a free shot at his mid-section. Ouch. That can leave welts.

Hansbrough got his competitive nature from his gene pool. His father Gene, a former high jumper at the University of Missouri, is an orthopedic surgeon. His mother, Tami, is a former Miss Missouri. His two brothers, Greg and Ben, tested him in pickup games on the hoop next to the garage of the family home. Younger brother Ben played basketball for Mississippi State and transferred to Notre Dame after one year.

Hansbrough draws most of his inspiration from older brother Greg, who is partially paralyzed on his left side after a neurosurgeon removed a slow-growing tumor at the base of his brain when he was just seven-and-a-half years old. Greg had to learn to walk and ride his bike all over again. He lifted weights in the family room, learned how to back Tyler down with his right arm in pickup games and eventually made the high school basketball team. He has gone on to run three marathons.

As a sophomore, Hansbrough scored 26 points and grabbed 17 rebounds during an 86-72 victory over Duke at the Smith Center. With 14.5 seconds remaining, Duke guard Gerald Henderson Jr. crashed into Hansbrough and hit him in the face with his right elbow, breaking Hansbrough's nose and leaving his face a bloody mess. Hansbrough went on to play with a face mask through that post season before ripping it off in the second half of a victory over Michigan State in the second round of the NCAA Tournament. He ripped the Spartans that day for 33 points.

Tyler Hansbrough

*ickie V's View:* The 2008 season was a great one · Tyler Hansbrough. Many projected him to be the ayer of the year in the preseason. Did he live up to pectations?

You bet he did, baby.

In my three decades of broadcasting, I have not en a player who played harder on every possession an this Tar Heel star. Man, I remember watching m on TV at the end of the Duke game at the Smith nter back in 2007. He scored 26 during a big-time rolina victory. There was blood all over his face er he caught an elbow from Gerald Henderson at e end of the game. But that didn't stop him from goal – to bring another W to the Tar Heels.

He has been sensational for North Carolina since e day he arrived from Poplar Bluff, Mo.– genuine superstar. You have to love his passion, love for the jersey he wears and the school he resents. He's an absolute coach's dream.

His story was very different than those of so any kids who declared for the draft early because ey know one stroke of the pen can change their es financially. Tyler was lucky. He didn't have that lemma. His family is financially stable, allowing m to enjoy a four-year solid-gold career.

I've heard numerous critics claim that he will ot be an outstanding pro. Don't bet on it. They aim he doesn't have the explosiveness and the uickness needed to be effective in NBA competition. eople also question his size. Give me a break. e're not in the Olympics in track and field. his is basketball and I know one simple fact – ler Hansbrough knows how to compete.

Also, I've heard where Michael Beasley of Kansas State, who was the second player taken in this year's NBA draft, does not have the 6' 9" size that people initially thought he possessed. Once again, I simply state, when it's all said and done, Beasley will quiet his critics and average 20 points a game in the NBA.

Something tells me Hansbrough will be a success on the NBA level when that time arrives. For now, let's cherish the moment of Hansbrough being a four-year college starter.

I have a feeling Hansbrough will taste that same big-time success.

**T**yler Hansbrough is the hardest working player I have seen in my 30 years of calling basketball games for ESPN/ABC. He is absolutely fearless inside.

## #45. TYLER HANSBROUGH, NORTH CAROLINA

|  | MIN | FG% | 3P% | FT% | RPG | APG | TPG | BPG | SPG | PPG |
|---|---|---|---|---|---|---|---|---|---|---|
| 05-06 | 30.4 | 57.0 | 50.0 | 73.9 | 7.8 | 1.3 | 2.5 | 0.7 | 1.2 | 18.9 |
| 06-07 | 29.9 | 52.5 | 25.0 | 76.8 | 7.9 | 1.2 | 1.9 | 0.4 | 1.1 | 18.4 |
| 07-08 | 33.0 | 54.0 | 0.0 | 80.6 | 10.2 | 0.9 | 2.1 | 0.4 | 1.5 | 22.6 |
| **TOTALS** | *31.1* | *54.5* | *37.5* | *77.1* | *8.6* | *1.1* | *2.3* | *0.5* | *1.3* | *20.0* |

# MASSACHUSETTS:

## Marcus Camby

7' 0"

215 pounds

Center

1993-1996

*Profile:* Marcus Camby grew up just a few blocks away from the Hartford Civic Center. As a child, he was a huge Connecticut fan and once waited outside the building after a game to get an autograph from former Huskies' star Cliff Robinson

Everyone just assumed he would go to Connecticut.

But because of circumstances that limited his exposure until the summer before his senior year in high school, the slender 7' 0" center wound up an hour-and-a-half away at Massachusetts. There he became the poster child for John Calipari's "Refuse to Lose" teams that advanced to the NCAA Elite Eight in 1995 and the school's first ever – and only – Final Four in 1996.

Camby was the most dominant player in the country his junior year. He averaged 20.5 points, 8.2 rebounds and 3.9 blocked shots, was a consensus first-team All-American and everybody's National Player of the Year. He was a shot-blocking machine who finished with 336 during his career and set an NCAA Tournament record for career blocks with 43 in 11 games.

Camby's mother sent him to Conard High outside the city as part of Project Concern, a voluntary program of school desegregation. During his freshman year, he grew an amazing 10 inches. Camby played varsity for only five games his junior year before transferring back to Hartford Public, his neighborhood school, where he had to sit out the rest of the season because of transfer rules.

Calipari's assistant, Bill Bayno, discovered him playing for coach Jackie Bethea at the Hartford Boys and Girls Club. Bayno brought back a scouting report that said Camby could be the next Bill Russell.

Calipari, who was still trying to build his program, thought he had found the world's biggest sleeper. The rest of the hoops world caught on when Camby showed up and dominated Sonny Vaccaro's ABCD camp, which was held that year in Southern California. But Calipari won a national recruiting battle because he had cultivated Camby from the start.

Camby more than lived up to expectations, even though he was overshadowed by Lou Roe his first two years.

But that all changed when he was a junior. Camby scored 32 points in an opening-game upset of top-ranked and eventual national champion Kentucky. He outplayed a fellow junior center, the 6" 11" All-American Tim Duncan of Wake Forest, for a 35-2 team that won 26 straight games and was ranked No. 1 most of the season.

After a midseason scare in which he collapsed in a game at St. Bonaventure, was unconscious for 10 minutes and had to be flown to Pittsburgh by helicopter for tests, Camby recovered to lead the Minutemen to a fifth straight Atlantic 10 title. Then he scored 23 points, grabbed eight rebounds and blocked seven shots during an 86-72 victory over Georgetown in the regional finals in Atlanta.

The story didn't have a totally happy ending.

Shortly after the season, word came out that, unbeknownst to Calipari, Camby had taken more than $28,000 from two agents. UMass was stripped of its Final Four finish. Camby, who was selected by the Knicks with the second pick overall in the 1996 draft, eventually repaid the school the $151,000 it had to return to the NCAA for his transgressions.

## #46. MARCUS CAMBY, MASSACHUSETTS

| | MIN | FG% | 3P% | FT% | RPG | APG | TPG | BPG | SPG | PPG |
|---|---|---|---|---|---|---|---|---|---|---|
| 93-94 | 21.9 | 49.4 | 0.0 | 59.6 | 6.4 | 1.2 | 1.7 | 3.6 | 0.6 | 10.2 |
| 94-95 | 22.6 | 55.0 | 100.0 | 64.3 | 6.2 | 1.2 | 1.8 | 3.4 | 0.8 | 13.9 |
| 95-96 | 30.6 | 47.7 | 0.0 | 70.0 | 8.2 | 1.8 | 2.5 | 3.9 | 1.0 | 20.5 |
| **TOTALS** | 25.3 | 50.1 | 7.7 | 66.1 | 7.0 | 1.4 | 2.0 | 3.7 | 0.8 | 15.1 |

*Dickie V's View:* Marcus Camby was always motivated to play against the best players. Coach John Calipari made sure he did, giving him the opportunity to play against Tim Duncan of Wake Forest early in his junior year in 1996.

Camby had an index card taped to the wall above his bed that read: "Dec. 6, 1995. TIM DUNCAN. National Player of the Year." Then he went out and outscored Duncan, 17-9, and outplayed him as UMass won, 60-46, in Worcester, Mass.

I just wonder where Camby got the idea to tape that index card with the date of the Wake game over his bed. John Calipari doesn't miss a trick. He's right on top of it.

He knew how good Camby was.

Apparently Hillary Rodham Clinton did, too. I had the good fortune of doing a book signing with the former First Lady in Lexington, Ky., shortly after Camby scored 32 points and UMass dominated Kentucky on the interior during an early-season victory in Detroit that was shown on ESPN.

We exchanged books and her first question to me was, "Is that Massachusetts team that good?"

I was shocked. The First Lady was following the hoops action.

UMass played in the Atlantic 10. The Minutemen weren't from an elite conference but they stepped up and showed they could play with the big boys. They were good enough to make it to the Final Four.

And Camby, who was a tremendous defensive force, was good enough to win the National Player of the Year award.

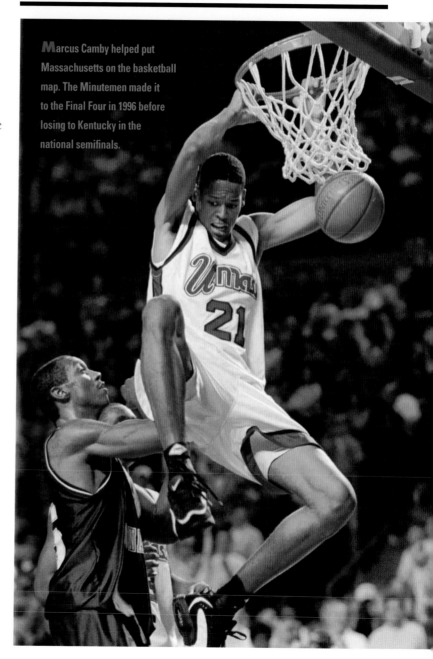

Marcus Camby helped put Massachusetts on the basketball map. The Minutemen made it to the Final Four in 1996 before losing to Kentucky in the national semifinals.

# SYRACUSE:

**PLAYER NUMBER 47**

## Derrick Coleman

6-9

230 pounds

Forward/
Center

1986-1990

*Profile:* Syracuse coach Jim Boeheim got a huge assist from former roommate Dave Bing, still arguably the program's best player ever, when he recruited Derrick Coleman.

Harry Hairston, Coleman's high school coach at Detroit Northern, took his young star – who had been raised fatherless and had two close friends shot – over to meet Bing, the president of Bing Steel, in the hope that he could mentor him. Bing took an interest in Coleman and even arranged for him to attend Boeheim's summer camp. He convinced the 6' 10" center to go to college. Coleman, who had blossomed into a McDonald's All-American, chose Syracuse over Michigan State.

Then he started to destroy the rest of the Big East.

"DC" – who averaged 15 points and 10.7 rebounds while shooting 56.8 percent during his four-year career – played with a swagger. He was a three-time All-Big East selection, a two-time All-American and was selected National Player of the Year in 1990. He averaged 11.0, 11.4 and 12.1 rebounds his final three years.

Coleman made an immediate impact as a freshman as a starting power forward when a young Orange team won the Big East title and made an unexpected run to the national championship game. Coleman, the Big East Rookie of the Year, averaged 10.5 points and 12.1 rebounds in six NCAA games, grabbing 19 rebounds against Indiana in the final.

Syracuse had a 73-72 lead, with 27 seconds left to play. Coleman went to the free throw line for a one-and-one. Converting the free throws would have sealed the victory, but Coleman missed the front end. Hoosier guard Keith Smart made a game-winning jumper just before the final buzzer.

Syracuse never made it back to the Final Four during Coleman's career, but it did win 113 games and advanced to the Elite Eight during Coleman's junior year when he moved over from power forward to center, replacing Rony Seikaly.

He was the most intimidating player in the Big East as a senior, averaging 17.9 points. He had 27 points and 13 rebounds against Georgetown – with twin towers Alonzo Mourning and Dikembe Mutombo – during an 89-87 victory on Senior Day, his final game at the Carrier Dome.

Coleman was later selected by the New Jersey Nets with the first pick overall in the 1990 draft.

*Dickie V's View:* I always felt – and I said this during his games – that Derrick Coleman was a guy who turned it on when the lights came on in the Carrier Dome. He was long and lean; and, oh, could he flat out rebound. He would go after every rebound like it was his last meal. And he grabbed more than anyone by the time he left school.

Coleman came to Syracuse from Detroit. And I have to believe Dave Bing had a vital part in the recruiting. Bing was a Hall of Famer and a legend in that city from the time he played for the Pistons. Before that, he played in the backcourt at Syracuse with Jimmy Boeheim. I always kid Jimmy. I tell him, "You and Bing scored 35 in college. What a combo. He'd get 34 and you'd post one."

Actually, Jimmy, you were better than that, baby. Dave was the CEO of a steel company and has been a role model for so many kids in Detroit. He loved Syracuse and had a terrific relationship with his former college teammate Jim Boeheim. I'm sure Derrick Coleman had it pointed out to him by Boeheim and his staff that Bing was an icon at Syracuse. To be honest, it didn't surprise me when he decided to enroll and play for the Orangemen.

Syracuse went to the Final Four in Coleman's freshman year, 1987. People like yours truly were saying on national TV that Syracuse had no shot against North Carolina in the East Regional finals. My feeling was that J.R. Reid would dominate the Syracuse baseline.

Well, my friends, how wrong I was.

Derrick and his buddy Seikaly were all over me on Bourbon Street. "Hey, Dickie V, where are the Tar Heels, baby? We're here in New Orleans. We're here to celebrate."

## #47. DERRICK COLEMAN, SYRACUSE

|  | MIN | FG% | 3P% | FT% | RPG | APG | TPG | BPG | SPG | PPG |
|---|---|---|---|---|---|---|---|---|---|---|
| 86-87 | 30.6 | 56.0 | 0.0 | 68.6 | 8.8 | 1.2 | 1.8 | 1.8 | 1.2 | 11.9 |
| 87-88 | 32.4 | 58.7 | 16.7 | 63.0 | 11.0 | 2.2 | 2.2 | 1.6 | 1.3 | 13.5 |
| 88-89 | 33.1 | 57.5 | 0.0 | 69.2 | 11.4 | 2.9 | 2.4 | 3.4 | 1.2 | 16.9 |
| 89-90 | 35.3 | 55.1 | 36.6 | 71.5 | 12.1 | 2.9 | 2.7 | 2.0 | 1.5 | 17.9 |
| TOTALS | 32.8 | 56.8 | 29.1 | 68.4 | 10.7 | 2.3 | 2.3 | 2.2 | 1.3 | 15.0 |

Derrick Coleman came from the Detroit area to make a difference for Jim Boeheim's Syracuse squad. He was a rebounder deluxe, a Windex man who really cleaned the glass.

# KENTUCKY:

PLAYER NUMBER 48

## Kenny Walker

6' 8"

222 pounds

Forward

1982-1986

*Profile:* Kenny Walker led Crawford County High in tiny Roberta, Ga., to a pair of state championships. The 6' 8" forward was voted Mr. Basketball and was selected to play in the McDonald's All-American game.

But when he mentioned that he wanted to go to the University of Kentucky, his high school coach, Clyde Zachery, seemed hesitant. "They play some big-time basketball over there," he told Walker.

"I can play anywhere," Walker announced.

No argument there.

Walker was a two-time All-American, a two-time SEC Player of the Year and a four-time All-SEC selection when he played for the Big Blue, dazzling crowds with his spectacular dunking ability.

His nickname was "Sky" – for good reason.

Walker averaged 15.8 points and 7.1 rebounds and scored 2,080 career points before the advent of the three-point shot, while shooting 57.1 percent from the field and 75 percent from the line.

Walker came from humble beginnings. When he was just five years old, his mother cut out the bottom of a bucket and nailed it to a tree in the yard so he could work on his game.

He never stopped. After Crawford County won its second state title, the first thing he did was ask his coach to keep the door to the gym open the next year so he could practice. Zachery simply handed him the keys to the building.

Walker was a four-year starter. He was a sophomore on the 1984 Kentucky team that went to the Final Four. But his game really took off the next year when he averaged 22.9 points and 10.2 rebounds – scoring 30 or more points seven times

and going off for 36 when Kentucky defeated a Danny Manning-led Kansas team on New Year's Eve in Louisville.

He became an All-American during what was technically a rebuilding year at the end of the Joe B. Hall era. Kentucky made it to the NCAA Tournament with a 16-12 record. The Wildcats then advanced to the Sweet 16 before losing to St. John's, 73-60, in a game where Walker scored 23 points. He was playing with a scratched cornea after being poked in the eye by Chris Mullin midway through the first half.

Walker continued on fire his senior year, becoming a consensus All-American after averaging 20 points and 7.7 rebounds for a team that was ranked No. 1 for part of the season. Kentucky went undefeated in the SEC and advanced to the NCAA Southeast Regional finals before being upset by 11th-seeded LSU in Atlanta.

The Knicks, who saw him as a potential heir apparent to Bernard King, selected him with the fifth pick overall in the 1986 draft.

*Dickie V's View:* There is a reason Kentucky fans will always refer to Kenny Walker as "Sky" Walker. He could really jump, he loved to dunk and he put on some big-time aerial shows when he played for the Big Blue.

Walker led Kentucky to a Final Four in 1984, and I thought the Wildcats might go back again during his senior year. They were ranked No. 1, had swept through the SEC undefeated – beating LSU three times that year.

But LSU coach Dale Brown found a way to slow Kentucky down during the regional finals with that

**K**enny "Sky" Walker became a legend in Lexington. The Kentucky Wildcat fans are the most passionate in college basketball and I have loved calling games at Rupp Arena.

## #48. KENNY WALKER, KENTUCKY

|  | MIN | FG% | 3P% | FT% | RPG | APG | TPG | BPG | SPG | PPG |
|---|---|---|---|---|---|---|---|---|---|---|
| 82-83 | 19.3 | 61.1 | | 66.2 | 4.9 | 0.6 | 1.1 | 0.6 | 0.4 | 7.3 |
| 83-84 | 31.2 | 55.5 | | 73.4 | 5.9 | 1.3 | 1.2 | 0.7 | 0.9 | 12.4 |
| 84-85 | 36.7 | 55.9 | | 76.8 | 10.2 | 1.3 | 1.7 | 1.2 | 0.9 | 22.9 |
| 85-86 | 34.8 | 58.2 | | 76.4 | 7.7 | 1.4 | 1.5 | 1.2 | 1.3 | 20.0 |
| **TOTALS** | **30.9** | **57.1** | | **75.0** | **7.1** | **1.2** | **1.4** | **0.9** | **0.9** | **15.8** |

*Photo Courtesy of Getty Images.*

reak Defense" he used. It was Upset City, baby.

But that certainly didn't detract from the lividual brilliance of Walker, who went on to ay in the NBA.

He made a big statement about his jumping lity at the NBA's slam dunk contest in 1989. Three days before the event, his father, Jerome, collapsed and died from a stroke. Walker's mother told him to compete anyway. Walker wound up winning, beating Clyde "The Glide" Drexler in the finals.

He said afterwards his dad was out there helping him.

# SYRACUSE:

PLAYER NUMBER

## Pearl Washington

6' 3"

190 pounds

Guard

1983-1986

*Photo Courtesy of the Big East Conference*

*Profile:* His name was Dwayne Washington, but from the time he was eight years old, everyone called him "Pearl" because his game resembled that of Knicks' star Earl "The Pearl" Monroe. He was a playground legend whose reputation reached mythic proportions long before he graduated from Boys and Girls' High and announced he would attend Syracuse in a nationally televised interview with Al McGuire.

The Pearl, who was the highest-recruited player in the country, was royalty at the outdoor summer league in a park in Harlem where fans stood on rooftops to watch the 6' 3" guard in action. In Brooklyn, they talk about the time he scored eight straight times on an opposing team, then ran by the coach and said, 'Yo, coach, you'd better call a timeout." At Syracuse, they still talk about the T-shirts that read: "On the Seventh Day God Created Pearl."

"Everybody says Patrick Ewing and Chris Mullin made the Big East, but Pearl made the league," Syracuse coach Jim Boeheim told his beat reporter, Mike Waters. "They were the best players, but Pearl was the player people went out to see and turned on their TVs to watch. We had the highest-rated games every year Pearl was there."

Washington averaged 15.6 points, shot 52.4 percent and led the Orange in assists and steals in each of his three years there. More importantly, he gave Syracuse credibility as a national power. He used the massive Carrier Dome as his own personal stage.

He was named Big East Rookie of the Year in 1984 and was a first-team All-Big East selection three times. He was a consensus first-team All-American during his final year, when he averaged 17.3 points and 7.8 assists.

Washington had spectacular shake-and-bake ball-handling skills and a flair for the dramatic. The was the time he beat Boston College, 75-73, as a freshman, when he took an outlet pass, took a coup of dribbles and launched a shot as he crossed half-court. The ball dropped through the net. A crowd o 30,293 at the Carrier Dome exploded. Fans stormed the floor. Washington just kept running off the cou and into the locker room, like he had planned it.

His performances against Georgetown in the Big East Tournament at the Garden were also noteworth As a sophomore in 1985, tensions between Washington and Patrick Ewing became so inflamed in a semifinal game that Ewing threw a punch that

rowly missed Washington. Neither player was
[sele]cted, and the Hoyas went on to win, 74-65.
Washington got his revenge the next season,
[scor]ing 28 points to lead the Orange to a 75-73
[ove]rtime victory in the semis. Washington was
[sele]cted MVP of the tournament even though
[Syr]acuse lost to St. John's in the finals.

Syracuse never really made a dent in the NCAA
[tou]rnament during Washington's career – but he was
[e]ntertaining to watch.

He declared early for the draft and was selected
[by] the Nets with the 13th pick overall.

*[Dic]kie V's View:* The Pearl brought show biz to
[the] Big East, baby. He was a Brooklyn kid who loved
[the] bright lights of Broadway. And he loved doing his
[thi]ng on his own stage at Syracuse.

The Big East was loaded with great players in
[tho]se days. It seems like everybody had a big-name
[coa]ch and a star – guys like Patrick Ewing of
[Geo]rgetown, Chris Mullin of St. John's, Ed Pinckney
[of V]illanova and Michael Adams of Boston College.
But there was only one Pearl.

Washington was the entertainer, and he turned
[hom]e games at the 34,000-seat Carrier Dome into
[mu]st-see events. It was like a rock concert, man, and
[he] was like Kenny Chesney, if you love country, or a
[Kan]ye West concert. He would have the place rockin'
[and] rollin'.

That was back in the days when Georgetown-
[Syr]acuse was considered the social event of the
[win]ter.

When you had Pearl, you always had a chance.
[He] could break your ankles off the dribble. During

my time at ESPN, there was nobody on the
collegiate level who could make the bounce pass
to the post as well as Pearl. He had instinct and
great peripheral vision and a special feel for the
game that he'd developed on the city playgrounds.
He was a flat out legend.

He was a key guy in the world of recruiting and
he brought so much attention to the program. He
became a soap opera star on ESPN when the Big East
was just making its name.

Dave Gavitt, the first commissioner of the Big
East, got a huge TV deal for the league. The Pearl was
on TV constantly. During my travels, people would
run up to me all the time and ask, "Hey, is that kid
Pearl as good as people say?"

Wow. I'd hear that all the time in airports.

He was another of the great ball-handling wizards
from New York City, along with guys like Kenny
Anderson and Kenny Smith.

That was back when the Big East was dynamite.
You had guys like Patrick Ewing and Chris Mullin
and Pearl – guys who stayed in school three or four
years. Now, players don't stay long enough to become
household names. They bring some charisma and
magic to the game; but, before you know it, they're
gone.

**Pearl Washington was
Mr. Excitement for Syracuse.
He helped make the Big
East a special conference
and I loved his energy and
enthusiasm.**

## #49. PEARL WASHINGTON, SYRACUSE

|  | MIN | FG% | 3P% | FT% | RPG | APG | TPG | BPG | SPG | PPG |
|---|---|---|---|---|---|---|---|---|---|---|
| 83-84 | 34.6 | 54.4 |  | 66.2 | 2.6 | 6.2 | 3.5 | 0.1 | 2.4 | 14.4 |
| 84-85 | 34.1 | 49.0 |  | 78.4 | 2.9 | 6.1 | 4.5 | 0.1 | 2.0 | 15.2 |
| 85-86 | 32.3 | 53.5 |  | 72.6 | 2.5 | 7.8 | 3.3 | 0.0 | 2.7 | 17.3 |
| **TOTALS** | 33.7 | 52.4 |  | 72.9 | 2.7 | 6.7 | 3.8 | 0.1 | 2.3 | 15.6 |

CONNECTICUT:

# Emeka Okafor

6' 10"

252 pounds

Center

2001-2004

*Profile:* When Connecticut coach Jim Calhoun first saw Emeka Okafor play in the spring of his senior year at an AAU event, he had no idea that the 6' 10" center would some day become the best big man in school history.

Okafor was the son of immigrant parents who escaped war-ravaged Nigeria. He was the first member of his family born in the United States and moved with his family from Houston to Bartlesville, Okla., when his father, Pius, took a job with Phillips Petroleum there. Okafor's father took him to the local YMCA when he was just eight years old to learn the sport. He quickly sensed his son had a gift.

Okafor averaged 22 points, 16 rebounds and seven blocked shots for Bellaire (Tex.) High, trying to pattern his game after Hakeem Olajuwon. He was a straight A student and wanted to go to Vanderbilt, Stanford or Rice, but none of them had a scholarship available.

Calhoun signed Okafor as a project. When Okafor first arrived in Storrs, he had limited offensive skills and no jump shot. But he displayed an instant knack for blocking shots.

Three years later, as a junior in 2004, after exhaustive individual instruction from the staff and extra workouts on his own, Okafor transformed himself into a consensus first-team All-American who won several national player of the year awards and was chosen National Defensive Player of the Year for a second straight season. Okafor averaged 17.6 points while shooting 59.9 percent for a Big East program that started and finished the season ranked No. 1. He also grabbed 11.5 rebounds and led the country

in blocked shots for a second consecutive year, wit 4.08 per game.

The Huskies had three other future pros – Ben Gordon, Charlie Villanueva and Josh Boone – on that roster. But Okafor was The Man.

Okafor was troubled by back problems all seaso and scored only two points in a painful 19 minutes during the Huskies' 87-71 Elite Eight victory over Alabama. But he came up huge when it counted, scoring all 18 of his points in the second half of a 7 78 victory over Duke in the 2004 NCAA semifinals at San Antonio – helping the Huskies erase a defici in the final 15 minutes. Okafor had 24 points and 15 rebounds – his 24th double double of the seaso – as UConn defeated Georgia Tech to win a second national title in six years.

Okafor, a two-time first-team Academic All-American, graduated in just three years with a 3.8 GPA and an honors degree in finance.

He finished his career near the top of the NCAA all-time leaders in blocked shots with a total of 44 1

He declared for the pros that year and was selected by the Charlotte Bobcats with the second pick overall in the 2004 NBA draft. He was invited to join the U.S. Olympic team that summer, which finished with a bronze medal in Athens.

*Dickie V's View:* I had to have Emeka Okafor in our top 50 because he epitomizes the student-athlete. He graduated in three years with a 3.8 GPA in finance. And he brought home the gold trophy as the Most Outstanding Player in the 2004 NCAA Tournament.

Okafor and Ben Gordon – the Huskies' other big star on that title team – roomed together for three years. Before they arrived on campus as freshmen, Gordon asked Okafor who was going to bring the TV.

Okafor seemed surprised. He didn't think they would have time to watch TV.

I can't believe it! Not even when I was on talking about the Huskies' superstar?

Okafor was a serious student. He used to get up at one o'clock in the morning and then study until a.m. before going back to sleep.

Gordon had to convince him to spend more time in the gym.

The results? Okafor had 24 double doubles his final year and dominated Georgia Tech's 7' 0"center Luke Schenscher in the lane in the finals.

Okafor did so many things impressively – blocking shots, affecting the way teams tried to penetrate in the lane, keeping people from scoring inside. He was the best shot blocker I'd seen in college since David Robinson and Patrick Ewing.

Is it any wonder Okafor and Gordon went two-three in the NBA draft that June?

## #50. EMEKA OKAFOR, CONNECTICUT

|       | MIN  | FG%  | 3P% | FT%  | RPG  | APG | TPG | BPG | SPG | PPG  |
|-------|------|------|-----|------|------|-----|-----|-----|-----|------|
| 01-02 | 30.0 | 59.0 | 0.9 | 62.0 | 9.0  | 0.8 | 1.4 | 4.1 | 0.7 | 7.9  |
| 02-03 | 32.9 | 58.0 | 0.0 | 59.9 | 11.2 | 0.5 | 2.3 | 4.7 | 0.9 | 15.9 |
| 03-04 | 32.4 | 59.9 | 0.0 | 51.8 | 11.5 | 1.0 | 2.3 | 4.1 | 1.0 | 17.6 |
| **TOTALS** | 31.8 | 59.0 | 0.9 | 56.4 | 10.6 | 0.8 | 2.0 | 4.3 | 0.9 | 13.8 |

Emeka Okafor made my top 50 because he exemplified the term "student-athlete." He came to Connecticut and was a shot-blocker and inside scoring threat, helping the Huskies win the national title in 2004.

I have great admiration
my recent play-by-play part
Dan Shulman. Like all
broadcast buddies, he is so w
prepared and easy to work w

# Up next...
## MY TOP 50 MOMENTS

# NORTH CAROLINA STATE *stuns Houston to win the 1983 NCAA championship*

## The Cardiac Pack

MOMENT NUMBER 1

North Carolina State 54
Houston 52
April 4, 1983

*Profile:* North Carolina State wasn't supposed to be there.

The Wolfpack wasn't supposed to be cutting down the nets after the 1983 national championship game. And Jimmy Valvano wasn't supposed to be running around, looking for somebody to hug, with all that craziness surrounding him in The Pit at Albuquerque.

But nobody told the "The Cardiac Pack" that Cinderella was just a fairy tale.

They found a way to win the ACC Tournament that season and earn an unexpected automatic bid to the NCAA Tournament. Then they went on a wild ride that ended with 6' 7" sophomore forward Lorenzo Charles flushing down a dunk at the buzzer to give State a stunning 54-52 upset victory over heavily favored Houston in a game no one outside the Wolfpack locker room thought they could win.

Houston presented a menacing presence. The Cougars were a group of serial dunkaholics whose nickname was "Phi Slamma Jamma" – center Akeem "The Dream" Olajuwon, forwards Clyde "The Glide" Drexler and Larry "Mr. Mean" Micheaux and guards Michael "Mr. Clutch" Young, Alvin Franklin and Benny Anders. These make-believe fraternity brothers were on a 25-game winning streak, just coming off a wild, rim-rattling 94-81 victory over Louisville in the national semifinals when they had 11 dunks in the second half.

"We figure the team with the most dunks will win," said Olajuwon, who finished that game with 22 points, 21 rebounds and four dunks down the stretch.

State, whose best NBA prospect was 6' 11" Thurl Bailey, may have appeared overmatched; but the Pack had underrated guard play with Sidney Lowe, Dereck Whittenburg, Ernie Myers and Terry Gannon. They had developed a strong sense of inside-outside balance during their NCAA Tournament run.

They also had Valvano's sense of confidence.

"We're trying to keep it close and hope there's some magic left in a very overused wand," Valvano said.

That's exactly what happened.

Houston had taken a 42-35 lead and looked like it had the game under control with 11 minutes to play. Then Houston coach Guy Lewis decided to take time off the clock – a decision that would forever haunt him. State started fouling, Houston started missing free throws and State worked its way to a 52-52 tie. With 45 seconds left, Franklin missed the front end of a one-and-one and State called a timeout to set up the final play.

Valvano was hoping Houston's defense would collapse on Lowe, leaving Whittenburg, Gannon or Bailey open for the final shot. He left Charles underneath in case of a miss. But the play broke down, and Whittenburg wound up firing a 30-foot air ball. Charles grabbed the rebound and instinctively dunked it over a stunned Olajuwon as time ran out.

The impossible dream suddenly had become a reality and March Madness was here forever.

*Dickie V's View:* Maybe I'm a little biased because of my affection for Jimmy V. Hey, he was always one step ahead. You talk about a guy who had a great feel for where his players were psychologically. Jimmy was special, just like the late Al McGuire of

Marquette. He could really feel the moment.

The week before NC State left for Albuquerque, he had his team practice cutting the nets down – that's right, cutting the nets down – so they would believe in a miracle.

Now, this sounds like 1980 in hockey, man. The Miracle on Ice. Is Al Michaels calling this, baby? But State's 54-52 victory over Houston was that special.

What made their NCAA run so magical was the fact they had to beat North Carolina with Michael Jordan, Virginia with Ralph Sampson and Wake Forest in the ACC Tournament just to get into the 52-team field. That wasn't exactly Cupcake City.

No way were they getting an at-large bid.

And, once they got to the NCAA Tournament, they fought all kinds of odds to survive and advance. The Pack had to go double overtime to beat Pepperdine in the first round and then escaped UNLV with a one-point victory. After a win over Utah, NC State had to beat Virginia – in what was Sampson's final college game – in the West Regional finals.

Nobody gave them a shot against Houston – a team with two future Hall of Famers, Akeem Olajuwon and Clyde Drexler, and all those stars from Phi Slamma Jamma – in the championship game.

But everybody remembers how they won it. They remember Lorenzo Charles' shot at the buzzer and they remember Jimmy V running around like a crazy man, looking for somebody to hug.

To me, their triumph epitomizes what college basketball is all about: the enthusiasm, the energy, the spirit of winning. You couldn't write a better script.

Movie time, baby. Where's the movie? Where's Pacino playing Jimmy V?

# CHRISTIAN LAETTNER'S *field goal at the buzzer gives Duke a double overtime victory against Kentucky in the 1992 NCAA East Regional final*

## Miracle Moment

MOMENT NUMBER

2

Duke 104
Kentucky 103 (2OT)
March 28, 1992

*Profile:* Duke's 6' 11" senior All-American center Christian Laettner made more big shots than anyone in the history of the NCAA Tournament.

But none resonated louder than the game-winning jump shot he made at the buzzer to give the Blue Devils a 104-103 double overtime victory over Rick Pitino's inspired Kentucky team in the 1992 NCAA East Regional finals at the Philadelphia Spectrum.

It is a moment that is played over and over again throughout the month of March. And some argue it may have been the best game ever played.

Laettner was a perfect player who played a perfect game that night, shooting 10 for 10 from the field and 10 for 10 from the line for 30 points.

Duke had won the national championship in 1991, but it looked like the Blue Devils' one-year reign might be over after Kentucky guard Sean Woods scored on a driving layup over Laettner with 2.1 seconds left in the game.

Duke's Bobby Hurley immediately called a timeout. Coach Mike Krzyzewski addressed the team in the huddle. "We're still going to win," he said.

Then he told them how.

Krzyzewski asked Grant Hill, the team's best baseball passer, if he could make a three-quarter-court pass to Laettner at the top of the key. Then he asked Laettner, who he expected to be double covered, if he could catch the pass flashing to the top of the key from the left corner.

"Yeah, coach, I can do it," Laettner said.

The pass from Hill, who was left unguarded on the inbounds play, was perfect. Laettner, guarded by Kentucky's John Pelphrey and Deron Feldhaus,

caught the ball, dropped his left shoulder, dribbled left, spun, then shot an 18-footer.

"I knew it was in as soon as he shot it," Krzyzewski said. "He had practiced that shot so many times, I knew it was in."

The ball ripped through the net. Then Laettner ran in a crazy half circle with his hands up, waiting for his teammates to embrace him.

"I didn't know I hadn't missed a shot," Laettner said later. "No one told me. I just felt, `Man, we're going to lose.' And I didn't want to lose. If we lose, we won't be able to repeat."

Two games later, the Blue Devils won again, beating Michigan in the national championship gam But the victory over Kentucky was the biggest step the road to the Final Four.

*Dickie V's View:* I was having dinner in an Italia restaurant, but I couldn't take my eyes off the TV se I was standing up with about 20 people, watching t game. I absolutely could not believe it when he mad that shot.

The Dukies in the place went nuts. The Kentuck fans were just devastated. The Commonwealth will be talking about that play forever. That particular Kentucky team was so special to everyone down there.

They were called "The Unforgettables" because four senior starters – Richie Farmer, John Pelphrey, Deron Feldhaus and Sean Woods – were all there when the NCAA slammed Kentucky with probatior in 1989, and the program was ineligible for post-season play for two years. A lot of their teammates

iled out, left, transferred. The Unforgettables
ere the end of the bench. They could have left,
o, but they stayed and helped Rick Pitino rebuild.

Three years later, they were back in the national
cture.

The school honored them by retiring all four
their numbers in a surprise celebration after the
ason.

As for Duke, the Blue Devils went on to win
nother NCAA title.

As special as Laettner's shot was, I think a lot
people forget about the great pass Grant Hill
d to make to set up the whole thing. There will
ways be a lot of discussion about Pitino's decision
t to guard the inbounds pass. Remember this,
y friends, anybody who may have been critical of
tino's decision: there are two basic theories. One
to play a center fielder, go five on four, and go for
e deflection and make it difficult for the shooter
take that shot. The other is to guard the baseline
y.

Let's not critique Pitino but rather give credit to
ill and Laettner for a great play.

Wow. That's like Eli Manning of the New York
iants finding Plaxico Burress for the score,
ocking the Patriots and winning the Super Bowl.

one of the greatest finishes
NCAA Tournament history,
ke's Christian Laettner hit the
inning shot to stun Kentucky
the 1992 East Regional final in
iladelphia.

# VILLANOVA *plays a flawless game to upset Georgetown in the 1985 NCAA championship game*

## The Perfect Game

MOMENT NUMBER

3

Villanova 66
Georgetown 64
April 1, 1985

*Profile:* Villanova picked a perfect time to play the perfect game.

Rollie Massimino's Big East Wildcats had made a Cinderella run to the 1985 Final Four in Lexington, beating such powerhouses as Michigan, Maryland, North Carolina and Memphis to reach the national championship game against Georgetown.

It looked like the ride was about to stop there.

The Hoyas, with senior All-American center Patrick Ewing, were huge 9 ½ -point favorites in the final. But not even John Thompson's 35-2 Hoyas had an answer for an inspired, superbly coached team that shot 78 percent for the game and nine for 10 in the second half of an improbable 66-64 victory.

The Wildcats' familiarity with Georgetown in the Big East regular-season wars helped.

Senior center Ed Pinckney, who had played against Ewing in the Five Star camp, scored 16 points, grabbed six rebounds, had five assists and was selected most outstanding player after holding his own against Ewing, who had 14 points and five rebounds. Senior forward Dwayne McClain led the Cats with 17 points, shooting five for seven and making six of seven free throws. Sophomore guard Harold Jensen came off the bench to shoot a perfect five for five and score 14 points; junior forward Harold Pressley shot four for six and had 11 points; while senior point guard Gary McLain committed only two turnovers against Georgetown's stifling pressure.

Pinckney, McLain and McClain – the Three Amigos – had formed a bond in summer camp when they were in high school and came to Villanova together with thoughts of winning a national title. But

after they lost to Pitt by 23 in their final regular-season game, there were thoughts they might not even receive a bid to the newly configured 64-team NCAA Tournament.

The Cats were a 10-loss eighth seed. But they didn't play like one in the championship game when they broke Georgetown's 17-game winning streak.

Jensen made a jump shot to give the Cats a 55-5 lead; Nova took control and put the Hoyas away fro the free throw line.

It was the end of an emotional day for the Cats. That morning, former Villanova coach Al Severance – a teacher for five of the Cats' 14 players – who had traveled to the Bluegrass with the team, died sudden ly in his hotel room. And then there was Jake Nevin Villanova's beloved long-time trainer, who had been restricted to a wheelchair after being diagnosed with Lou Gehrig's disease. He was seated on the sidelines by the bench to witness what some call a miracle.

"I told them that on a one-shot deal, we could beat anyone in the United States," Massimino said.

*Dickie V's View:* I knew Rollie well. He was a hig school coaching legend at Hillside High School, up North Jersey, where I came from. I heard him speak at camps and clinics. He was always so enthusiastic as a leader. He just treasured that national champior ship moment, the same way Jimmy V and Al McGui did when they won it at NC State and Marquette.

My guy Rollie pitched a perfect game against Georgetown. He was just like Don Larsen of the Yankees in the 1956 World Series. Execution – make every pass count, every shot count. Villanova was playing a club against which you couldn't make any mistakes. If you did, the party was over. It was finished.

But he wouldn't allow that to happen. He had his team dreaming.

A lot of people talk about this being a bigger upset in the NCAA Tournament than in 1983 when NC State beat Houston. But here's something they don't realize. Villanova had played Georgetown close twice during the regular season and the Wildcats went into that big game with a certain air of confidence. They took it to Ewing, and his Hoya teammates, thus denying Georgetown its second straight national title.

In the national title game, Villanova would have deal with Georgetown's intensity and especially suffocating defense. It was amazing to me the way Villanova was able to spread the floor and get great shots. The Wildcats shot 78 percent for the game.

I always thought Massimino belonged at Villanova, like Lou Holtz belonged at Notre Dame or like Krzyzewski belongs at Duke. Certain guys fit certain places. After leaving Villanova in 1992, it just wasn't a good fit for him at Vegas. I would have liked to see him finish his career on the Main Line.

His energy and enthusiasm were so infectious to everyone around the Villanova program. Oh man, did love his enthusiasm.

Rollie, Lou Carnesecca, John Thompson, McGuire, Valvano. Where have they all gone?

I remember going to a Villanova practice once, and Rollie started screaming at me as soon as I walked in, "How come I wasn't in your Rolls Royce to five coaches in America, baby?"

I said, "Rollie, they must have cut it. You were number six."

**V**illanova's Dwayne McClain throws his fist in the air in celebration as his Wildcats pitched the perfect game in winning the 1985 NCAA championship over Patrick Ewing and the Georgetown Hoyas.

# KEITH SMART *makes the game-winning shot as Indiana defeats Syracuse in the 1987 NCAA championship game*

## Get Smart

MOMENT NUMBER 4

**Indiana 74**
**Syracuse 73**
**March 30, 1987**

*Profile:* It was the same year "Hoosiers" debuted – a movie about a small-town Indiana high school that comes out of nowhere to win the state's all-class basketball championship.

Keith Smart helped Indiana write a Hollywood script of its own that season, making a 16-foot jumper from the left wing with five seconds remaining to propel the Hoosiers to a 74-73 victory over Syracuse in the 1987 NCAA Tournament championship game at the Louisiana Superdome.

The 6' 1" junior guard was familiar with his surroundings. Ten years before that one shining moment, he was a Boy Scout from Baton Rouge who used to work as a volunteer usher for New Orleans Saints home football games in the nosebleed seats at the Dome.

He was center stage the night Hall of Fame coach Bob Knight won his third national title.

Smart took an uncharacteristic route to Bloomington. He was a junior college star from Garden City (Kan.) Community College. Knight had never recruited the junior college circuit before, trying to steer away from what he considered to be marginal student-athletes with only two years of eligibility. But because the talent pool had temporarily dried up in the state, he felt he had to expand his horizons. Knight signed two junior college recruits – Smart and 6' 10" Dean Garrett – who would both become starters on his championship team.

Smart was only the fifth-leading scorer on the team. But he took the game over down the stretch, scoring 12 of the Hoosiers' final 15 points.

Smart's chance to create Hoosier hysteria came i a tight game after Syracuse's 6' 9" freshman forward Derrick Coleman missed the first part of a one-and-one with 27 seconds left. Had he made it, that coul have given the Orange a three-point lead. Forward Darryl Thomas grabbed the rebound and IU pushe the ball up the floor, looking to get Steve Alford, wl scored 23 points, freed up for an open shot. Alford ran off multiple screens, but couldn't shake Syracus point guard Sherman Douglas. The ball eventually went to Smart, who made the game winner.

Smart finished with 21 points, six assists and fiv rebounds and was named Most Outstanding Player of the Final Four. Thomas had 20 points and seven rebounds and Garrett finished with 10 points and 1 rebounds for the winners, who were 4-0 in one-poi games and 13-2 in games decided by five points or less. Center Rony Seikaly and Coleman combined f 26 points and 29 rebounds for Syracuse.

*Dickie V's View:* Hey, I was teasing my guy Bobb Knight – one of the great coaches of all time – on o ESPN show. We both felt that John Calipari should have called a T.O., baby, to set up a defense to prevent a three-point shot at the end of regulation in the 2008 championship game versus Kansas. Remember, Mario Chalmers made the biggest trifecta in Jayhawk basketball history to send the championship game into overtime.

I turned to the General and said, ``Wait a minute. Wait a minute. This brings back memories. How come you allowed Keith Smart to take the last shot in your 1987 championship game against Syracuse when you had Steve Alford, the best shooter in the nation?"

Well, as only the General can do, he began to laugh. And Digger Phelps, who was on the set with us, broke up as well.

And then we shared the moment about how Alford was covered like a blanket and Smart's shot was an absolute baseline beauty. I can still see him, taking a pass and making that tough, mid-range 16-footer from the baseline to beat Syracuse.

Smart was one of two junior college players – along with center Dean Garrett – who played on Knight's third national championship team. A lot of people thought Knight made a mistake – that he was going against his principles when he went after junior college players. They felt he should take only high school kids who could be four-year program players.

But he thought Smart and Garrett were both quality kids who could make that transition academically and athletically. I know he wouldn't tolerate it any other way. In numerous conversations with the General, he constantly mentions how proud he was that both Smart and Garrett not only produced on the basketball floor, but also demonstrated that they were genuine student-athletes by receiving their Indiana diplomas.

**W**hile many people thought Steve Alford would take the last shot for the Hoosiers in the 1987 championship game, it was Keith Smart who earned the role of hero. Syracuse fans were left heartbroken down in New Orleans.

# FRESHMAN

*Michael Jordan makes the game-winning jump shot as North Carolina defeats Georgetown in the 1982 NCAA championship game*

## Michael's Magic

MOMENT NUMBER 5

North Carolina 63
Georgetown 62
March 29, 1982

*Profile:* University of North Carolina Hall of Fame coach Dean Smith had taken the Tar Heels to the NCAA Final Four on six previous occasions, reaching the title game three times during that period. But each trip ended in disappointment.

Smith's storied ACC program finally had a major breakthrough in 1982 when UNC defeated powerful Big East champion Georgetown and its young 7' 0" star, Patrick Ewing, 63-62, in the national championship game before a crowd of 61,612 at the Louisiana Superdome. It was Carolina's first title since 1957.

But the outcome hung in the balance until the final moments.

Georgetown took a 61-60 lead after All-American guard Sleepy Floyd – who was from Gastonia, N.C., and a high school rival of UNC's 6' 9" star forward James Worthy, who was also from Gastonia – hit a jumper with less than a minute left. Smith was forced to call a timeout with 25 seconds to play when his team appeared disoriented. Smith drew up the final play. Most people thought it might be designed to go inside to Worthy, who had already scored 28 points.

But as the team broke the huddle, Smith looked over to his 6' 6" tongue-wagging freshman prodigy, Michael Jordan. "If it comes to you, Michael, knock it in," Smith said.

The Tar Heels inbounded the ball against Georgetown's collapsing zone, and point guard Jimmy Black floated a cross-court pass to Jordan, who caught it on the left wing and nailed a 16-foot jumper that swished through the net with 16 seconds to play.

*Photo Courtesy of Getty Images.*

"I actually closed my eyes," Jordan admitted. [so]mething I'd never done before. I didn't know [th]e shot had gone in until Georgetown took the ball [reb]ounds."

The Hoyas still had one last chance to win the [ga]me, but Worthy assured the victory with a [gam]e-saving steal. Georgetown opted to push the [bal]l up court instead of calling a timeout. Hoyas' [po]int guard Freddie Brown pulled up at the top of [the] key and faked a pass. Worthy lunged for a steal, [the]n Brown threw a soft pass into Worthy's chest by [mi]stake.

Afterwards, Jordan, who finished with 16 points [an]d nine rebounds, said he actually thought about [bei]ng in position to take the last shot when he was [rid]ing over to the game on the team bus. "All I could [thi]nk about was whether I would make it or miss it," [he] admitted.

It was Jordan's first of many brushes with great[ne]ss. Jordan became an instant celebrity in Chapel [Hi]ll. The next fall, the picture of his shot appeared [on] the cover of the local phone directory, and he had [a s]andwich named after him at the Four Corners [res]taurant on Franklin Street.

**[M]ichael Jordan was Mr. Clutch early in [his] college career. He showed a glimpse [of h]is future success in crunch time, hitting [the] winning shot against Georgetown in [the] 1982 championship game.**

*Dickie V's View:* It was an incredible moment for North Carolina – Dean Smith's first national championship after taking the Tar Heels to the Final Four in 1967, 1968, 1969, 1972, 1977 and 1981 and coming away empty.

People were starting to wonder when Smith was going to win one.

The players knew it. Before the 1982 NCAA semifinals against Houston, James Worthy and Jimmy Black, the team captains, called a meeting among their teammates. "Let's win it for coach," Worthy said.

And then it all came true when this special freshman, Michael Jordan, squared his body, went up and made that game-winning shot against Georgetown in the final moments of the national championship game.

Everybody talks about Worthy intercepting that pass from Freddie Brown on the final possession, but let me tell you, my friends, North Carolina wasn't cutting the nets down unless Jordan came through in the clutch.

That's what the guy was all about his whole career – creating magical moments.

Interestingly, Jordan's late father, James, stole some of that magic after that game. As reporters waited outside the Carolina locker room, some spotted James pretending to kick an imaginary object down the hallway.

"What are you doing?" one asked.

"It's the monkey off coach Smith's back," he said, with a grin. "I'm kicking it out of here."

# UCLA'S

# Edney's Dash

*Tyus Edney goes coast to coast for a game-winning field goal in a 1995 NCAA second-round victory over Missouri*

MOMENT NUMBER

**6**

UCLA 75
Missouri 74
March 19, 1995

*Profile:* Tyus Edney paved the road to UCLA's 1995 national championship.

The 5'10" senior point guard from Gardenia, Calif., playing with a sore ankle suffered two days earlier in a first-round win over Florida International, made what is still considered the greatest play in Bruins' history when he saved his Pac-10 champion team from disaster in a 75-74 NCAA Tournament second-round game against Missouri in Boise.

The Bruins were down by a point with just 4.8 seconds to play in regulation when Edney took the inbounds pass and raced the length of the floor through a maze of defenders. With his speed and creative ball handling, Edney found an opening and made a four-foot bank shot that set the stage for this hallowed program to win its 11th national championship and the first since the end of the John Wooden era in 1975.

"I heard the buzzer after the shot," Edney said afterwards. "Sweet sound. It was just a great feeling, knowing the shot went through and we were still in the tournament."

Edney's dash to glory was the culmination of a sustained comeback. The Bruins had to rally from an eight-point halftime deficit and from nine points down with 16:02 remaining in the game. Missouri gave UCLA the ultimate obstacle to overcome after Julian Winfield scored a field goal with 4.8 seconds, giving the Tigers a 74-73 lead. Harrick called a timeout and decided to go to Edney instead of All-American senior forward and team captain, Ed O'Bannon, the program's MVP in the '90s and the Wooden Award winner.

UCLA had prepared for this kind of situation throughout the season – running a drill that called for the players to go the length of the floor in six seconds. Edney had less time, but he felt he could get to the rim for a shot before the game ended. He took an uncontested inbounds pass from teammate Cameron Dollar 10 feet up the court, then took off up the left side. Missouri's Jason Sutherland attempted to trap him at midcourt, but Edney avoided pressure with a behind-the-back dribble. After reaching the key, 6' 8" forward Derek Grimm slid over in an attempt to stop the guard. Edney adjusted his shot around Grimm and banked it in.

The Bruins went on to win it all, defeating Arkansas, 89-78, in the finals at Seattle. Ironically, Edney, who had a great tournament run with 76 points, 38 assists and only nine turnovers, played only three minutes against the Hogs after he sprained his right wrist in the first half of a semifinal win against Oklahoma State.

*Dickie V's View:* There's no way in the world a coach is designing a play like that. It was a miracle moment for UCLA coach Jimmy Harrick. And it was Heartbreak City for all the Missouri fans.

That game looked like it was Lock City for the Tigers, but you couldn't tell it to this little guy from UCLA. He pulled a Danny Ainge, duplicating what the BYU guard did against Notre Dame back in the 1981 NCAA Tournament. He just broke the defense down – one defender after another – and went from one end of the floor to the other like a jet and completed the play.

Then it was celebration time for the Bruins and Heartbreak City for Missouri. The Tigers' two 7-foot twins, Sammie and Simeon Haley, kept shaking their heads and waited around at midcourt, hoping the officials would rule the shot was too late. But it didn't happen.

Harrick knew what it felt like to be on the losing end of a game like this. He was there a couple of times earlier in his career. In 1983, he was coaching Pepperdine and had NC State down by six points with less than a minute left – and lost in double overtime. Then in 1993, UCLA led Michigan's Fab Five by 19 – and lost again. Edney ironically wore the goat's horns in that Michigan game. With the game tied, he stole the ball at half court and passed to Ed O'Bannon when he could have scored a layup himself. Jimmy King intercepted the ball and the Wolverines won in overtime.

Edney had to wait two years, but he finally got a chance at redemption.

Teams are going to have those scares during a tournament run, but that was the ultimate scare – and Edney's play became a treasured moment in the history of UCLA hoops.

**T**alk about a dramatic ending. UCLA's Tyus Edney drove the length of the court and scored the winning basket against Missouri in the second round of the NCAA West Regional in 1995. The Bruins moved on with a 75-74 victory.

# KANSAS

*star Mario Chalmers' three-point shot sends the 2008 NCAA championship game into overtime as the Jayhawks go on to defeat Memphis for the title*

# Mario's Moment

MOMENT NUMBER 7

**Kansas 75**
**Memphis 68 (OT)**
**April 7, 2008**

*Profile:* It was the shot heard 'round the heartlands and the most dramatic shot in the history of Kansas' storied basketball program.

Junior guard Mario Chalmers, a McDonald's All-American from Anchorage, Alaska, made a life-altering, historic three-point jump shot with 3.6 seconds left in regulation to force overtime and give the Jayhawks the momentum they needed for a 75-68 victory over Memphis in the 2008 national championship game at the Alamodome in San Antonio.

Chalmers had been there before – in his dreams.

Four years earlier, Chalmers and his father, Ronnie, made the trip to the 2004 Final Four in this same town to watch Connecticut defeat Georgia Tech in the finals.

At one point during the game, Chalmers turned to his father and wistfully remarked, "One day, I'm going to be out there winning the national championship."

He was. He did. And his father, the director of Kansas' basketball operations at the time, was on the bench to see it.

Chalmers, who scored 18 points and was selected Most Outstanding Player of the Final Four, created a moment that will last forever on TV replays.

Memphis, which led by nine points with just 2:12 remaining, suffered a meltdown at the foul line, with Chris Douglas-Roberts, the Tigers' junior All-American guard, missing three straight to leave the door ajar for the Jayhawks to win their first championship in 20 years.

Memphis' freshman prodigy, Derrick Rose, still had a chance to lock up the game when he stepped to the line for two shots with 10.8 seconds to play. He missed the first but made the second,

sending the Tigers up 63-60.

Then Memphis coach John Calipari made a decision that may haunt him for the rest of his career. He decided not to call a timeout to give Kansas coach Bill Self a chance to set up a last shot. At the same time, he never got a chance to remind his players a foul would have prevented any shot that could result in a game-tying three-point goal.

Kansas guard Sherron Collins pushed the ball up the floor, avoiding Memphis defenders who tried to foul him. He almost lost the ball, before shoving a pass to Chalmers, coming off the wing.

Chalmers caught the ball, squared up, then nailed a three.

The overtime was anti-climactic.

Memphis' 6' 9" senior forward, Joey Dorsey, the Tigers' best interior defender, had fouled out. And the Jayhawks cruised home.

*Dickie V's View:* Hey, in a lot of ways, Kansas coach Bill Self was getting ripped like so many other coaches who have come close but aren't able to cut the nets down and win it all. We live in a world of instant gratification. Win, win, win – or you're a failure.

Are you kidding me? Self had all kinds of success at Tulsa, Illinois and Kansas as he made four journeys to the Elite Eight before the 2008 season. But now he was getting a reputation as the best coach never to win a national championship.

Wow. They were talking about Bill Self like they used to talk about Bud Grant of the Minnesota Vikings, who got criticized for not winning it all. I want to know how many other guys got to number two?

Well, anyway, Bill Self ended that talk. He finally grabbed the brass ring when his team rallied to beat

mphis, 75-68, in overtime to win the 2008 NCAA mpionship in San Antonio.

But it wouldn't have happened without Mario almers, who made that huge three with just 3.6 onds left in regulation to force the game into ertime.

He was under relentless, unbelievable pressure. had a hand in his face when he put up the shot, he never lost his poise. And he gave Rock, Chalk, hawkland another reason to be proud.

I spoke with Calipari the day after the game and told me he had a couple reasons for not signaling imeout after Rose's second free throw went through net. First, the Tigers work on end-of-game situations all the time. Second, with the Jayhawks out of timeouts, Memphis did not want to give Self a chance to draw up a play. He also said this: "If Chalmers doesn't make an amazing shot, are we even talking about this?"

By the way, after the season, Oklahoma State tried to lure Self back to his alma mater, but he said no to overtures about replacing Sean Sutton as head coach of the Cowboys.

Was I surprised?

Not at all. Oklahoma State has tradition, but Kansas is one of the solid gold programs in America and they now have another gold trophy for the display case in Allen Fieldhouse.

**M**ario Chalmers hit the dramatic game-tying three-point shot that really stunned Memphis late in the 2008 national championship game. The Jayhawks left San Antonio with their first national title since 1988.

# DUKE GUARD

## A-Capel-A Music

*Jeff Capel makes a 40-foot shot to push the 1995 Duke-North Carolina game into a second overtime*

MOMENT NUMBER 8

North Carolina 102
Duke 100 (2OT)
February 2, 1995

*Profile:* Duke had been such a dominant program – reaching the Final Four seven times in the previous nine years – that no one saw this coming.

But by the middle of the 1995 season, Mike Krzyzewski had left the team with back problems. The Blue Devils, coached on an interim basis by Pete Gaudet, were going through their worst season in recent memory. They were 0-7 in the ACC and facing the prospect of an upcoming visit from powerful neighborhood rival North Carolina at Cameron Indoor Stadium.

But for part of one enchanted evening, that was all a distant memory. Duke summoned up enough emotional courage to push the Tar Heels – who went to the Final Four that year – to the limit during a 102-100 double overtime loss.

For a while in that game, it looked like the Tar Heels might embarrass Duke. They made their first nine shots and jumped out to a 26-9 lead, fueled by two ESPN *SportsCenter* dunks – an alley oop to Rasheed Wallace and a reverse jam by Jerry Stackhouse over two Blue Devils.

Duke – which got 18 points on six threes from freshman guard Trajan Langdon and 89 points from their five starters – actually rallied to take a 12-point lead in the second half before Carolina staged a rally of its own to force the first overtime.

The Tar Heels looked like they had a chance to put the game away in the first overtime. They led 95-92 and their big center, Serge Zwikker, stepped to the line to shoot a pair of free throws. But Zwikker missed both and the wheels were set in motion for guard Jeff Capel to make one of the most memorable shots in Duke history – a running 40-foot heave that dropped through the net to tie the score as the buzzer sounded, forcing another overtime.

For one of the few times that season, Cameron erupted.

Carolina got 25 points on 10-of-11 shooting from Wallace before he fouled out with 10 seconds left in regulation; 25 from Stackhouse and 24 from senior guard Donald Williams. In the end, the Tar Heels had too much firepower for the outmanned Blue Devils.

The game was still tied late in the second overtime when Williams scored for the Heels. Then guard Jeff McInnis stole the inbounds pass for an easy layup to send Carolina ahead, 102-98.

Duke had a chance to force a third overtime or win the game outright on the final possession, but Steve Wojciechowski missed a jump shot and center Greg Newton shot an air ball on the putback reducing Capel's miracle shot to one of those glorious moments in a glorious rivalry.

*Dickie V's View:* Jeff Capel's 40-foot shot to force second overtime in the Blue Devils' 102-100 double overtime loss to North Carolina was Hail Mary time, but it was one that will always be remembered.

I was doing the game for ESPN in a little cubicle in the rafters of Cameron Indoor Stadium, and I got so excited when he hit that shot, I hit my head against the pipes and it caused me to bleed. But I

In't care. Blood was running down my neck. But I
In't care. I didn't want the game to end. I wanted to
 there all night long, as Lionel Richie would say.

My buddy, Mike Patrick, who loves ACC
sketball, stared at me with an incredible look
en he saw me bleeding. But I simply looked
ck and said, "Simply roll on, my friend, and let's
pe for six OTs as I have no place to go and want
enjoy this moment forever."

It was one of those dramatic games and it was just
e of those moments where that Duke team, which
d been struggling all year, stepped up to make it
mpetitive against its neighborhood rival.

What's that line people use: Throw the records
ay. You've got to believe that happens when you
k about the greatest rivalry in all of college sports.
s, Michigan-Ohio State and all you football lovers,
ke-North Carolina basketball is the best rivalry in
 of college sports. It is simply number one. Once
u watch one of those battles between the Dukies
d the Tar Heels, you'll understand that the emotion
d excitement are unparalleled.

But to the residents of Tobacco Road, it's just life
usual.

**In 1995, records meant nothing
when Duke and North Carolina
met. When Jeff Capel hit a
dramatic long-range shot, I thought
we would be there all night long,
as Lionel Richie would say.**

*Photo Courtesy of Duke Sports Information.*

# CHAMINADE *stuns No. 1 Virginia in 1982*

**No Island Hospitality**

MOMENT NUMBER

**9**

Chaminade 77
Virginia 72
December 23, 1982

*Profile:* Virginia was ranked No. 1 in the country and had just come off two huge victories over Georgetown and Houston. Towering 7' 4" All-American center Ralph Sampson outplayed Patrick Ewing as the Cavs defeated the Hoyas, 68-63, in Landover, Md. Then Virginia dispatched the powerful Cougars in Tokyo even though Sampson sat out after being diagnosed with pneumonia.

A pre-Christmas trip home from Japan through sunny Hawaii to play a little-known opponent sounded like the perfect reward.

But Chaminade – a tiny NAIA school with an enrollment of just 800 students – took all the fun out of the road trip, stunning the Cavs, 77-72, before a crowd of 3,500 at Blaisdell Arena in Honolulu, in what is still considered the biggest upset in the history of college basketball.

The Silverswords, who had started up their program only seven years earlier, were coming off a deflating loss to Wayland Baptist and did not look like they would offer much resistance to the ACC's mighty Cavaliers. Their coach, Merv Lopes, said he would consider it a moral victory if his team could stay within 20 points of the Cavs.

But no one bothered to tell that to Chaminade's 6' 8" center Tony Randolph.

Randolph had grown up in Virginia and played for Robert E. Lee High in Staunton, an archrival of Sampson's Harrisonburg High. He was a tough kid who was forced to grow up quickly after his parents died when he was in grade school. After spending two years at Panhandle Junior College in Oklahoma, he wound up at Chaminade so he would be closer to his brother, who lived on the islands.

Randolph had played against Sampson in high school and pickup games and knew his game. But no one expected him to hold his own against the big guy.

Randolph had 19 points and five rebounds, taking Sampson outside. Sampson finished with 12 points and 17 rebounds.

Virginia looked like it had taken control of the game early in the second half when it went on a 7-0 run to bust open a 42-42 tie, but the Silverswords refused to go away. They took a 70-68 lead on a field goal by Randolph with 90 seconds to play, then put the Cavs away from the free throw line.

The game ended at 2 a.m. – so late the news didn't hit the mainland until the next morning. But in a season when NC State won the national championship, it showed that no one in college basketball was invincible.

*Dickie V's View:* This was one of those shocking stories in the history of college basketball. Every time Chaminade plays a team from the mainland in a preseason tournament, people bring it up. They always wonder whether we're going to have a Chaminade moment.

I wasn't there. But when I saw it flash across the TV screen, I couldn't believe it. Virginia was No. 1 and they had Ralph. Chaminade didn't have anyone knew about. The question I ask is this: How many of those kids playing for Chaminade would be offered scholarship to play in the ACC? Zero.

But it shows what happens if you play together and the other team isn't playing with the same passion. Chaminade 77, Virginia 72. If they played again, Virginia would probably beat them by 30, man.

But not that night, man. It was all Chaminade.

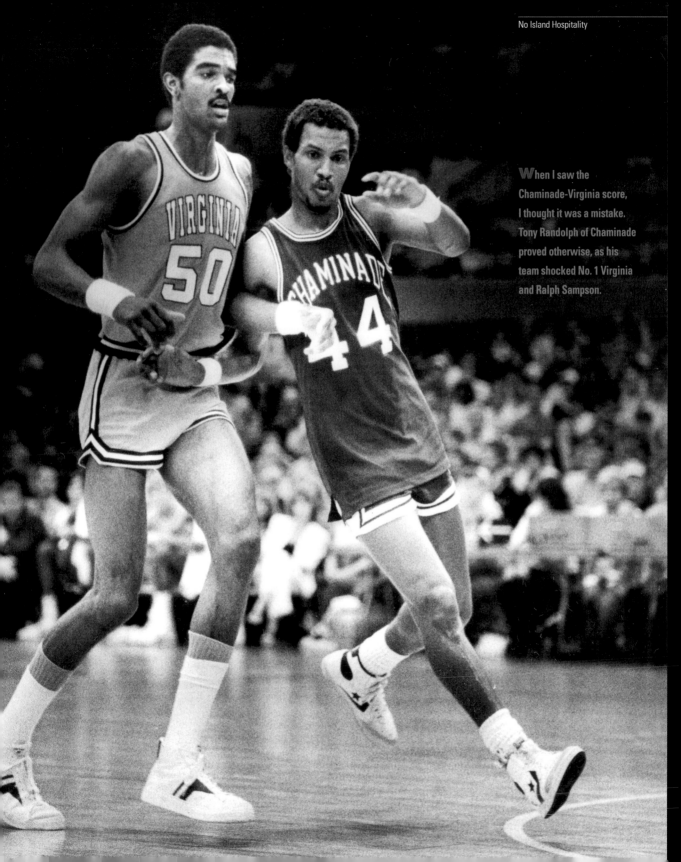

When I saw the Chaminade-Virginia score, I thought it was a mistake. Tony Randolph of Chaminade proved otherwise, as his team shocked No. 1 Virginia and Ralph Sampson.

# MID-MAJOR CINDERELLA

*George Mason makes the 2006 Final Four, beating Michigan Sta UNC and Connecticut along the way*

**Patriot Games**

MOMENT NUMBER
10

George Mason 86
Connecticut 84 (OT)
March 26, 2006

*Profile:* George Mason made an improbable run to the NCAA Final Four in 2006, flexing its mid-major muscles to beat three traditional powers – 2005 Final Four participant Michigan State, defending national champion North Carolina and pre-tournament favorite Connecticut – along the way.

Jim Larranaga's Patriots weren't even expected to be in the bracket after losing to Hofstra in the semifinals of the Colonial Athletic Association Tournament in Richmond. But the selection committee gave the Patriots an at-large bid, seeding them 11th in the East region.

It figured to be a short stay.

But Mason – an undersized team with good senior leadership and three shooters – liked the idea of staying around. The Patriots stunned Michigan State, 75-65, in a first-round game in Dayton, despite the fact that their starting guard, Tony Skinn, had been suspended for the game after punching Hofstra star guard Loren Stokes in the groin during the NCAA Tournament. The Patriots advanced by holding the Spartans scoreless over a seven-minute stretch.

Their string of upsets continued when they rallied from a 16-2 deficit to defeat North Carolina, 65-60, in the second round. Guard Lamar Butler led the way with 18 points. The Patriots, whose biggest players – Jai Lewis and Will Thomas – were only 6' 7", limited the Tar Heels' 6' 9" freshman All-American Tyler Hansbrough to just 10 points on five-of-12 shooting and held Carolina to less than 30 percent shooting.

But the pièce de résistance came when Mason defeated mighty Connecticut, 86-84, in overtime in the regional finals at the Verizon Center in Washington, D.C. The day of the game, Larranaga

began whistling the theme from "Mission Impossibl on the bus ride over to the Verizon Center. Then he sang it in the locker room.

The Patriots had a built-in advantage before the game. They were playing just 20 miles from campu. and the building had a home-court feel to it. Mason deserved everything it got that day. Swingman Folan Campbell scored 27 points for the Patriots, which put all five starters in double figures. Thomas and the 275-pound Lewis combined for 39 points and 1 rebounds against the taller Huskies; and the Patriots shot 61 percent after halftime.

Mason outscored UConn, 40-31, in the second half and, at one point, built a 12-point lead. But UConn came storming back and forced overtime when Denham Brown hit a last-second layup.

Mason's Cinderella carriage could have turned into a pumpkin then, but it didn't.

There was some suspense at the end after Lewis missed two free throws with six seconds left, and Brown had a chance to make a game-winning three on the final play. But the ball clanked off the front o the rim.

Mason had broken through the glass ceiling to claim the glass slipper.

*Dickie V's View:* Are you kidding me? Was I dreaming? Or did it really happen that George Maso went to the Final Four?

On Selection Sunday, people in the studio were surprised to see the Patriots in the field of 65. At the time, George Mason was 23-7, including two losses to conference rival Hofstra, which went to the NIT. This was a team that was taken to overtime by

Georgia State in the first game of the Colonial Athletic Association Tournament. The Patriots lost to Wake Forest, Creighton, Old Dominion and Mississippi State. And none of those squads made it to the Big Dance.

My friends, Jim Larranaga's squad was the biggest Cinderella story ever. I know you can make a case for Jimmy V knocking off Phi Slamma Jamma in 1983. And Villanova had its amazing run in 1985, upsetting Patrick Ewing and Georgetown in the championship game in Lexington. Danny and the Miracles were an amazing story when Kansas beat Oklahoma in 1988.

But George Mason tops them all.

Think about it. During this impossible run to the Final Four, the Patriots had to beat three elite programs in Michigan State, North Carolina and Connecticut. That meant that Larranaga had to battle the likes of three coaches who have national championship rings – Tom Izzo of Michigan State, Roy Williams of North Carolina and Jim Calhoun of UConn. My friends, I don't think we'll ever see anything like this again.

In the regional finals, they weathered a 12-point comeback from a Connecticut team picked by many cut down the nets in Indianapolis.

George Mason sent out a message loud and clear that in the NCAA Tournament, the little guy is capable of pulling off surprise after surprise in this day and age.

Later, I saw that they were selling T-shirts that read: "Coach L for President." If he's not interested in that job, they should at least erect a statue of him on campus.

Jim Larranaga and George Mason made an incredible run in the 2006 NCAA Tournament. The Patriots beat Michigan State, North Carolina and Connecticut en route to the Final Four as an 11th seed!

# MICHAEL JORDAN *leads North Carolina to a comeback victory over Virginia with Ralph Sampson in a 1983 ACC showdow*

## Jordan Rules

MOMENT NUMBER

## 11

North Carolina 64
Virginia 63
February 10, 1983

*Profile:* Ever since Michael Jordan knocked down the game-winning shot against Georgetown in the 1982 national championship game, he began developing a flair for the dramatic.

It really blossomed during his junior year. Jordan made a 24-footer at the buzzer against Tulane to tie the game, and North Carolina went on to win in triple overtime. In a game against Maryland, he charged from the top of the key to swat away a potential game-winning unguarded layup by the Terps' Chuckie Driesell.

But nothing will ever top his performance in the second meeting between the Tar Heels and Virginia that season. Carolina, which was ranked No. 1, had won the first game between the two ACC powers in Charlottesville, 101-95, to break the Cavs' 34-game home court winning streak. The Heels took an 85-62 lead with 9:41 remaining, holding off the Cavs when Jimmy Braddock and Jordan each made a pair of late one-and-ones.

The second-ranked Cavaliers, with their 7' 4" National Player of the Year Ralph Sampson, appeared to be on the verge of a huge revenge win in the rematch. Sampson hit a baseline jumper to send Virginia up 58-42 with 8:30 to play. The Cavs were still up, 63-53, with 4:12 remaining before Carolina staged one of the more impressive comebacks for which Dean Smith had become famous – scoring the last 11 points of the game in the 64-63 victory.

And Jordan, who scored 12 of his 16 points in t[he] second half, was right in the middle of it.

Jordan cut the Cavs' lead to 63-62 when he tipp[ed] in a missed three-pointer by Braddock with 1:07 le[ft] on the clock.

Then as Virginia guard Rick Carlisle was bringin[g] the ball up court and was nearly at the halfcourt lin[e] Jordan flicked it away and went in untouched for a monster dunk that gave Carolina its first lead of the second half and sent Carmichael into hysteria.

Virginia still had plenty of time to win and calle[d] a timeout with 23 seconds to play. Carlisle missed what could have been a game winner from the top [of] the key with three seconds left, and a possible tip in was averted when Jordan rose over Sampson to grab the rebound with only one second remaining.

Braddock scored 14 points for Carolina. Matt Doherty had 12 and Sam Perkins added 10 as the Ta[r] Heels solidified their spot atop the ACC. Sampson finished with 15 points and 12 rebounds for Virgini[a]

*Dickie V's View:* Oh, what a special game this wa[s] Talk about being pumped up. I remember I was rea[lly] excited about doing a game between the two great players in college basketball – Ralph Sampson and Michael Jordan.

Yes, my friends, Ralph was dominating college. And this new young star, Michael Jordan, was starti[ng] to make waves. And how special a battle it was.

The game was played in Carmichael. The noise was unbelievable. The place was going bananas. And Dean Smith was his usual Michelangelo self at the end of a big game.

For years, I remember telling people, "When the Heels are down, don't leave, baby. Don't leave the tube because he finds a way to do some unbelievable things."

Like he did that night.

In fact, that brings back a memory. Jimmy V was putting a hurt on North Carolina and I kept screaming, "Don't turn your TV off. Dean Smith's a master."

Well, after the game, I get a buzz from my buddy, Jimmy V, and he says, "Here we are, playing brilliantly – and we're winning. And all I'm hearing about is 'Dean this, Dean that.' Thanks a lot, buddy."

I began to laugh.

Dean was at it again in this game, and Carolina found a way to win because of none other than Michael the Magnificent." Mr. Jordan was simply sensational down the stretch, but then again, my friends, what else is new?

**It's Rejection City as MJ blocks a shot by Virginia's Othell Wilson in a 1984 match-up. I loved watching Jordan and Ralph Sampson on the same court under pressure in ACC action.**

# VIRGINIA

*defeats Georgetown in a 1982 classic between All-American centers Ralph Sampson and Patrick Ewing*

## Clash of the Titans

**MOMENT NUMBER 12**

**Profile:** The ultimate matchup of big men in college basketball occurred in 1968 when UCLA played Houston at the Astrodome in the Game of the Century and Lew Alcindor squared off against Elvin Hayes. Hayes scored 39 points as the No. 2 Cougars upset the top-ranked Bruins, 71-69, that night, taking advantage of the fact Alcindor was suffering from a severely scratched cornea that affected his vision.

That was one for the ages.

Virginia-Georgetown in 1982 was a close second.

WTBS, which outbid CBS for the rights to produce the dream game, promoted it as a matchup between two Goliaths – Virginia's 7' 4" senior All-American, Ralph Sampson, and Georgetown's 7' 0" sophomore, Patrick Ewing, who led the Big East Hoyas to the 1982 national championship game.

The hype took on epic proportions, even though neither Georgetown coach John Thompson nor Virginia's Terry Holland allowed their stars to talk to WTBS for the pre-game show. The universities were located just 125 miles apart. Top-ranked Virginia was the king of the ACC. Georgetown was the Beast of the Big East. And Sampson and Ewing were the chief attractions in the first major college basketball blockbuster to appear on basic cable TV.

Sampson had dominated every center he had played against – including the Russian national team's center in a preseason exhibition game. But he developed a case of the flu that required him to be pumped full of fluids after the battle was over.

He didn't play like he was sick.

He outplayed Ewing, outscoring him 23-16, and outrebounding him 16-8, blocking seven shots to Ewing's five as the veteran Cavs won, 68-63. There was a sellout crowd of 19,043 at the Capital Centre in Landover, Md., that was split down the middle with Virginia and Georgetown fans.

If Sampson imposed his will on the game with his finesse, Ewing did the same with his raw power. At one point, with the Cavs leading, 57-51, Sampson spun around Ewing for a dunk. On the next possession, an unhappy Ewing threw down a thunderous slam over Sampson, giving the horde of NBA scouts there a sense of his ability.

The score was tied at 59-59 with 3:48 to play. With Virginia ahead, 63-61, Ewing had a layup stuffed by Craig Robinson. And Anthony Jones – in a terrible shooting slump – missed the first part of a one-and-one. The Cavs, who scored only one field goal in the last 10:51, managed to hang on, making nine of their final 10 free throws.

Sampson was gracious in victory, calling Ewing "a great, great player."

Ironically, neither team advanced to the Final Four that season.

**Dickie V's View:** I remember watching that game on TV. It was a heavily hyped matchup, pitting the physical intimidation of Patrick Ewing of Georgetown against the offensive skills of Ralph Sampson of Virginia.

Virginia 68
Georgetown 63
December 11, 1982

Sampson got the best of Ewing that night and Virginia won, 68-63, in Landover. It was Goliath vs. Goliath – something we don't see today because players of that stature are just one-and-done. They're out, gone to the pros.

It's become a real farce, a mockery. There's no way that the current system lends any credence to the term "student-athlete" as it is simply a situation where a player is forced to play college basketball when he really has no desire to be on a college campus.

The NCAA talks about the student-athlete, but all this 19-and-under deal has been is a dress rehearsal for the NBA. I just wonder what happens when these kids are done playing in March.

In my mind, the NCAA should adopt a rule similar to the one it has in baseball. Kids – the LeBrons, the Kevin Garnetts, the Kobe Bryants – should be able to go right to the NBA out of high school. Like my guy, Sonny Vaccaro, the sneaker guru, says, they shouldn't be denied from making a living.

But after that, any kid who enters college should have to stay in school for three years. Why? Because there are benefits – the pro game benefits, the college game benefits. And, most of all, the individual athlete benefits. Stability, stability, stability. It's something that doesn't exist right now in the NBA or in the college game.

Oh well, I just thought I'd get that off my chest, baby.

The 1982 showdown between Georgetown's Patrick Ewing and Virginia's Ralph Sampson had a Final Four feel. There was so much national attention given to the battle of the big men, which Sampson's Cavaliers won, 68-63.

# DANNY MANNING *leads Kansas to an upset victory over Oklahoma in the 1988 NCAA championship game*

## Danny's Miracles

**MOMENT NUMBER 13**

Kansas 83
Oklahoma 79
April 4, 1988

*Profile:* Danny Manning's senior year could have evaporated before it started.

When the versatile 6' 10" consensus All-American center decided to return to school for his senior year in 1987-88, expectations were high. But injuries and eligibility issues hampered the Jayhawks. Kansas, which lost five players throughout the season, started out 12-8, and had to rally just to earn a spot in the NCAA Tournament.

Kansas was the sixth seed in the Midwest Region. But Manning made them seem unbeatable when it counted, averaging 26.4 points and 8.7 rebounds during the Jayhawks' improbable run to the national championship.

He had 25 points and 10 rebounds in a win over Duke in the semifinals.

But he saved the best for last in the national championship game against Oklahoma in Kansas City, just 40 miles from KU's campus in Lawrence. Manning scored 31 points, grabbed 18 rebounds, made five steals and brought the ball up the floor against OU's pressure during an 83-79 victory over the heavily favored, top-ranked 35-3 Sooners, who had won the Big Eight title and beaten Kansas twice during the regular season.

Kansas coach Larry Brown wanted to slow the ball down against the Sooners, but Manning spoke up in the huddle prior to the game. "Let's run and show them we're not afraid of them," he said.

That's exactly what happened.

The game was tied at 50-50 at halftime of the tournament's 50th anniversary title game. Brown told the team about the 1980 national championship game when he was coaching UCLA, and the Bruins lost to Louisville, 59-54, when high-flying Darrell Griffith went off for 23 points. He looked at Manning. "Griffith was the best player on the court and he was not going to let Louisville lose that game," Brown said. "You have to do the same."

Brown slowed the tempo in the second half. And the Jayhawks started looking for Manning, who showed why he was an easy choice for the National Player of the Year, scoring 17 of his team's final 33 points and taking over the game down the stretch. He made a running hook to give the Jayhawks a 69-68 lead and another hook to increase the lead to 75-71. Manning put the finishing touches on the victory over his Big Eight rival by making a pair of free throws with five seconds left.

Kansas finished 23-11 and became the first team with more than 10 losses to win the NCAA Tournament.

That Jayhawk team became known forevermore as Danny and the Miracles, an appropriate nickname for this March Cinderella.

*Dickie V's View:* This is a terrific story about how a gifted, talented player took a well-coached basketball team that had struggled initially and led them all the way to the championship.

Kansas started the year out 12-8. But all of a sudden, the beauty of college basketball was really displayed by Danny and the Miracles.

**D**anny Manning (facing camera left of center) had reason to celebrate when his Jayhawks upset Oklahoma in the 1988 national championship game, 83-79. Manning totaled 56 points in two Final Four games.

When you come to tournament time, everybody really unbeaten. Each team gets a chance to compete against the best in pursuit of the dream and NCAA title. Danny Manning and his gang went an unbelievable six-game run.

He was just a PTPer, a Prime-Time Player. Larry Brown, a disciple of Michelangelo, built everybody's game around Danny.

Looking back, maybe that was the last time a player told his teammates to jump on his back and simply carried them to the winner's circle.

Glen Rice averaged 30.7 points when Michigan won it all the next year, but the Wolverines had five future NBA players.

The closest might have been Syracuse freshman Carmelo Anthony in 2003. The Diaper Dandy scored 20 or more points in 15 of his last 18 games, and he was absolutely sensational in the Final Four. But he had a little help, too. Hakeem Warrick was a future All-American and a first-round pick. And guard Gerry McNamara was a terrific three-point shooter, hitting six trifectas against Kansas in the finals.

Danny had a bunch of blenders around him. The Miracles without Smokey Robinson are not the same. You need Smokey there to give them that great, great tune. Well, the Jayhawks needed Danny and, oh, did Danny deliver.

I thought it was interesting that 20 years after Danny Manning put on that big show against Oklahoma, he was back cutting down the nets against Memphis in 2008. Only this time he was wearing a suit and tie, working as an assistant coach on Bill Self's staff.

After spending 15 years in the NBA, Manning clicked his heels three times and he was back in Kansas.

# LOYOLA MARYMOUNT

*guard Bo Kimble shoots free throws left-handed in a 1990*
*NCAA Tournament run in honor of his fallen teammate, Hank Gath*

## Bo's Tribute

MOMENT NUMBER

14

Loyola Marymount 111
New Mexico State 92
March 16, 1990

*Profile:* Hank Gathers and Bo Kimble were inseparable from the time they were teammates at Dobbins Vocational in North Philadelphia.

They signed with USC, and then transferred to Loyola Marymount, where they helped coach Paul Westhead transform the tiny West Coast Conference school near Los Angeles into a national power with a fast-paced, three-point-oriented offense that set an all-time NCAA Division I record by averaging 122.4 points per game in 1990. In a game against U. S. International, the Lions went off for 186 points.

Gathers and Kimble – "The Hank and Bo Show" – were the stars of this wild ride.

The 6' 7" Gathers, an All-American forward, led the country in scoring in 1989, averaging 32.7 points as a junior. He averaged 29 points the next year. The 6' 4" Kimble averaged 35.3 points in 1990, which also led the nation.

Together, they felt they could make a run at the NCAA championship during their senior year in 1990.

Sadly, Gathers collapsed and died during the first half of the WCC Tournament semifinal against Portland at LMU's Gersten Pavilion. The rest of the conference tournament was postponed. The Lions were given the league's automatic bid because they won the regular season.

Despite its national ranking, the NCAA selection committee seeded Loyola 11th in the West Regional.

But Kimble stepped up in a special way when Loyola took the court against New Mexico State in a first-round game. Kimble, who was right-handed, shot his first free throw left-handed in honor of his friend. Gathers, a right-hander who had trouble

shooting free throws, had switched to his left hand before the season started.

Then Kimble personally shredded the Aggies wi[th] 45 points, providing the Lions with the momentum for an emotional run that carried them to the Elite Eight.

Kimble shot his first free throw with his left han[d] for the rest of the NCAA Tournament, leaving colle[ge] basketball fans with a lump in their throats. He ma[de] all three of his attempts.

Kimble's inspirational gesture carried over to his teammates.

Guard Jeff Fryer made 11 threes and scored 41 points during LMU's 149-115 second-round victory over Michigan. The Lions got by Alabama, 62-60, in the Sweet 16 before losing to eventual national champion UNLV in the regional finals, despite 42 points from Kimble.

*Sports Illustrated* celebrated Kimble's act of remembrance with a cover photo and a headline that read, "This is for you, Hank."

*Dickie V's View:* Hank Gathers and Bo Kimble ha[ve] been close friends and teammates ever since they played together on the Dobbins Vocational team tha[t] won the Philadelphia Public League.

They both wound up at Loyola Marymount. Wi[th] Loyola and Paul Westhead, you needed a computer to tally up the points. It was run, baby, run. And b[oth] Bo and Hank were capable of getting 30 any time they wanted.

When Hank died so suddenly from a heart ailment in the 1990 WCC Tournament, it crushed [me] and everybody else in his old neighborhood of Nor[th] Philly. Hank thought they had a shot to make histo[ry]

winning the national championship.
wanted to make sure no one forgot about
buddy in the Lions' first-round NCAA
rnament game against New Mexico State.
It was an emotional night for everyone
olved. Both teams wore black patches in
or of Gathers.
When Kimble stepped to the line for his first
throw attempt, he decided to shoot
handed because Hank shot them
handed. It was an emotional

moment, a moment dedicated to a fallen
comrade. Bo was showing the passion he had
for his teammate. This was his tribute –
his way of saying, "I love you and
I'm not going to forget you."
And he went one step farther –
he swished it.
Then he went out and scored
45 points as Loyola marched on
with a blowout victory.

*Photo Courtesy of Loyola Marymount Athletics.*

**W**hat a tribute!
Loyola Marymount's
Bo Kimble shot his first free
throw of every 1990 NCAA
Tournament game left-
handed in honor of his fallen
teammate, Hank Gathers.
Kimble's squad made it to
the Elite Eight before falling
to UNLV.

# KENTUCKY *rallies from 31 points down to stun LSU in a 1994 SEC game in Baton Rouge*

## Nine Lives

MOMENT NUMBER

15

**Kentucky 99
LSU 95
February 15, 1994**

*Profile:* Kentucky's dramatic 99-95 victory over LSU in 1994 was known as "The Mardi Gras Miracle." It is considered by many to be the greatest comeback of all time. The fact that Rick Pitino's Wildcats rallied from 31 points down in the second half to stun the Tigers in a late-night ESPN televised game in Baton Rouge has become a rich part of Kentucky folklore.

"I can't believe it," Pitino said. "I know I've never, ever seen anything like it."

Kentucky, coming off a trip to the Final Four the previous year, was ranked sixth in the country but had lost two straight games – to Arkansas and Syracuse. The Cats looked like they were headed for calamity after LSU, which shot 68 percent in the first half, made an 18-0 run to take a 68-37 lead just five minutes into the second half.

But the Cats refused to wilt inside the hot arena.

Pitino called a timeout and senior guard Travis Ford spoke to the team. "We're down 31 points and we're not leaving this building without a win," he told them. "We're going to win no matter what it takes. I'll stay here all night."

From that point, everyone stepped up.

Kentucky scored 24 of the next 28 points to get back in the game. Guard Tony Delk hit a three, and forward Walter McCarty hit another from the corner with 19 seconds remaining to play to give Kentucky a 96-95 lead – its first since 1-0 – and finally deflate the Tigers.

The Kentucky players mobbed one another at the end.

The LSU players were too stunned to speak.

The 7' 0" McCarty, who started the second half for Rod Rhodes, was the Cats' biggest star. He shot nine for 14, scored 23 points, grabbed eight rebounds and made four of seven three-pointers. Backup guard Jeff Brassow scored 14, center Gimel Martinez had 13, and Ford added 10 to offset the fact that LSU freshman guard Ronnie Henderson scored 36 points and Clarence Caesar had 32.

The Wildcats made 13 of 24 three-point shots in the final 12 minutes while LSU missed 11 of its final 12 free throws.

Like many Cat fans, McCarty's father, Steven Lindsey, fell asleep during the comeback. He didn't want to watch a blowout. McCarty called home afterward to tell him about Pitino's latest miracle.

*Dickie V's View:* Rick Pitino, who was really the first to use the three-point shot, had to be ecstatic with the way his kids were knocking down threes during that amazing comeback against LSU in Baton Rouge.

Are you kidding me? They were down 31 big ones.

I didn't do the game. I was watching the game periodically, but turned off the tube early in the second half as it looked like it was going to be Blowout City. Poor Rick Pitino. Embarrassing, humiliating. He's got to be going nuts inside because I know he has such unbelievable pride. Then I came back and turned on *SportsCenter* to get some of the final scores. And I couldn't believe what I saw.

I'm saying to myself, "This can't be true. It has to a joke."

No, it wasn't a joke. It was a fact. We're talking out the comeback of all comebacks.

Kentucky hit three after three. They hit 13 in the al 12 minutes. It just showed how quickly the me can change when a team gets on fire from hind the three-point line. It had to be Shock City Dale Brown.

Even Pitino looked like he couldn't believe it when he walked off the court. It was just another chapter – just like his 1987 Providence team with Billy Donovan, and "Pitino's Bombinos" down there at Kentucky – in his superb coaching legacy, which should eventually land him in the Hall of Fame.

He'd definitely get my vote if I were eligible to cast a ballot.

## JIMMY VALVANO *gives a moving farewell speech at the 1993 ESPY Awards*

# Never Give Up

MOMENT NUMBER

# 16

ESPY Awards
March 4, 1993

*Photo Courtesy of The V Foundation.*

*Profile:* Jimmy Valvano was on top of the world when he coached North Carolina State to the 1983 national championship. And he had become a popular studio analyst with ESPN once he left the game after the 1990 season.

But his world began to crumble in 1992.

Valvano had complained of back pain at the Final Four that year. When he visited the doctor on June 12, he was diagnosed with acute and aggressive bone cancer that began to sap the life out of one of the most vibrant men on the planet.

Valvano was given a year to live. He felt remorse for not spending more time with his family and lamented that he had spread himself so thin he didn't have enough time for his players at State.

Valvano tried to fight. But he was in constant pain, getting treatment for the disease at the Duke Medical Center.

He made a special trip back to NC State's Reynolds Coliseum for a celebration of the 10th anniversary of the Cardiac Pack's victory. He had to carry a small, hand-held pump with him that shot morphine into his body. He was swallowing 24 Advil tablets a day and walked around with a bottle of holy water from Lourdes, hoping for some divine intervention.

On March 4, 1993, ESPN planned to honor him with its first annual Arthur Ashe Courage Award at the inaugural ESPY ceremony at Radio City Music Hall in New York City.

Valvano almost didn't make it. But he flew to the city with his wife, Pam, because he had something to say to the audience and anyone fighting the dreaded disease.

Hobbling to the stage with the help of Duke coach Mike Krzyzewski, Joe Theismann and Dick Vitale, Valvano took the microphone and offered a stirring speech, delivering these lines:

"Cancer has taken away a lot of my physical ability. But what cancer cannot touch is my mind, my heart and my soul. Those three things will carry on forever.

"There are three things we all should do every day. We should laugh every day. We should spend time in thought. We should have our emotions moved to tears – it could be from happiness or joy. If we laugh, we think and we cry, that's a full day. That's a heckuva day."

Valvano ended his speech with the following words of encouragement: "Don't give up. Don't ever give up."

Valvano died April 28, 1993. He was 47.

But his inspiration for the birth of The V Foundation for Cancer Research that has raised millions of dollars for cancer research lives on.

*Dickie V's View:* When Jimmy Valvano was 17, he started writing down his life goals on an index card. He wanted to become a coach, win a game in the Garden and cut down the nets after the national championship game.

Shortly before his death, his wife, Pam, found another index card in the pocket of one of Jimmy's sports coats.

He had made a new list. He wanted to learn how to paint, play the piano and find a cure for cancer.

I remember sitting in the green room the night of the ESPYs, getting ready to introduce Jimmy as the recipient of the first Arthur Ashe Courage Award. I remember being so nervous and asking for advice. Standing there was one of the great actors of our time, an All-Rolls Roycer – Dustin Hoffman. His job was to explain what the Arthur Ashe Award is all about. Arthur Ashe was a champion in so many ways – a winner both on and off the tennis court.

I still get goose bumps when I think about that moment – about how Jimmy struggled to make the journey from Raleigh to New York City. Mike Krzyzewski and his wife, Mickie, were on the flight with Jimmy, who was ill on the plane. He had to be in a wheelchair at the hotel.

I remember talking to Pam. She told me Jimmy was down after learning at his regular checkup that the cancer had spread throughout his body. I spoke with Jimmy and he shared his feelings about his children – Nicole, Leann and Jamie – and how much he loved them and would miss them.

He was so upset he almost didn't come to the event.

But once he got on stage, he rocked the house with an inspirational speech as he poured his heart out about battling cancer. I – along with so many others – was moved to tears.

The V Foundation for Cancer Research was set up by his friends to help fight the dreaded disease that took my friend.

The sign of greatness in a man is not just winning a basketball game but affecting generation after generation once you're gone. The V Foundation for Cancer Research has raised more than $75 million for cancer research in the name of Jim Valvano.

His legacy is going to go on and on and on.

I will never forget Jimmy V's speech at the inaugural ESPY awards. The V Foundation for Cancer Research has made a difference in the lives of so many people. Jim's legacy has gone way beyond the sport of college basketball.

# DUKE *stuns unbeaten UNLV in the 1991 NCAA semifinals*

## Rebels Be-Deviled

MOMENT NUMBER 17

Duke 79
UNLV 77
April 1, 1991

*Profile:* The 1991 UNLV team looked like it was on the verge of immortality heading into its national semifinal matchup against Duke in Indianapolis.

The Runnin' Rebels, who were coming off a national championship season, were 34-0, ranked No. 1 in the country, and had been challenged only twice during a perfect season. They were being compared to some of the best teams of all time – the 1976 Indiana Hoosiers and all the great UCLA teams.

The swaggering Rebels, with three top 12 NBA draft picks in their lineup – All-American forwards Larry Johnson and Stacy Augmon and point guard Greg Anthony – had every reason to be confident. They had blown away Duke, 103-73, in the championship game the previous year.

No one gave Duke much of a shot.

But Jerry Tarkanian was nervous.

He realized the Blue Devils, who had won 30 games, also had three first-round draft picks – 6' 11" All-American senior center Christian Laettner, sophomore forward Grant Hill and junior point guard Bobby Hurley. And Mike Krzyzewski would make a point of reminding them they had been embarrassed.

His worst fears were realized when the Blue Devils stunned Tark's best team ever, 79-77, at the RCA Dome in Indianapolis. UNLV couldn't stop Laettner, who went off for 28 points. The Devils, who shot 51.8 percent, also got a great effort from the gritty Hurley, who had been sick and ineffective with a stomach flu in the 1990 title game, but responded this time with 12 points, nine assists and only two turnovers.

Krzyzewski told his players if they could keep it close at the end, Vegas might lose its comfort zone because the Rebels hadn't been challenged before.

That's exactly what happened.

UNLV lost its leadership on the floor when Anthony fouled out with 3:56 to play. The Rebels still had a 76-71 lead and looked like they might have the game under control when Hurley hit a huge three – which is still considered one of the biggest shots in program history – to show the Rebels Duke wasn't going anywhere. With 15 seconds left and the score tied at 77, Laettner was fouled on an offensive rebound and drained two free throws to put the Devils up two. UNLV had the last shot, but Johnson – their rock – passed on a three, passing instead to guard Anderson Hunt, who had to chase the ball down and wound up putting a desperation shot that didn't come close.

The Devils broke into celebration, but Krzyzewski calmed them down. "We still have one more," he said.

They got it two days later when they defeated Kansas, 72-65, to give Krzyzewski his first national title.

*Dickie V's View:* Think about it. This great game almost didn't take place. Everybody knows about the way the NCAA and Jerry Tarkanian were battling.

In his book, "Runnin' Rebel," Tarkanian claimed that, at one point, the NCAA was threatening to suspend UNLV – the defending national champions from the 1991 NCAA Tournament for past infractions.

But saying all that, Tarkanian was at his best when he was in the gym. Yes, "Dr. Tark," as I like to call

, was the master of getting the most out of
ple.

And, oh my friends, did he get the most out of
1991 team. You better believe it. People were
ing about this team as being the ultimate college
ketball team.

But they had one little dilemma. They ran into
am from Durham, N.C. – a Duke team they had
zed by 30 the year before in the title game.

But Christian Laettner, Bobby Hurley and Grant
l had a great sense of pride. And you just knew
y were going to give it their best shot in this
nce to get back at the Runnin' Rebels.

Krzyzewski made sure they didn't forget what
opened. He showed his players a tape of that game,
nting out that even though the final score looked
sided, the Blue Devils had made many uncharac-
stic mistakes that helped Vegas along the way.

Duke had a little chip on its shoulder when it
k the court.

And it had one huge plus – the matchup on the
ide with Laettner, as he had no equal. UNLV's 6'
' center George Ackles had no chance. It was an
, No Contest, baby, as Laettner put 28 on the
rd and used his talent to go inside and outside.

Two more things got a little overlooked. Hurley
l been sick the year before and he was healthy for
rematch. No excuses. Vegas was clearly the better
m in '90 and dominated. In 1991, Hurley had that
three late in the game and forward Greg Koubek,
underrated player, did a good job slowing down
superstar Larry Johnson defensively.

Oh, what a magic moment for the Dukies.

Christian Laettner (32) blocks a shot attempt by UNLV's Larry Johnson during the 1991 NCAA semifinals. One year after losing in the championship game by 30 points, the Dukies were not intimidated and scored a stunning upset over "Tark the Shark" and his Runnin' Rebels.

## STEVE FISHER *replaces Bill Frieder and coaches Michigan to the 1989 NCAA championship*

The Substitute Teacher

MOMENT NUMBER 18

*Profile:* There was an air of uncertainty surrounding the University of Michigan as the talented Wolverines prepared for the 1989 NCAA Tournament. Just two days before the team was to leave for its first-round game, coach Bill Frieder had flown to Tempe and accepted the head coaching job at Arizona State, effective at the end of the season.

Frieder thought he still would be allowed to coach Michigan in the postseason, but AD Bo Schembechler was so upset that Frieder had not told him personally that he fired Frieder on the spot. "A Michigan man coaches Michigan," he said.

That man was Frieder's assistant, Steve Fisher, a former high school coach with no experience on the Division I level. Fisher, who was named interim coach, inherited a team of four future pros.

And he made the most of it.

Senior All-American forward Glen Rice went off, averaging 30.7 points, and the Wolverines went on a wild ride, winning six straight games. The Wolverines defeated ACC power North Carolina, 92-87, in the Sweet 16 at Lexington; Big Ten regular-season champion Illinois, 83-81, in the national semifinals; and Big East champ Seton Hall, 80-79, in overtime to win the championship in Seattle.

Rice scored 34 points against UNC, 28 against Illinois and ripped the Hall for 31 points and 11 rebounds. He was an easy choice for Most Outstanding Player in the NCAA Tournament, but the title game still came down to the final moments.

Guard John Morton, who scored 35 points for Seton Hall, gave the Pirates a 79-76 lead with 2:50 remaining. Michigan still trailed by a point when Morton put up an air ball in the final seconds. Rice grabbed the rebound and fed a pass to Rumeal Robinson, who drove down the floor, sticking out his elbows and hips, trying to draw contact with Seton Hall guard Gerald Greene.

The whistle blew. The call could have gone either way. But official John Clougherty sent Robinson to the line for two free throws with 3.1 seconds remaining and a chance to win the game.

Seton Hall called two timeouts trying to ice Robinson, but Robinson would not be denied, making both attempts. Michigan won its first national championship in men's basketball.

When Fisher arrived back at Ann Arbor, Schembechler rewarded him by naming him head coach on a full-time basis.

*Dickie V's View:* This was a team that was really put together by Bill Frieder. They had four future pros – Glen Rice, Sean Higgins, Rumeal Robinson and Terry Mills.

I felt Frieder really got a raw deal. I really do. He should have been allowed to coach that team before moving on to Arizona State.

Having said all that, Steve Fisher, the assistant at the time, took over and had Frieder's kids playing with a single-minded purpose – to win a national

Michigan 80
Seton Hall 79 (OT)
April 3, 1989

championship. They responded in a very positive way to a new coach.

Robinson will always be remembered for making those two game-winning free throws against Seton Hall at the end of the championship game after a controversial call.

He's such a great story – a Prop. 48 non-qualifier from Cambridge, Mass., who not only graduated in three-and-a-half years but also went on to do some work on a master's degree at Harvard's business school.

I remember he said to me that the Prop. 48 label embarrassed him. He told me, "You walk into class and it's like you've got a big sign on your chest. Everybody's looking at you like you're different."

There are a lot of kids like Robinson, who have the potential academically. All they need is someone to direct them, give them an opportunity.

I'll never forget, after Michigan won the title, walking up to Steve Fisher and telling him it doesn't get any better than this. "Steve," I said. "You're 6-0. Retire, baby."

**Steve Fisher showed that a Michigan man could lead the Wolverines to the promised land. The Maize and Blue beat Seton Hall in Seattle to win the national championship in 1989, shortly after Fisher replaced Bill Frieder as head coach.**

# CONNECTICUT'S *Tate George hits a buzzer beater to defeat Clemson in a 1990 NCAA Sweet 16 gam*

## By George!

MOMENT NUMBER

19

Connecticut 71
Clemson 70
March 22, 1990

*Profile:* The University of Connecticut had gone from unranked in the preseason to winning its first-ever Big East regular-season and tournament titles in 1990. But the Huskies' dream season was in danger of evaporating during an NCAA Sweet 16 game against ACC giant Clemson at the Meadowlands before senior guard Tate George intereded.

George, who had been booed by the UConn crowd just three weeks earlier because of a disappointing performance in Hartford, became an instant hero. He made a dramatic 16-foot jumper from the right corner off a 90-foot pass from freshman teammate Scott Burrell just before time expired to bail out the Huskies from near disaster and give them a 71-70 victory over the Tigers.

The victory propelled UConn to its first East Regional final. But it didn't come without some moments of doubt.

The Huskies went from being in total control to falling behind 70-69 after Clemson went on a 30-10 roll to make up a 19-point deficit in the final 12 minutes. Forward Sean Tyson gave the Tigers the lead on a three-pointer from the left corner with 11.3 seconds left. UConn looked like it was finished when George missed a jumper from the left of the key, and Burrell fouled Tyson with 2.6 seconds to play. Tyson missed the first part of a one-and-one. Burrell grabbed the uncontested rebound, calling a timeout with just one second to play.

In the huddle, the UConn coaches kept telling the players, "It's not over. It's not over."

UConn Hall of Fame coach Jim Calhoun had practiced what he called a home run play just for this type of occasion. And he had the perfect weapon –

the 6' 7" Burrell – to make the inbounds pass.

Burrell, from nearby Hamden, Conn., had the arm. He had been drafted by the Seattle Mariners out of high school and offered a $100,000 contract Notre Dame and Miami had also recruited Burrell a a quarterback. But assistant coach Howie Dickenma convinced him to play basketball for the Huskies.

Clemson's 6' 11" Elden Campbell guarded Burre at the baseline. He lofted a soft length-of-the-floor overhand pass to George on the far baseline. George caught the ball, had the presence of mind to regrou spun and shot over the 6' 7" Tyson, who had backe off because he was concerned about committing a foul. The ball sailed through the net as the buzzer went off. The officials signaled it was good.

The next day, the headline in the *Hartford Courant* read "It's late. It's great. It's Tate."

It was a heartbreaking loss for Clemson coach Cliff Ellis and the Tigers, who seemingly had the game won. Ironically, two days later, UConn lost to Duke, 79-78, in the regional finals when Christian Laettner made a last-second shot of his own.

*Dickie V's View:* That was a huge breakthrough game for Jim Calhoun as he built the Connecticut program into a national power.

The Huskies came out of nowhere to win their first Big East championship in 1990. Then they fou a way to keep a magical season alive, making a last-second miracle play to beat Clemson, 71-70, in the NCAA Sweet 16 at the Meadowlands.

I'm sure Tate George's shot was the talk of Storr and everywhere else in the state of Connecticut next day. It was celebration time. That was miracu-

It was the pass heard 'round Connecticut. Tate George and Chris Smith (13) celebrate as the Huskies scored in the final second to stun Clemson in the 1990 East Regional semifinals at the Meadowlands.

s. But the thing I'll always remember most about t game was Scott Burrell's perfect length-of-the- or pass to the right corner to set it up.

Everybody talks about the shot. But there have n some memorable passes throughout the tory of the NCAA Tournament: Grant Hill hitting ristian Laettner with a three-quarter-court pass for t miracle shot in the 1992 Duke-Kentucky East gional final. Jamie Sykes making that inbounds pass to Bill Jenkins, who flipped the ball to Bryce Drew off a hook-and-lateral for the game-winning three-point jumper at the buzzer as Valparaiso upset Ole Miss in the first round of the 1998 NCAA Tournament.

Burrell was the perfect guy for UConn's Mission Impossible.

He was a major league pitching prospect coming out of high school and he threw a perfect strike, baby.

# ROY WILLIAMS *leaves Kansas after 15 years to return to his roots as North Carolina's head coach*

**Tar Heel Born**

MOMENT NUMBER

**20**

Lawrence, Kansas/
Chapel Hill, North Carolina
April 17, 2003

*Profile:* Moments after Kansas' heartbreaking 81-78 loss to Syracuse in the finals of the 2003 NCAA Tournament in New Orleans, CBS reporter Bonnie Bernstein asked Roy Williams the question that seemed to be on everybody's mind: Was there any truth to the widespread speculation he would leave Kansas after 15 years and return to coach North Carolina, his alma mater?

She caught Williams, who was visibly upset, at the wrong time.

"I don't give a (bleep) about North Carolina," he told a national TV audience.

A week later, Williams walked into a 9 p.m. press conference in Chapel Hill to announce he was indeed coming home to the place where he had gotten his start in coaching as an assistant for 10 years to Hall of Famer Dean Smith.

Smith not only hired Williams, but he also recommended him to Kansas AD Bob Frederick when Larry Brown left Kansas in 1988 after coaching the Jayhawks to the NCAA championship.

Williams inherited a Kansas team that was about to go on NCAA probation.

But he persevered and took the Jayhawks to unprecedented heights during his time in Lawrence. He coached that storied program to 418 wins – an average of 27.8 wins per year; nine Big 12 titles; 14 straight NCAA bids and four Final Fours.

Williams had been targeted and romanced by North Carolina to replace Bill Guthridge, who retired in 2001. But he couldn't decide before flying back to the Midwest and told Carolina officials he needed time to think it over. A week later, Williams announced he was staying at KU in front of 16,000 cheering Kansas fans at Memorial Stadium.

But after Carolina dismissed Matt Doherty following a 19-16 non-NCAA Tournament season that included accusations he had alienated his players, Williams couldn't say no again to the legendary Smith, despite his love for the Kansas program.

"I was a Tar Heel born and I'll be a Tar Heel when I die," Williams said at his press conference. "But, in between, I was Tar Heel and Jayhawk bred."

The Kansas faithful did not take it well, viewing the decision as a betrayal. T-shirts were printed that read, "Benedict Williams."

The Carolina nation viewed Williams as a savior.

Williams inherited a young, promising, but sometimes dysfunctional team that had future star power with 6' 9" center Sean May and guards Raymond Felton and Rashad McCants. Two years later, after adding 6' 8" freshman Marvin Williams, the Tar Heels won the national championship that had eluded Williams at Kansas, defeating Illinois, 75-70, in St. Louis. May, the tournament's Most Outstanding Player, led the Tar Heels with 26 points and 10 rebounds in the final.

Four stars from that team – May, Felton, Williams and McCants – were taken in the first round of the June draft. Williams was elected to the Naismith Memorial Basketball Hall of Fame two years later.

*Dickie V's View:* I always felt Roy Williams was treated a little unfairly by some Kansas alums and fans who were upset when he left to go home again.

He accomplished so much in Lawrence, averaging close to 28 wins a year for 15 seasons. He took four of his Kansas teams to the NCAA Final Four – in 1991, 1993, 2002 and 2003. He fell short in some eyes because he didn't win a national title.

But to me, you don't have to do that to validate
urself as a great coach because there are only a
udful of guys who get that gold ring.

In my mind, I've always believed the mark of a
at athlete or a great coach is consistency. If you can
sistently stay at the top year after year – like Fran-
Albert Sinatra, who dominated the entertainment
ld one decade after another – that's greatness.
That's what Roy Williams, Bob Knight, Mike
yzewski and Dean Smith did over the years. That's
y they're all in the Hall of Fame.
I hope the people of Kansas realize it was simply

a question of going home. Roy loved his stay, loved
his time in Lawrence. But when his alma mater came
calling, there was no way he was going to say no a
second time.

I've often said you couldn't get a better fit than
Roy Williams and North Carolina. He is absolutely
North Carolina through and through. He graduated
from there, served 10 years as a second lieutenant
under Dean Smith there, and his kids went to school
there. So how could anyone begrudge him making
the move? As they say, my friends, since his arrival,
nothing could be finer than to be in Carolina.

**H**all of Famer Roy Williams
proved you can go home
again. He returned to take
over the head  coaching
reigns at North Carolina and
celebrated the 2005 national
championship when the
Tar Heels beat Illinois in
St. Louis.

# CARMELO ANTHONY *leads Syracuse to the 2003 NCAA championship*

Melo Yellow

MOMENT NUMBER 21

Syracuse 81
Kansas 78
April 7, 2003

*Profile:* Jim Boeheim had coached Syracuse to the NCAA championship game twice before, only to come away disappointed. Indiana's Keith Smart broke his heart, making a 16-foot baseline jumper with five seconds to go to give the Hoosiers a 74-73 victory at the Louisiana Superdome in 1987. Then Rick Pitino's most talented Kentucky team ever defeated the Orange, 76-67, in 1996 at the Meadowlands.

But Boeheim never had a franchise player like Carmelo Anthony on either of those teams.

The 6' 8" Anthony was a 19-year-old freshman phenom from Baltimore who signed with the 'Cuse largely because of the recruiting efforts of assistant Troy Weaver, who had roots in the D.C. area and had watched Anthony's star rise since ninth grade.

Anthony grew up in a crime-infested housing project and commuted to Towson Catholic for his first three years in high school. When Weaver persuaded Boeheim to watch Anthony, who had grown five inches the summer after his sophomore year, play in 11th grade, Boeheim quickly sensed he might be watching the best prospect in the country. Anthony committed to Syracuse that spring, then transferred to Oak Hill (Va.) Academy, where he got his grades in order and made the McDonald's All-American game, winning the slam dunk competition.

He spent only one year in college, but wasted little time carving out his legacy.

Anthony averaged 22.2 points and 10 rebounds, rapidly emerging as the Orange's number one option on offense. He was selected Big East Rookie of the Year and was the only freshman to make the 2003 first-team All-Big East. He was the dominant personality in the NCAA Tournament that March, leading a young, ever-improving third-seeded team

– which had just one senior and six freshmen and sophomores playing key roles – to the school's first national championship.

Anthony averaged 17 points and 8.7 rebounds during the first four games of the tournament. Then in the national semifinals against Texas at the Superdome, he took off, scoring 33 points on 12-of-19 shooting against Longhorn defensive stopper Royal Ivey. He also grabbed 14 rebounds during that 95-84 victory.

Anthony was just as influential in the championship game against Kansas two nights later, scoring points, grabbing 10 rebounds and contributing sev assists as the Orange jumped out to an 18-point le then held on for an 81-78 victory. Freshman guard Gerry McNamara drilled six threes for Syracuse in that game, which came down to the final possessic

Syracuse was clinging to a three-point lead but 6' 8" sophomore forward Hakeem Warrick missed two free throws with 24 seconds left. Warrick mad up for those mistakes by swatting away Michael Le three-point attempt out of bounds with 1.5 second left. Kansas guard Kirk Hinrich missed a desperat three at the buzzer.

Afterwards, Boeheim said that Anthony, who w named the NCAA Tournament's Most Outstanding Player, was "by far the best player in college basketball."

Who could argue?

Originally, Anthony had planned to spend two three years in college; but having accomplished his ultimate goals, he declared for the NBA draft with Boeheim's blessing.

He was selected by Denver with the third pick the draft.

**C**armelo Anthony was a difference-maker for Syracuse from the first day he stepped onto the college campus. He helped the Orange win a national championship in New Orleans in 2003.

*ckie V's View:* Hey, let's face reality. Early in ..my Boeheim's coaching career at Syracuse – and ..n later on – a lot of local critics were all over his ..e. It was like they were never satisfied. But if you ..ck out the stats, he was always winning 25 games .he tough Big East, always challenging for the ..mpionship. And he took two teams to the NCAA ..al Four, in 1987 and 1996. But it never seemed to .enough.

Now, here comes this kid, Carmelo Anthony, a ..uine Diaper Dandy from out of Baltimore. You ..ldn't tell he was a freshman.

I remember talking to him before the first game of . career, just telling him to relax. Well, all he did in . debut was score 27 points and grab 11 rebounds . a loss to John Calipari's Memphis Tigers at the ..rden – the Mecca in the eyes of some for college ..sketball. With numbers like that, you knew he was .ng to be special.

I just didn't know in my heart if Syracuse had .trong enough supporting cast to challenge for a ..ional title.

Well, my friends, Carmelo just kept getting better .d better. He was just brilliant throughout the 2003 .AA Tournament. And he did get a lot of help in . championship game against Kansas, especially ..m freshman guard Gerry McNamara, who hit six ..ee-pointers, and forward Hakeem Warrick, a ..ure All-American who made a game-saving block .he end of the 81-78 victory.

But don't forget about the leadership from Mr. ..my Boeheim, who, in his own quiet way, kept his .yers poised throughout that six-game tournament ..

Jimmy looked like he was on cloud nine when he and his beautiful wife, Julie, walked into a restaurant where we were celebrating at our ESPN wrap-up party. Jimmy had the smile of a champion and who could blame him, as he became the toast of the basketball world on that special, memorable night? By the way, for all those critics, who now have become huge Jimmy B fans, you can find him in the Naismith Memorial Basketball Hall of Fame in Springfield, Mass. My friends, he has an NCAA championship and recently added an Olympic golden moment as Coach K's second lieutenant with the USA's "Redeem Team."

# THREE
*second-round shockers – St. Joseph's stuns No. 1 DePaul, U.S. Reed hits a shot from behind midcourt to g[ive] Arkansas a victory over Louisville, and Rolando Blackman leads Kansas State to a victory over Oregon [State]*

# Wild Weekend

MOMENT NUMBER

22

St. Joseph's 49
DePaul 48

Arkansas 74
Louisville 73

Kansas State 50
Oregon State 48

March 14, 1981

*Profile:* It was the day the wheels came off for the favorites during second-round games in the newly expanded 48-team NCAA Tournament in 1981.

St. Joseph's – a tiny Catholic school in Philadelphia with just 2,340 undergrads – stunned top-ranked, top-seeded DePaul, 49-48, in a Mideast subregional at Dayton. Guard U.S. Reed hit a shot from beyond midcourt at the buzzer to give Arkansas a 74-73 win over defending national champion Louisville at Austin, Tex. Guard Rolando Blackman, a 1980 Olympian from Brooklyn, hit a game-winning 16-foot jump shot with two seconds left as Kansas State upset second-ranked and top-seeded Oregon State out West in Los Angeles.

All of these wild finishes ended within seconds of one another – and March Madness was born.

Jimmy Lynam, the young coach of St. Joseph's – a Jack Ramsay disciple – made a national name for himself when his Hawks outplayed the more talented, but less motivated Blue Demons. Lynam did a good job controlling tempo with his four-to-score offense; and the Hawks did a good job containing DePaul's cocky star, Mark Aguirre, holding him to just eight points and six shots.

DePaul still had a chance to put the game away when Skip Dillard – who was named "Money" because he was an 85-percent foul shooter, went to the line with DePaul up one, 48-47, to shoot a one-and-one with 13 seconds remaining. But Dillard missed.

St. Joseph's guard Bryan Warrick raced down court finding freshman forward Lonnie McFarlan open in the right corner. McFarlan then passed to forward John Smith, who was all alone, for a last-second game-winning layup.

The enduring images of the end of that game w[ere] Lynam's 15-year-old daughter racing onto the floor to embrace her father and Aguirre walking off the court and out the door, with his earphones on and the game ball in his hands – which he threw into t[he] river.

Louisville looked like it might advance, too, wh[en] the late Derek Smith scored a go-ahead basket in th[e] final moments. But Arkansas coach Eddie Sutton to[ld] his players to get the ball to Reed on the final possession, and he made a game-winning shot that wa[s] measured at 49-feet, four-and-4/5 inches.

Finally, Kansas State rallied from 12 points dow[n] to beat what might have been the best Oregon Stat[e] team ever. The game began to turn when Oregon State's 7' 0" big man, Steve Johnson, fouled out with 3:23 to play. The score was tied at 48-48, but the Beavers still had a chance to take control when Charlie Sitton stepped to the line to shoot a one-and-one with 11 seconds left. He missed. And Blackma[n] wrote Oregon State's tournament obituary with a jumper from the right corner with two seconds left.

After all that suspense, the country needed a chance to exhale.

*Dickie V's View:* Who would have thought it? The No. 1- and 2-ranked teams in the country and the defending national champions, all gone in the blink of an eye. It was a topic of conversation the next morning and it created a buzz that pushed the NCAA Tournament forward.

I remember watching those games on TV. Reed and Blackman can both dine out on those shots for the rest of their lives.

I was always impressed by Kansas State coach Jack Hartman, a coach's coach and a purist in every way; Arkansas' Eddie Sutton, who had greatness written all over him from the time I first met him at a clinic we both worked when he was at Creighton and I was coaching the University of Detroit; and St. Joseph's coach Jimmy Lynam.

Most people had heard about Hartman and Sutton. Lynam was more of a new kid on the block. I knew about him from Five-Star camp. Wow, talk about a great clinician. He coached St. Joseph's all the way to the regional finals, then went on to become an assistant with the NBA Portland Trail Blazers, working for Jack Ramsay, one of my favorite coaches of all time. I still have Dr. Jack's book on pressure basketball. It was one of my bibles that I utilized in my coaching career.

**A**rkansas teammates U. S. Reed (24)
and Darrell Walker (20) raise their arms
after Reed nailed a last-second shot
from beyond midcourt. Louisville
was sent packing during an amazing
string of Shock City performances in
the 1981 NCAA Tournament.

# DUKE *becomes the first team since UCLA to win consecutive NCAA championships in 1991 and 1992*

## Back to Back

**MOMENT NUMBER**

**23**

Duke 71
Michigan 51
April 6, 1992

*Profile:* When Duke's players arrived back on campus after winning the school's first national championship in 1991, they were in a mood to celebrate.

But their coach, Mike Krzyzewski, wanted to talk about the future. He challenged them to become the first team to repeat since UCLA completed its remarkable seven-year run with titles in 1972 and 1973.

He told the players he was going to postpone giving out their championship rings until they won a second title. Then he instructed them never to use the word "defend" when they spoke about the championship. "The word 'pursue' is what we will use," he said.

And what a glorious pursuit it was.

Duke had all the stars back from the previous year – senior center Christian Laettner, junior point guard Bobby Hurley and sophomore forward Grant Hill – and most of the supporting cast. The multi-talented Hill made tremendous improvement between his freshman and sophomore years. Laettner was the best player in the country for most of the season. And Hurley was the gritty glue that held the pieces together.

The result was a gem of a 34-2 season where all five starters – Laettner, Hill, Thomas Hill, Hurley and Brian Davis – averaged double figures. The Blue Devils achieved their stated goal by polishing off Michigan's Fab Five, 71-51, before a crowd of 50,379 at the Metrodome in the NCAA championship game.

This was definitely Krzyzewski's best team ever.

When history judges the Blue Devils, their two championships and seven trips to the Final Four in nine years from 1986 through 1994 will compare favorably with UCLA – which created its dynasty long before the NCAA Tournament expanded to 64 teams and never had to leave the West Coast before playing in the Final Four.

Duke spent the entire season ranked No. 1, but that is not to say there weren't problems.

After winning the first 17 games of the year, Duke lost to North Carolina, 75-73, in Chapel Hill. Hurley broke his foot. He returned in three-and-a-half weeks. Then Grant Hill got hurt.

But they were all 100 percent for the stretch run when Duke buried Carolina, 94-74, in the ACC Tournament finals to avenge an earlier loss, and to make their way through another gauntlet of teams ready to chip away at their legacy.

Their most difficult test during their six-game NCAA Tournament run that year was Kentucky. The Cats looked like they had the Devils beaten in the East Regional final in Philadelphia after guard Sean Woods scored over Laettner with 2.1 seconds to play to give UK a 103-102 lead in double overtime. But Laettner, one of the great clutch players in the history of March Madness, had the final say, draining a miracle 18-footer at the buzzer to give Duke a 104-103 victory. He finished a perfect night with 30 points. His line read 10 for 10 from the field and 10 for 10 from the line.

Hurley was the hero of Duke's 81-78 victory over Indiana in the national semifinals in Minneapolis, scoring 26 points to pick up the slack for an exhausted Laettner.

Laettner's tank still looked like it was running on empty in the first half of the Blue Devils' national championship game against Michigan's Fab Five two days later. Hurley implored Laettner to step up in the second half. And, with eight minutes left, he finally

Duke coach Mike Krzyzewski had reason to smile as his Blue Devils cut down the nets after winning the 1991 NCAA championship at the Hoosier Dome in Indianapolis. The semifinal upset over UNLV was a classic battle.

, scoring over Chris Webber, Juwan Howard and
c Riley – three future NBA players – to ignite a run
en Duke scored on 11 of its next 12 possessions to
ry the young Wolverines, limiting them to just 20
ond-half points.

Laettner, who had just five points and seven
novers in a horrible first half, responded with
of his 19 points in the second half. Hurley was
ned Most Outstanding Player of the Final Four.

Someone once asked Krzyzewski what he
ught was his best win during those two years of
mination – the win over UNLV in the 1991 nation-
semifinals or the miracle victory over Kentucky?
s answer surprised many. He said it was Kansas in
1991 national championship game because of go-
g to the Final Four four times before that and never
nning. It was a unifying experience for everyone
o had been connected with his Duke teams.

ckie V's View: Any time you've built a tradition
e the New York Yankees in baseball or Notre Dame
football, people either love you or hate you. To me,
t's a sign that you've made it, baby. People don't
icize situations that involve non-achievers. Reggie

Jackson of the Yankees said it best: "They don't boo nobodies."

Duke hears a lot of boos, takes a lot of hits from opposing fans across the nation because there's a lot of envy out there. But it's hard to argue with what the Blue Devils accomplished in 1991 and 1992. The Blue Devils set a standard of excellence for their program when they won back-to-back titles. People were using Duke's success as a standard to attain. It wasn't until 2007, when Florida won two straight, that anyone was able to duplicate what the Blue Devils achieved in 1991 and 1992. Hey baby, now add to Coach K's resume an Olympic gold medal, as his leadership skills helped to unite a bunch of super stars into a passionate USA team.

Let's simply look at the facts. Duke has done it the right way. Everyone in the college basketball landscape would certainly agree it is a first class program that starts with brilliant leadership in Mike Krzyzewski, who recruits genuine student-athletes. Krzyzewski will be the first to let you know, "It's great graduating a high percentage of players. But heck, we're supposed to graduate them. We're Duke. We're getting the crème de la crème, the best of the best."

When Krzyzewski walks into the living room of a blue chip prospect today, that kid is looking at him in awe. Coach K has three championship rings and you better believe many of the youngsters he's recruited are looking at him with the feeling of "Can I have your autograph, coach?"

This takes me down memory lane when I was recruiting for the University of Detroit. I would walk into the home of a prospect and I would need 20 visits before he would lift his head and acknowledge I was even there.

Bobby Hurley (11) and Christian Laettner celebrate as the Blue Devils beat Kansas to win the 1991 national championship in Indianapolis. Hurley could flat out dish the rock and he held the NCAA career assist record for a long time.

# THE WILDCATS *rally from 18 down to defeat Duke in the 1998 NCAA South Regional finals*

## Payback Time

MOMENT NUMBER

24

Kentucky 86
Duke 84
March 22, 1998

*Profile:* It had been six years since Duke's Christian Laettner broke Kentucky's heart with a last-second jump shot at the NCAA East Regional finals in Philadelphia.

But no one connected with the Wildcat program had forgotten about that moment.

Fast forward to the 1998 NCAA South Regional finals at Tampa. The selection committee had placed top-seeded Duke and second-seeded Kentucky in the same region again, and the two Goliaths were set to face each other for the right to advance to the Final Four.

Rick Pitino was gone from the Bluegrass, along with Derek Anderson, Ron Mercer and Anthony Epps – much of the star power that had fueled Kentucky to a 1996 national championship and Final Four run the next season.

But first-year coach Tubby Smith endeared himself to the Wildcat nation in the sequel as the Cats rallied in the second half to stun Duke, 86-84, before 40,589 at Tropicana Field and opened the door for the school's fifth national title.

Senior guard Jeff Sheppard scored 18 points and grabbed 11 rebounds for the Cats, who put five players in double figures. Duke, which got 19 points and eight rebounds from forward Roshown McLeod and 18 from All-American guard Trajan Langdon, also put five players in double figures. The Blue Devils played a near-perfect first half, shooting 54.8 percent, to take a 49-39 lead. Their lead expanded to 18 points with 11 minutes to play before the Cats came to life, turning point guard Wayne Turner –

who was the quickest player on the floor – loose and clamping down defensively.

With Turner – the South Regional's Most Outstanding Player – penetrating and distributing the ball to open shooters, the Devils' huge lead started to evaporate. Forward Scott Padgett, who – along with walk-on guard Cameron Mills – grew up in the Bluegrass and watched the 1992 game on TV, nailed a three-pointer off a pick-and-roll with 39.4 seconds left to break an 81-81 tie. And the Cats held on from there.

Duke had a shot to pull off another miracle on the final play of the game. The Cats held a two-point lead with 4.5 seconds left when Duke inbounded the ball under its own basket. Unlike 1992, Smith chose to guard the inbounds pass, and Duke was forced to inbound the ball in the backcourt to William Avery, who raced up the floor and launched a prayer that fell short.

*Dickie V's View:* This was the one game, more than any other, that gave Tubby Smith instant credibility in the eyes of Kentucky fans.

Tubby was the sixth of 17 children born to sharecroppers Guffire and Parthenia Smith in Great Mills, Md. He got his nickname because he was fond of staying in the washtub where the kids got their baths. He tried to shake the nickname when he was younger, but it stuck like glue.

Smith got his first taste of Kentucky basketball when Rick Pitino hired him as an assistant in 1989. Pitino was brought in to rebuild a scandal-plagued program that had been whacked by NCAA probation and player defections.

When Pitino succeeded in a big way, Tubby, along with Ralph Willard, another assistant, became hot commodities. Willard got the Western Kentucky job and Smith went to Tulsa in 1991. His 1994 and 1995 Tulsa teams advanced to the NCAA Sweet 16 and Smith moved on to Georgia, where he became the school's first African-American coach.

When Rick moved on after a 1997 Final Four season to coach the Boston Celtics in the NBA, Tubby proved you could come home again.

Pitino had coached the Wildcats to three Final Fours and a national championship in 1996 and was building a dynasty. And it could have been catastrophic when he left.

Tubby was under a big microscope all season by many UK fans who were still mesmerized by Pitino and felt Tubby had big shoes to fill.

He and the Wildcats showed up big-time against Duke, surprising the Blue Devils with their incredible comeback victory in the regional championship final. When the final buzzer sounded, there was hysteria and jubilation in the Wildcat basketball nation. It was repeated by many of the Kentucky faithful, "Wow, this guy can really coach."

Kentucky went on to become the first team ever to win the national championship without a first-team All-American or a future NBA lottery pick.

And Tubby Smith was the toast of Lexington on that special night in 1998.

**Y**ears after suffering through Christian Laettner's game-winning shot in the 1992 East Regional final, Kentucky got a measure of revenge. The Wildcats beat the Blue Devils in the 1998 NCAA South Regional final, 86-84.

# BOB KNIGHT *surpasses Dean Smith to become the winningest coach in Division I men's basketball history in 2007*

## Good Knight Story

**Profile:** Bob Knight became even more of a legend in college basketball on New Year's Day in 2007, surpassing the legendary Dean Smith of North Carolina as the all-time winningest coach in Division I men's basketball history.

This milestone – 880 career victories – did not occur in Bloomington, Ind., the place where Knight won three national championships at Indiana in 1976, 1981 and 1987. But it did happen on Indiana Ave., even though it was in out-of-the-way Lubbock, Texas. The administration at Texas Tech – looking to infuse energy into a stagnant Big 12 program – had given him a second chance in 2001 after Knight had been fired six months earlier for what Indiana labeled "a pattern of unacceptable behavior."

The then-66-year-old Knight, wearing a black Texas Tech sweater, has always been a lightning rod for controversy. But he had one of the – if not the single – finest college basketball coaching minds of his generation.

Tech had prepared for this day for close to two weeks.

There had been one false start – a loss to UNLV – two nights earlier.

But Knight got it done when his team built up a huge 20-point lead against New Mexico, then had to rally from a 64-60 deficit in the last 6:25 to defeat the Lobos, 70-68, before a sellout crowd at the United Center.

Guard Jarrius Jackson led the Red Raiders with 22 points – scoring the go-ahead basket with just 2:04 remaining – but the outcome was still in jeopardy until a three-point attempt by the Lobos' J.R. Giddens bounced off the rim at the buzzer allowing fans,

players and even Knight a chance to exhale.

Pat Knight, his son, assistant and heir apparent, put his arm around his father's neck as they walked over to shake hands with New Mexico coach Ritchie McKay. Both looked relieved to have the hoopla surrounding this record behind them.

The crowd was already on its feet. The cheers became louder as Knight did his TV interview and the sound system blared Frank Sinatra's "I Did It My Way" – a fitting tribute to a man who marched to the beat of his own drum. Red confetti fell from the ceiling.

Knight motioned to his wife, Karen, to join him at midcourt. "The first 15 minutes were Karen's game plan," he said. "The rest of it was mine, unfortunately. I just say thank you."

He thanked both Tech's president at the time, David Schmedly, and AD Gerald Myers for giving him the opportunity to coach again. A series of video tributes followed – with former player and assistant Mike Krzyzewski of Duke saying, "You're the best that's ever been. I'm so glad you've been my coach and my friend. No one who played for you or coached with you is surprised by this."

Knight coached the rest of that season, then retired February 5, 2008, midway through the season. This set the wheels in motion for his son to succeed him on a full-time basis.

His final record was 902-371 in 42 years, 29 of them at Indiana. He was selected National Coach of the Year four times. He coached the United States to gold medals in the 1979 Pan Am Games and the 1984 Olympics. His Indiana teams won 20 games or more 29 times and 11 Big Ten championships.

MOMENT NUMBER

25

Texas Tech 70
New Mexico 68
January 1, 2007

It was a Happy New Year's Day 2007 in Lubbock as The General, Robert Montgomery Knight, earned record-breaking career win No. 880. Texas Tech edged New Mexico, 70-68, in that special game.

like to have hit 62 home runs," Knight said, ⌐ecting on his moment in history. "Then I think I ⌐ld have accomplished something. I hope those ⌐s that played for me at Army back in '65 watched ⌐ game and can look at themselves or their ⌐ndchildren and say, 'I was there when that son ⌐ bleep started.'"

⌐kie V's View: Robert Montgomery Knight has to ⌐mentioned with the coaching greats of all sports. ⌐en you mention Casey Stengel in baseball, Bear ⌐ant and Joe Paterno in college football, Vince ⌐nbardi and Don Shula in the NFL, Red Auerbach ⌐he NBA, and John Wooden and Dean Smith in ⌐lege basketball, Knight has to rank right up there. ⌐se guys are the chairmen of the board of the ⌐ching fraternity.

⌐ I did that historic game for ESPN.

⌐ I don't think Knight thought this game would be ⌐dramatic as it was. But you could feel the emotion ⌐ring the game, watching him on the sidelines. ⌐ere was definite pressure. Trust me, he felt like a

million bucks afterwards. This was a special moment.

The post-game ceremony was absolutely unbelievable. It would have been even more special if someone from Indiana's administration had been present to honor the General for his achievements in Hoosier Country. Think about it – all he did was win 662 games, numerous Big 10 titles, three national championships and, oh yes, raised thousands and thousands of dollars for scholarships and for the school library. Isn't it sad, in a way, that the egos of some administrators would keep Knight from being a member of the university's hall of fame? To me, personally, a hall of fame at the university can't have validity without Knight being a member.

There are so many beautiful fans in that state who have a passion and love for their basketball. They appreciate what he did at IU with the three national titles, graduating all his players and never getting into any trouble with the NCAA.

It's time to let bygones be bygones. I've always thought Assembly Hall in Bloomington should be re-named the Bob Knight Assembly Hall.

# FLORIDA *completes the double, winning its second straight NCAA championship in 2007*

Gator Bait

MOMENT NUMBER

**26**

Florida 84
Ohio State 75
April 2, 2007

*Profile:* No one could have blamed forwards Joakim Noah and Corey Brewer and center Al Horford – three of the stars of Florida's first national championship team in 2006 – if they had left for the NBA following their sophomore years.

What more was there left to accomplish?

But Noah, Brewer and Horford told coach Billy Donovan they all wanted to stay and make history. It was an unselfish act that epitomized this team. And together, along with senior guard Lee Humphrey; another junior, point guard Taurean Green; and 6' 8" senior sixth-man Chris Richard, they did just that – duplicating Duke's back-to-back title runs in 1991-1992.

The Gators – who were the first team with the same starting five to win back-to-back titles – methodically advanced through the NCAA Tournament, finally defeating Ohio State and its 7' 0" freshman phenom, Greg Oden, 84-75, in the title game in Atlanta in 2007.

"I think this team should go down as one of the best teams in college basketball history," Donovan said. "Not as the most talented and not on style points – but because they encompassed what the word 'team' means."

No one on the team averaged more than 13 points. But Brewer, Horford and Noah were all lottery picks, and Green and Richard were both drafted.

Brewer was selected Most Outstanding Player of the Final Four. The 6' 9" Horford had 18 points and 12 rebounds. Green scored 16 in the title game for the Gators, who finished 21-0 in the month of March over a two-year period. Humphrey set an

all-time NCAA Tournament record for three-point goals made with 47. The colorful 6' 11" Noah – th Most Outstanding Player of the 2006 Final Four – finished with eight points and three rebounds.

But points were never an issue on this team.

Donovan, who won his second national title at age 41, opted to play Oden straight up when the Gators were in man-to-man. Oden – the eventual first pick in the 2007 NBA draft – responded with points and 12 rebounds. But the defensive strategy allowed the Gators to put more pressure on the Buckeyes' shooters, who were just four for 23 from three-point range.

Florida became the first athletic program to hol both the NCAA Division I college football and coll basketball titles in the same academic year.

*Dickie V's View:* Joakim Noah, Corey Brewer, Al Horford and Taurean Green could have taken the easy path and left Florida after winning it all as sophomores to cash in on the riches of the NBA. B they decided to stay – to be part of something spec

And, my friends, they made hoops history at a football school.

Billy Donovan decided to stay put, too. He was courted by Kentucky – the Big Blue, the Yankees o the college basketball world, a place where he usec work as an assistant to Rick Pitino – after the seaso But Florida AD Jeremy Foley gave him his first big job when he was just 30, and I was convinced his heart was in Gainesville. Let me tell you, Jeremy Foley is magic to work for. If you do the job, this A will provide all the resources to be a success. And

**C**orey Brewer was one of five returning starters for the Florida Gators when Billy Donovan's team went for back-to-back national championships. It is so rare to see a group return, especially when there was so much money put out by the NBA to lure them away from campus.

ly has a great relationship with Jeremy.

A couple of months later, the Orlando Magic from NBA came calling. Initially, Donovan accepted the d coaching job there; but after a weekend of l-searching, he changed his mind.

I was not shocked at all – surprised, but not cked – when he decided to stay in Gainesville. He fits the Gators like Mike Krzyzewski fits at Duke and Roy Williams fits at Chapel Hill.

There's something to be said about being happy where you are. Besides, college basketball needs all the great young coaches it can get.

As the late Jimmy V used to say, "Don't mess with happiness."

# RICK PITINO *utilizes the three-point shot to take Providence to the 1987 Final Four*

Pitino's Touch

MOMENT NUMBER

**27**

Providence 88
Georgetown 73
March 21, 1987

*Profile:* Rick Pitino's most successful coaching efforts have always come when expectations were the lowest.

When he left Hubie Brown's staff with the New York Knicks to take the head coaching job at Providence in 1985, the Big East Friars were coming off a dismal 11-20 season and had finished last or next-to-last in conference play five of the previous six years.

Two years later, the Friars were in the Final Four.

And Pitino was being hailed for his revolutionary use of the three-point shot, which had just been implemented that season.

The Friars did not have any marquee talent when the season started.

But senior point guard Billy "The Kid" Donovan, senior guard Ernie "Pop" Lewis and junior guard Delray Brooks made a reputation for themselves on a 25-win team that made 280 of 660 three-point attempts from outside the 19' 9" arc. Both of these stats were school records.

Pitino was young and demanding. But his roster of overachieving players bought into his philosophy during that magical season, practicing three times a day at times to get into condition to play his up tempo system. The once-chubby Donovan – who considered transferring to a Division II school when Pitino arrived – lost 20 pounds and turned into a first-team All-Big East selection for the Friars, who

received an at-large bid to the NCAA Tournament.

Pitino almost missed the ride.

On the way home from the Big East Tournament he was informed his six-month-old son, Daniel, who suffered from congenital heart problems, had just died. Pitino contemplated leaving the team, but his wife, Joanne, discouraged it.

The players turned that tragedy into triumph, winning four straight games to advance to the school's first Final Four since 1973, when Marvin Barnes and Ernie DiGregorio were playing for Dave Gavitt.

Providence, a sixth seed, needed overtime to beat Austin Peay in the second round.

But the Friars were at their best in the Southeast Regional. Donovan made five threes, scored 26 points and had 10 assists. Brooks added 23 as the Friars shot 14 of 22 from three-point range during a 103-? blowout of SEC champion Alabama in the Sweet 16.

Then the Friars took apart Big East rival George-town – a team that had beaten them two out of three times earlier that season – in the Southeast Regional final. They took advantage of the fact the Hoyas concentrated on taking away the three to effectively get the ball inside to big men Dave Kipfer, Darryl Wright and Steve Wright during an 88-73 victory.

Pitino went on to coach two other teams – Kentucky and Louisville – to the Final Four later in his career.

*Dickie V's View:* I've said it once. I've said it twice. Rick Pitino is a genius in the world of college basketball.

I'll never forget my phone ringing. It was my buddy, Richie Adubato – who was an assistant with the New York Knicks – telling me Pitino was leaving Boston University to join Hubie Brown's NBA staff.

After watching Pitino for a couple of days, he called me back and he said, "Dickie V, take this to the bank. This guy is going to be one of the special coaches of all time."

Adubato went on to say he'd never seen anybody with the energy and the ability to communicate with the players like Pitino. Oh, my friends, Richie Adubato was 100 percent on the mark.

Pitino left the Knicks' staff in 1985 to take the head coaching job at Providence. Who can forget the job he did with the Friars in 1987, taking them to the Final Four? That team did not have many big-name players. They had, like, none.

But Pitino was always on the cutting edge. He utilized the three-point shot quicker than anyone else. A lot of guys were fighting the rule and were afraid to use the shot. But Pitino said, "Hey, man, we're going to take advantage of it."

And they did in a big, big way.

By the way, I still kid Billy Donovan – who was the star of that Final Four team – telling him he may not even have been the best guard on the campus. It might have been Doris Burke, who does such a great job for us on ESPN, and who starred for the women's team back then.

Rick Pitino was the first coach to truly take advantage of the three-point shot. Having Billy Donovan helped as the Friars made it to the Final Four in 1987.

# BYU GUARD

*Danny Ainge drives the length of the floor for a game-winning layup as the Cougars stun Notre Dame in the 1981 NCAA East Regional semifinals*

## Beat the Clock

MOMENT NUMBER

28

BYU 51
Notre Dame 50
March 18, 1981

*Profile:* Before Danny Ainge enrolled at BYU, he was selected by the Toronto Blue Jays in the 1977 amateur baseball draft and signed a $500,000 contract. Ainge made it to the big leagues as a second baseman two years later when he was just a sophomore. His father, Don, said he thought Ainge's best sport was football, where he was an all-state wide receiver on a two-time state championship team at North Eugene High in Oregon.

But for two glorious weeks in the 1981 NCAA Tournament, Ainge reached legendary status as a basketball player.

The 6' 4" senior All-American guard had gone off for 37 points during a second-round victory over UCLA. But it was the coast-to-coast dash he made for a game-winning layup during a 51-50 victory over Notre Dame in an NCAA Sweet 16 game at the Atlanta Omni that will be forever known as his signature moment in college basketball.

Ainge averaged 24.4 points that season and was a unanimous first-team All-American. He set an NCAA record with 112 consecutive games in double figures. But Notre Dame coach Digger Phelps came up with a box-and-one that quieted Ainge for most of the game.

But everything changed in the final eight seconds.

That was when Ainge broke Phelps' heart in this battle of two religiously affiliated powers. Kelly Tripucka had just hit a jumper to send the Irish up 50-49 when Ainge took the inbounds pass, raced up the right sideline and slashed through three defenders at midcourt while dribbling behind his back. Then

he blew by a fourth at the foul line and flipped in a layup over 6' 8" Orlando Woolridge just before time ran out.

The 94-foot dash stunned the second-seeded Irish – whose senior class included future pros Tripucka, Tracy Jackson and Woolridge.

Afterwards, BYU coach Frank Arnold rushed up to Ainge's dad and gave him a hug. "Don," he said, "I just want to thank you for sending us your son."

It was a Mormon miracle.

BYU lost to Virginia in the regional finals two days later and Ainge made his way to spring training.

But he tired of baseball.

Ainge was drafted by the Boston Celtics in the second round of the 1981 NBA draft and joined the NBA franchise for the 1982-83 season after the Celtics bought out his contract with the Jays after a long legal battle.

*Dickie V's View:* Hey, I see that highlight all the time. We always tease Digger Phelps about it in the ESPN studios, especially around NCAA Tournament time. Whenever we want to bring him to his knees and knock him down a peg, we just scream at the producers, "Get us the tape. Get us that Danny Ainge play. It's time for Danny."

I always remind Digger that the first principle in a defensive transition is to stop the progress of the basketball. Then I simply get on his case by stating, "How did you let Ainge go coast to coast and send you to the loser's locker room?"

Digger usually responds by saying, "Thanks a lot, ¦dy. I really need to watch that tape. I really need ¦you to remind me of the Ainge moment."

It was just like that Tyus Edney moment, when ¦hey went coast to coast against Missouri to keep UCLA's title quest alive in the 1995 NCAA Tournament. Ainge went the length of the court for the game winner in the 1981 NCAA Sweet 16.

Can it be that long ago?

Today, he's the general manager – the architect – of the Boston Celtics. He's the executive of the year – the guy who is responsible for retaining Doc Rivers after the disastrous year the Celtics had in 2007. That, my friends, was the start of something big for Celtic basketball. Kevin Garnett and Ray Allen and the Celtics were on their way to becoming NBA champs in 2008.

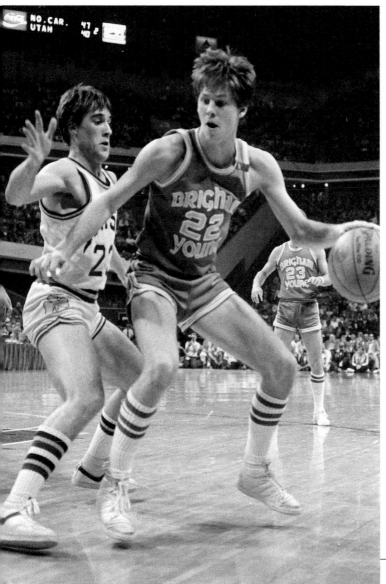

**P**oor Digger Phelps. He will always have to put up with the video of Danny Ainge going to the basket and beating his Irish in the 1981 NCAA Tournament.

# JIM CALHOUN *turns Connecticut into a national power, winning the 1999 NCAA Tournament*

## UCan't Stop UConn

MOMENT NUMBER

29

Connecticut 77
Duke 74
March 29, 1999

*Profile:* The first New England team to win an NCAA Tournament was Holy Cross, with Tom Heinsohn and Bob Cousy, in 1947. That region of the country had to wait 52 years for a second champion.

But Connecticut, a blue-collar team from the Big East, barged through the door, defeating seemingly invincible ACC colossus Duke – one of college basketball's blue bloods – 77-74, to win the school's first NCAA Tournament in 1999 at St. Petersburg, Fla.

"We wanted to shock the world," senior guard Ricky Moore said.

And they did.

That Huskies' team played with a great sense of purpose against a 37-2 team that was the first school in the history of the NCAA to have four players from the same team – Elton Brand, Trajan Langdon, Corey Maggette and William Avery – selected in the first round of the NBA draft.

UConn's junior All-American guard Richard "Rip" Hamilton scored 27 points and was chosen the tournament's most outstanding player. He was playing for his late grandfather, Edward, a former steelworker who had lost his battle with lung cancer the previous summer.

Moore had a special motive, too.

He scored 13 points in the first half and then made the game-winning defensive stop against Duke's All-American guard Trajan Langdon in the final 15 seconds when the Huskies were trying to protect a one-point lead.

He carried a pocket-sized card with the 23rd Psalm printed on it that had been given to him by Sheila McGinn in memory of her son, Joe, a 26-year-old former UConn team manager, who had died of a long illness that spring.

And Jim Calhoun was coaching to prove his program could be so much more than just a refuge from the Yankee Conference when he took over in 1986.

Calhoun had re-energized this program, previously coaching the Huskies to three Elite Eight in the '90s, but had always been denied a trip to th Final Four.

The one that hurt the most was a heartbreaking one-point loss to Duke when Christian Laettner hit game winner at the buzzer.

"We had our hearts broken that night," Calhoun said. "But we kicked some butts here and broke so hearts."

Calhoun got his first college head coaching job Northeastern University, where he took his team to three straight NCAA appearances from 1983-1986, before taking on the challenge at UConn.

His record there speaks for itself. He has coache the Huskies to 10 Big East regular-season titles through the 2008 season, six Big East Tournament championships, 15 NCAA bids, 11 Sweet 16s, seve Elite Eights and, perhaps most importantly, two national championships in 1999 and 2004. Calhou was inducted into the Naismith Memorial Basketba Hall of Fame in 2005, along with Syracuse coach Ji Boeheim. Twenty-four of the players Calhoun has coached at UConn have gone on to play in the NB/

*kie V's View:* People in the basketball
mmunity realize the impact Jim Calhoun had on
onn, turning an also-ran in the Big East into a
ional power.

But the average fan may not realize how far
onn has come. Think about where that program
d to be before he arrived. Connecticut, to
, back when I started at ESPN in 1979, was a
gram I associated with the Yankee Conference.
ny people thought the school would be a
ormat in the Big East.

But you couldn't tell it to Calhoun. He was so
npetitive. He worked relentlessly, selling his
duct.

ESPN gets an assist here. Calhoun took
antage of the visibility of the sport and the fact
network offices were so close to campus. When
former Big East commissioner Dave Gavitt cut a
liant deal with ESPN, the teams from that league
ame household names.

Calhoun told me he sold prospects from across
country on the idea their families could watch
m play on TV. He recruited players like Ray
en from South Carolina, Khalid El-Amin from
nnesota, Emeka Okafor from Texas, Caron Butler
n Wisconsin, and Rip Hamilton and Donyell
rshall from Pennsylvania.

Then he coached them to the highest level
h his competitive spirit, winning national
mpionships in 1999 and 2004.

Who would have thought that 20 years ago?

Jim Calhoun has been a Frank Lloyd Wright in coaching, a true
architect of an outstanding program. Connecticut was a Big
East also-ran before he arrived in Storrs. He built a national
powerhouse and true champion.

# GEORGETOWN *coach John Thompson leads a 1989 BCA boycott against NCAA Proposition 42*

## BCA Boycott

MOMENT NUMBER

## 30

January 14, 1989

*Profile:* Georgetown coach John Thompson was philosophically opposed to Proposition 48 because he felt the college boards were culturally biased against minority athletes, and the NCAA was using them to determine eligibility for athletes.

But his anger turned to outrage in 1988 when the NCAA passed Proposition 42, a controversial piece of legislation that prevented any partial qualifier who failed to meet either a 2.0 cumulative grade point average or achieved less than a minimum score on the SAT or ACT from receiving athletically related financial aid as a freshman.

Thompson, one of the most influential voices among black educators, decided to stage a demonstration.

Of one. Himself.

He announced he would walk off the court when his team played a Big East home game against Boston College at the Capital Centre January 14, 1989, in protest of the NCAA vote.

This was not the first time Thompson had taken on social issues.

In 1981, he had his players wear green ribbons remind people that black children were being killed in Atlanta.

Thompson said he didn't want his actions to be
viewed as racially motivated. But at a pre-game press
conference, he said the athletes who would be most
affected would be from the "lower socioeconomic
segment of society."

Just before tipoff, Thompson got out of his chair
and walked off the court toward the locker room – to
a standing ovation. He left the building and drove
into the city, listening to the game on the radio.

Thompson also decided to boycott his team's road
trip to Providence four days later. He never left D.C.
His assistants coached the game. But his trademark
white towel was draped over his empty chair in the
middle of the Hoyas' bench as a reminder.

Thompson's protest had an effect.

A day after the Providence game, Albert White,
the president of the NCAA, and Martin Massengale,
the chairman of the Presidents Commission, announced they would recommend legislation aimed at
postponing any changes in Prop. 48 until the NCAA
had done more homework on the relationship between a student's high school GPA and board scores.

Thompson, convinced the NCAA was sincere,
returned to the bench the next game against UConn.

A year later, the NCAA decided it did not need
Prop. 42 in its then-current form. The rule was
modified to allow students ineligible to participate
as freshmen to receive institutional aid so they could
continue their education. They could not be on
athletic scholarships, but they would not be denied
the opportunity to stay in school.

*Dickie V's View:* John Thompson is a very proud
man, proud of what he's achieved. And he does not
like to see injustices done.

His decision to walk off the court before the start
of the Georgetown-Boston College game in 1989 was
a protest against the NCAA's attempts to put a scarlet
letter on kids who were ineligible to participate in
athletics as freshmen because they didn't project
academically.

Prop. 48. Prop. 42.

Why not just hang a sign around their necks?
That was John's crusade, to tell people out there that
kids shouldn't be stereotyped.

During that era, an athlete who was declared
a Prop. 48 student was totally humiliated and
embarrassed. Everyone on the campus knew
that he did not make the necessary scores for
eligibility. Let's face it. Some kids just don't score
well on standardized tests, but yet, if given an
opportunity, with proper guidance and direction,
they can succeed in the classroom. When you're an
athlete and you're a Prop. 48, it's publicized. It's highlighted. And it's an embarrassment to the individual.

Wow, do we need more people like John
Thompson, people who stand up for what they
believe, especially when it's the right thing to do.

Aren't we in the business of helping kids instead
of hurting them? When I think about my daughters, I
was lucky. I had the financial means to hire tutors to
work with them in getting ready for the SATs. Many
youngsters from large urban areas or from the rural
areas don't have the luxury of having the same golden
opportunity.

**F**ormer Georgetown coach
John Thompson is a proud
man who has always taken
a stance on major issues.
He was not afraid to lead a
personal boycott when he
questioned Prop. 42.

# GEORGETOWN *nips Ivy champion Princeton in the first round of the 1989 NCAA Tournament*

## Taming Tigers

MOMENT NUMBER 31

**Georgetown 50**

**Princeton 49**

**March 17, 1989**

*Profile:* Princeton advanced to the NCAA Final Four in 1965 with Bill Bradley, who set a tournament single-game scoring record with 58 points in the third-place game. Penn made a surprise appearance there in 1979. But 10 years later, there was a growing concern about the Ivy League's ability to remain competitive on the national scene.

Princeton won the Ivy League that year but was seeded 16th in the East Regional and was matched up against Big East champion Georgetown – the number one seed in the East – at the Providence Civic Center on St. Patrick's Day.

The young, out-manned Tigers were listed as 23-point underdogs in Vegas and the game had all the makings of a blowout.

But, as it turned out, Georgetown was lucky to escape with its tournament life. The Hoyas managed to eke out a 50-49 victory but not before Pete Carril's Tigers threw a major scare into them, controlling tempo by milking the shot clock, scoring 15 layups off a spread offense that pulled Georgetown's 6' 10" freshman shot-blocking center Alonzo Mourning out to the foul line, and limiting the Hoyas to a season low in points.

Senior Bob Scrabis, the Tigers' captain and Ivy Player of the Year, led Princeton with 15 points. Forward Matt Lapin came off the bench and scored 12 points. Guards Jerry Doyle, George Leftwich and Troy Hottenstein suffocated Hoyas' All-American

point guard Charles Smith, limiting him to four points. Perhaps most importantly, 6' 7" center Kit Mueller had nine points and eight assists and refused to be intimidated by Mourning.

Princeton held the lead for 30 minutes and never trailed by more than two points the entire game. But the Tigers couldn't stop Mourning from taking over the game in the final minute. Mourning scored seven of the Hoyas' final nine points, making a free throw to give Georgetown a one-point lead.

Then Mourning, who led the country in blocked shots, swatted away consecutive Princeton field-goal attempts by Scrabis and Mueller in the final six seconds. There are still Princeton fans who swear Mueller was fouled in the final seconds, but Georgetown escaped.

"I'd be foolish to suggest the NCAA take away the Ivy League's bid after I came out of there fighting for my life," said Georgetown coach John Thompson, whose son, John III, had played for Princeton and was a first-year assistant on Carril's staff. "They need two automatic bids."

Georgetown beat Notre Dame and NC State before losing to Duke in the regional finals.

*Dickie V's View:* That game really became part of my TV career, a moment I'll always remember.

I was so confident John Thompson's club would have no trouble with Princeton, I said on TV,

"Let me tell you something. If Georgetown gets beat by Princeton, I'll hitchhike from Bristol to Providence. And I'll put on a Princeton cheerleader's outfit and cheer for the Tigers in their second-round game."

Tom Odjakjian – who used to work at Princeton and was the guy in charge of programming for ESPN – ran out, got a Princeton sweatshirt and put it on me. Oh, were we lucky to have Odjakjian working at ESPN, as he was responsible for many of our special basketball matchups.

Now, back to the game - if it hadn't been for Alonzo Mourning, who came out of nowhere to make that game-saving blocked shot on a play that a lot of people thought was a personal foul, it would have been an incredible upset win for Princeton.

A lot of people in the studio – producers, cameramen – were going, "Dickie V, get ready to hitchhike, baby."

**P**rinceton coach Pete Carril was a master at driving opponents crazy with his disciplined offense and back-door cuts. I will never forget the night in the studio in 1989 as his Tigers almost shocked Goliath Georgetown, falling 50-49.

# THE FAB FIVE *leads the Wolverines to the Final Four in the 1991 NCAA Tournament*

**Fashion Forward**

MOMENT NUMBER

**32**

Michigan 75
Ohio State 71 (OT)
March 29, 1992

*Profile:* The tangible evidence of the accomplishments of Michigan's Fab Five are rolled up and tucked away in Michigan's Bentley Historical Library.

The two NCAA Final Four banners were taken down from the rafters of Crisler Arena in 2002, after the school's self-imposed sanctions following revelations that four UM players – most notably 6' 9" All-American forward Chris Webber – had accepted illegal loans from the late Ed Martin, a booster, while they still had college eligibility left.

But no one can take away the fact that the Fab Five – the nickname given a group of five freshmen starters: Webber, center Juwan Howard and guards Jalen Rose, Jimmy King and Ray Jackson – led the Wolverines to their first of two consecutive NCAA championship games when they defeated Ohio State, 75-71, in overtime to win the South Regional championship in Lexington.

They wore baggy shorts and black sneakers and socks. They gave college basketball a taste of hip hop, playing with a brash style that turned them into rock stars and heroes to a younger generation of fans. But they weren't as popular with older hoops adherents, who weren't used to watching a trash-talking team whose players strutted like they were playing on a playground instead of in front of thousands in college arenas and millions on TV.

The one thing everyone could agree on was the Fab Five's polarizing effect on college basketball.

"We were so much either loved or hated and judged by the way we looked," Rose said. "Oh, look at these hoodlums – these thugs, these gangsters – because we had big shorts, black shoes and black socks. But then once Michael Jordan and the Bulls started wearing them, once mainstream America started to wear them and corporate America embraced it, then I guess it became cool."

Michigan's freshmen had no problem with confidence heading into the tournament showdown with Ohio State, the Big Ten regular-season champion, which had beaten the Wolverines twice in the regular season. "We realized from Day One that we were a Final Four team," Rose said to the media. "You guys are just now starting to realize it."

Webber led the way with 23 points and 11 rebounds. Rose had 20 and the Fab Five scored 73 of their team's 75 points against the Buckeyes.

Unlike the previous two meetings when Ohio State wore Michigan down with pressure, the Wolverines refused to lose. Ohio State actually had a chance to win the game in regulation, but Rose tipped a potential game-winning shot by All-American forward Jimmy Jackson to force overtime. The Wolverines looked like the more experienced team in the final five minutes, taking a 70-65 lead on an 18-foot jumper, a three-point basket and two free throws by Rose.

Jimmy Jackson finished with 20 points but committed nine turnovers and the Buckeyes couldn't limit Webber's or Howard's size inside.

Next stop: The Final Four and a date with Cincinnati in the national semifinals in Minneapolis.

*Dickie V's View:* It was unprecedented and unheard of – having five freshmen take a team to the Final Four.

I know they took some heat over the years. But let me tell you this, show me five freshmen who can come out of high school in June and, in less than eight months, be able to jell as a unit and make a serious run for a national championship. That's a major achievement for the kids involved and certainly the coaches, who were able to get them to blend together as a unit.

We talk about Chris Webber, but let's not forget about Jalen Rose, Juwan Howard, Ray Jackson and Jimmy King. These guys really liked one another, had great chemistry and a feel for the game.

And they were way ahead of everybody else in the world of marketing. They were so creative – with those long shorts, black sneakers and socks, the whole bit. Like them or not, they created an incredible trend, baby.

Sad in a way that the legal problems involving Chris Webber and his relationship with Ed Martin tarnished what these young kids achieved as Diaper Dandies.

**J**alen Rose was a vital member of Michigan's Fab Five. I don't think we will ever see a team of five Diaper Dandies go back to the Final Four the way Michigan did.

# DAVIDSON'S *Stephen Curry lights a fire in the 2008 NCAA Tournament*

**Spicy Curry**

**MOMENT NUMBER 33**

Davidson 74
Georgetown 70
March 23, 2008

*Profile:* Stephen Curry grew up in Charlotte, N.C., with the same sweet shooting touch as his father, Dell, who was a 16-year NBA veteran and one of the great long-range shooters in league history.

But nobody in the ACC was paying attention.

Curry went unnoticed when he attended Duke's summer camp. He wanted to follow in the footsteps of his father at Virginia Tech, but the best Seth Greenberg could do was an offer to walk on as a freshman and earn a scholarship the following year.

Most coaches thought the baby-faced Curry, who was only 5' 11" as a senior at Charlotte Christian, was too frail to survive at the highest level of the sport. Curry wound up choosing Davidson – a picturesque, 1,700-student liberal arts school 20 miles north of his hometown – over Virginia Commonwealth and Winthrop.

Then he made sure every coach who had passed on him knew they had made a mistake.

Curry grew to 6' 3". By his sophomore year, he had emerged as the best pure shooter in college basketball. He averaged 25.5 points, 4.7 rebounds and 2.8 assists. He made an NCAA-record 160 three-pointers as a sophomore for a 10th-seeded 29-7 Southern Conference school that escaped from the shadow of the ACC and advanced all the way to the 2008 NCAA Midwest Regional finals.

Curry put on an unparalleled series of performances during the Wildcats' four-game NCAA Tournament run. He gave fans in Charlotte a preview of coming attractions when he made eight of 10 threes and went off for 40 points during an 82-76 victory over Gonzaga in a first-round game. He got 30 points in the second half as the Cats rallied from an 11-point deficit.

Two days later, he did in powerful Georgetown scoring 25 of his 30 points in the final 14 minutes Davidson rallied from 17 down for a stunning 74-7 second-round victory.

Georgetown coach John Thompson III shut Cu down early, forcing him to miss 10 of his first 12 shots. But once he got it going, it was just a matter of time. The Hoyas tried four defenders on him in man-to-man, switched immediately on screens and even mixed in some various zones. But nothing worked. Curry hit six of his last nine shots and made five of six free throws in the final 23 seconds

Curry and Davidson had the country's attention and that of LeBron James, who was in the stands when Davidson played Wisconsin in the Sweet 16 Detroit's Ford Field. Curry lit up Michael Flowers, one of the best on-the-ball defenders in the country for 33 points and six threes as the Wildcats cruised a convincing 73-56 victory.

Davidson was just one step away from its first Final Four. Curry gave it his best shot in the region finals, scoring 25 points against Kansas, but the Jayhawks held on for a 59-57 victory.

Davidson had the ball, down two, with 21 seconds remaining and a chance to win the game. But Kansas covered Curry so tightly, he couldn't ge a shot off in the closing seconds – leaving him no choice but to dish to point guard Jason Richards, who launched a 25-footer from the top of the key that bounced off the backboard. And the Jayhawks escaped.

Curry, who has the words, "I can do all things" written in red trim on his shoes, was selected second-team All-American.

_ckie V's View:_ Stephen Curry. Are you kidding ? I haven't seen a series of performances like his he 2008 tournament in all my years at ESPN. n anyone remember any player carrying a d-major team on his back the way Curry did?

The Wildcats made the Elite Eight and were so se to – just seconds away from – advancing to Final Four.

Curry was brilliant. He stood the test of time h four exceptional performances, including ns over Gonzaga, Georgetown and Wisconsin, well as a heartbreaking loss to eventual national ampion Kansas in the regional finals.

He put on quite a show, baby. The script was itten for him to hit the game-winning trifecta. t give Kansas credit for its defense at the end of game. Sherron Collins helped double Curry, he had to pass the ball to Jason Richards on the al sequence.

A lot of his talent comes from the genes of his d, Dell, who was such a great shooter at Virginia h and later in the NBA. In fairness to high ool talent evaluators like Bob Gibbons, Norm venson, Clark Francis, Dave Telep, Van Coleman d Tom Konchalski, who do such a great job, nember this: You're not going to be perfect in ur assessments all the time.

Think about misses like David Robinson –The miral – at Navy or Tim Duncan at Wake Forest, o developed in school.

In the case of Curry, here's an example of a kid o slipped through the cracks. He went to David- n because the ACC didn't seriously recruit him. eryone questioned his size and his strength. They forgot about the greatest art he possessed – the ability to put the ball in the basket. Shooting the rock has a way of making up for a lot of liabilities.

And, oh, he made them pay. He plays with a little chip on his shoulder, proving to all the biggies they flat out made a mistake. He enjoys going head-to-head with all the Diaper Dandies and PTPers.

He was forgotten when his college career started. But believe me, under the guidance of Bob McKillop who has a great feel for the game and knows how to utilize Curry effectively, this kid is going to be one of the superstars of the 2008-09 college basketball landscape.

Davidson's Stephen Curry put on an amazing show during the 2008 NCAA Tournament. He led the Wildcats to victories over Gonzaga, Georgetown and Wisconsin before falling just short against Kansas.

# ARIZONA *defeats three top seeds en route to winning the 1997 national championship*

## Desert Swarm

MOMENT NUMBER 34

Arizona 84
Kentucky 79 (OT)
March 31, 1997

*Profile:* No one could have anticipated Arizona's 1997 run to the national championship.

The Wildcats were 19-9 entering the NCAA Tournament and were coming off consecutive road losses to Stanford and California. They finished fifth in the Pac-10, behind UCLA, Stanford, Southern California and Cal. And they had a history of first-round losses since 1992 – blowing up against East Tennessee State, Santa Clara and Miami of Ohio.

Lute Olson's fourth-seeded Wildcats started slowly, barely escaping South Alabama in the first round. But once they caught stride, they shocked the world when they knocked off three No. 1 seeds – Kansas, North Carolina and finally Kentucky – to win it all.

Olson, who kept preaching that the Pac-10 was better than the media cynics thought, had the perfect group of guards – juniors Miles Simon and Michael Dickerson, sophomore Jason Terry and precocious freshman point guard Mike Bibby – to orchestrate his palace coup in March. They had the ability to spread the floor, knock down shots and consistently beat teams off the dribble.

And the Cats possessed their own relentless "Desert Storm" mentality that allowed them to rally from 13 points down with 3:28 remaining and stun top-ranked Kansas, 84-83, in the Sweet 16. The Cats slowed down the Jayhawks' All-American center Raef LaFrentz and Bibby calmly made a pair of free throws with 21 seconds left.

The Wildcats then made 11 threes to beat North Carolina, 66-58, in the national semifinals at the RCA Dome in Indianapolis, using a smaller, quicker combination of front-court players – Bennett Davison, A.J. Bramlett, Eugene Edgerson and Donnell Harris – to make Tar Heels' All-American Antawn Jamison struggle for his 18 points.

Two days later, the Cats' 84-79 overtime victory against mighty Kentucky belonged to Simon and Bibby. Simon, who missed the first 11 games of the season because of academic suspension, scored 30 points and got to the line 17 times in a tense game where the lead changed 18 times. Bibby had 19 points, three assists and three steals, becoming the first freshman point guard in modern history to lead his team to a national title. Dickerson shut down Kentucky's All-American guard Ron Mercer, limiting him to 13 points.

U of A had to work extra hard to deny Rick Pitino a second consecutive championship. Kentucky forced overtime when Anthony Epps made a clutch three-pointer with 13 seconds left in regulation.

But it was all Arizona in overtime. The Wildcats, who made 85 percent of their free throws, scored 1 points – all from the line – and held a tired Kentucky team to just one field goal until the final six seconds. Afterwards Davison sneaked up behind Olson and mussed up his perfectly styled white hair.

It was finally time to exhale.

*Dickie V's View:* I don't think people back East realized how tough the Pac-10 was that year.

But Arizona got on a roll and shocked the world knocking off Kansas, North Carolina and Kentucky – three No. 1 seeds – to win it all. They also sent a

ssage with the trend they utilized – a three-guard
nse with Miles Simon, Michael Bibby and Michael
kerson with Jason Terry as the first guard off the
ich.

Lute Olson did a terrific job spreading the court
l spacing his guards 15 to 17 feet apart against
defenses they faced. He did a fantastic job getting
guards to beat their defender off the dribble. All
ir perimeter players had the ability to make the
ee-point shot. Simon had the ability to become
gical in marquee games. He had 30 against
ntucky in the national championship game.

To be fair, everybody in that tournament got a
major break because Kentucky's senior guard
Derek Anderson wasn't healthy. We're talking about
a big-time star here. I really believe if he hadn't
gotten hurt, Kentucky would have won three
straight national titles in 1996, 1997 and 1998.

One more thing: That Kansas team Arizona beat
was one of my favorite teams during my tenure at
ESPN. They never won an NCAA title, but Roy
Williams loved coaching this team as they had
quality people in Jacque Vaughn, Scot Pollard, Jerod
Haase, Raef LaFrentz and Paul Pierce. They were
35-2 and they were a classic group of student-athletes.
Each of the seniors on that team received his degree.
You'd have to put them in the same category as two
other runners-up – Georgetown in 1985 and
UNLV in 1991 – as some of the best teams never to win
an NCAA title.

Besides, nobody said bringing home the gold
trophy was easy.

**A**rizona coach Lute Olson had a lot to
celebrate over as his Wildcats beat Kentucky,
84-79, in overtime to win the 1997 national
championship. Arizona beat three different
No. 1 seeds in that tournament.

# PRINCETON *upsets defending national champion UCLA in the first round of the 1996 NCAA Tournament*

## Tiger Tale

MOMENT NUMBER

**35**

Princeton 43
UCLA 41
March 17, 1996

*Profile:* No one wanted to play Princeton Hall of Fame coach Pete Carril in March – particularly in the NCAA Tournament.

And it was easy to see why.

Carril made every team he faced sweat it out with his unique, slow, low-scoring style of play that emphasized movement without the ball, back-door cuts and his famed tenacious defense. His Ivy League Tigers pushed Georgetown to the limit in a 50-49 first-round loss in 1989 and almost got eventual Final Four participant Arkansas the next season, losing by four points in another first-round game.

In 1996, UCLA – the defending national champion – couldn't escape from the sauna.

Carril got his long-overdue, one shining moment when his 13th-seeded Tigers stunned the fourth-seeded Bruins, 43-41, in a first-round game at Indianapolis. It was considered one of the greatest upsets of all time and it was the Tigers' first NCAA win since 1983.

The Tigers ran the back-door to perfection against a more talented team that loved to run but seemed helpless to defend itself against a squad whose cerebral players benefited from a higher basketball I.Q.

Princeton, which was trailing by seven points with 6:31 to play, shut the Bruins out the rest of the way. As the game wound down, Princeton scored the go-ahead basket on a classic back-door play off a pass

from center Steve Goodrich to guard Gabe Lewullis who got behind Charles O'Bannon for a layup with four seconds left to play. UCLA guard Toby Bailey had a chance to force overtime, but missed a 15-foot jump shot at the buzzer.

Appropriately, the headline in the next morning Daily Princetonian read: "David 43, Goliath 41."

The 65-year-old Carril– who coached Princeton for 29 years and was the only coach to win at least 500 games without the aid of scholarships– announced his retirement after the Tigers' second-round loss to Mississippi State. He finished with 513 wins at Princeton. He came back for a nationally televised encore when he appeared on *The Tonight Show With Jay Leno*. Interestingly, one of the assistants on that particular Tigers' team was John Thompson III, a former Princeton player who coached Georgetown the 2007 Final Four using a slight variation of Carril style of play.

*Dickie V's View:* UCLA had that fantastic feeling coming off its NCAA championship in 1995. The Bruins had a strong nucleus coming back. But it all ended so quickly after they ran into Princeton and that incredible motion game – and all those back-door cuts – in the first round of the 1996 NCAA Tournament.

People never wanted to see the Tigers when the brackets were posted – Jim Harrick included.

He was right to be nervous, man.

The Tigers executed their offense to perfection and sprang the big upset, beating the Bruins, 43-41, in Indianapolis.

Pete Carril's Ivy League teams had come close before in post season. In 1989, they had that defining moment against Georgetown in the first round of the NCAA Tournament when it looked like they were going to upset the Big East champs. But Alonzo Mourning ruined their dreams by blocking a shot at the end.

And the Tigers had to settle for a moral victory.

But it wasn't just a moral victory this time. It was absolute celebration time, baby.

Among his peers, the W solidified Carril's reputation as an absolute genius. Carril's in the Hall of Fame now with all the other big names.

It reminds me of that old saying: You can't catch a Tiger by the tail. And if you do catch him, hold on for dear life.

**D**efending national champion UCLA fell victim to Princeton's back-door cuts and slowdown offense during the first round of the 1996 NCAA Tournament. Mitch Henderson of the Tigers jumps for joy after the 43-41 shocker.

# BRYCE DREW'S *last-second shot gives Valparaiso a victory over SEC champion Mississippi in the first round of the 1998 NCAA Tournamen*

## All in the Family

MOMENT NUMBER

## 36

Valparaiso 70
Ole Miss 69
March 14, 1998

*Profile:* At Valparaiso, it will always be known as "The Shot." But it was also the ultimate father-and-son bonding moment in NCAA basketball history.

Valparaiso senior guard Bryce Drew was a Mr. Basketball in Indiana. But he opted to play at Valparaiso – a tiny Lutheran school with 4,000 undergrads, located 55 miles southeast of Chicago. His father, Homer, was the coach; and his older brother, Scott, was an assistant there.

The Crusaders, a 13th seed representing the Mid-Continent Conference, had never won an NCAA Tournament game and were facing fourth-seeded Ole Miss from the powerful SEC in a first-round game at Oklahoma City.

But on game day, the stars were aligned in Valparaiso's favor.

Drew drained a lean-in, 30-foot three-point goal as time expired to give the relatively unknown Crusaders a 70-69 victory over the Rebels in dramatic fashion, an ending that is replayed constantly during March Madness telecasts. The shot put Valpo on the basketball map forever.

Drew, a three-time Mid-Continent Conference Player of the Year, still holds the school records for career points, three-pointers and assists. He had a chance to give the Crusaders a one-point lead with six seconds to play, but missed an open shot and was forced to foul Ole Miss' best player, Ansu Sesay. But Sesay missed two free throws, and Ole Miss forward Keith Carter knocked the ball out of bounds.

Homer Drew had 2.5 seconds to set up his version of the Christian Laettner miracle. All season

long, he had his team practice a last-second play – "The Pacer" – a sort of hook-and-lateral to free up a shooter. But the Crusaders had never used it in a game – until now.

Jamie Sykes, a 5' 11" guard who inbounded the ball, was guarded by the 6' 4" Carter on the baseline but he was still able to unleash a bomb to Bill Jenkins. Jenkins caught the ball, spun and tipped a short pass forward to Drew to set up the game-winner – just like his dad had diagrammed.

Drew, who finished with 22 points, eight assists and four steals, was swarmed by his excited teammates. But it was the hug he received from his dad that meant the most. For that moment, they were coach and player, but father and son.

Valparaiso's Cinderella run lasted two more games as the Crusaders defeated 12th-seeded Florida State to advance to the Sweet 16 of the upset-riddled Midwest Regional.

Houston selected Drew with the 16th pick in the 1998 draft. His heroics lived on when the ESPY honored "The Shot" as the play of the year.

Drew became so popular, seven babies in Porter County that year were given the name Bryce. In 2005, Drew returned to his alma mater to join his father's coaching staff.

*Dickie V's View:* Bryce Drew came from a basketball family. His father, Homer, was his coach at Valparaiso. His older brother, Scott, who is now the head coach at Baylor, was an assistant coach on that staff.

Bryce was the star of that team.

There was a time when Bryce didn't know he uld be playing in college.

During his high school career, he developed a id heartbeat that required three surgeries to air. Despite that, he led his team to the state mpionship game and was selected Mr. Basketball ndiana in 1994 – just like Steve Alford and mon Bailey before him.

Drew was recruited by dozens of schools, but he nted to stay home and play for his father. And he ame a hometown hero when he made that shot at buzzer to beat Ole Miss in the first round of the 98 NCAA Tournament.

Hey, what a dramatic moment – father helping son and son helping father. Oh, if you could only see the tears in Homer's eyes after Bryce made that big, big shot that was heard all over the nation.

That was one of the special moments in college basketball history. For Valparaiso to challenge an SEC team – not only challenge but beat Ole Miss in dramatic fashion – is what the NCAA Tournament is all about.

That shot turns up on instant replay every year during March Madness.

As it should, my friends, as it should. It's a classic.

# DUKE RALLIES *from a 22-point deficit to beat Maryland in the 2001 NCAA semifinals*

**Knockout Punch**

MOMENT NUMBER

**37**

Duke 95
Maryland 84
March 31, 2001

*Profile:* While the Duke-North Carolina rivalry is generally regarded as the best in college basketball, the four games between the Blue Devils and Maryland in 2001 were as dramatic as any in ACC history.

Duke won three of the four games, but in each case the Blue Devils had to come back from a double-digit deficit. They beat the Terps in overtime after rallying to tie the score in the final minute of regulation at Cole Field House in January. Then they won again on a last-second tip-in by forward Nate James in the ACC Tournament semifinals at Greensboro.

But it was Duke's 95-84 comeback victory over Maryland in the NCAA Tournament semifinals in Minneapolis that put an exclamation point on its national championship season. Duke had to rally from a 22-point deficit – the largest in Final Four history – to advance to the title game against Arizona.

Maryland – which was a year away from winning its first national championship – felt it could play with Duke. The Terps, coached by Gary Williams, had two emerging stars in junior guard Juan Dixon and junior center Lonny Baxter and a talented freshman point guard, Steve Blake, who had caused Duke's first-team sophomore All-American guard Jason Williams unexpected problems offensively.

The Terps came out smoking, building a 34-17 lead at the TV timeout with 7:55 to go in the half. "You're losing by so much, you can't play any worse," Duke coach Mike Krzyzewski screamed at his team. "What are you afraid of – that we'll lose by 40? Just

settle down and do the things that got us here."

After the timeout, Blake stretched the Terps' lead to 39-17 with a long three-pointer. But Duke refused to fold, getting back in the game by pounding the ball inside to 6' 8" junior center Carlos Boozer, who was playing just his third game after breaking a bone in his foot in the Devils' lone loss to Maryland earlier in the season at Cameron Indoor Stadium.

Boozer scored 19 points off the bench. Senior All-American forward Shane Battier, the tournament's most outstanding player, scored 25 points and grabbed eight rebounds. Williams, who had shot just one for seven in the first half, came to life in the second half when he scored 19 of his 23 points. Then there was the 6' 7" James, who shut down Dixon, holding him to three points in the second half after the Maryland guard had gone off for 16 in the first half.

Williams, who had missed his first nine threes of the game, nailed a big one to give Duke its first lead at 73-72 with 6:52 to play. The Devils built the lead to five and put the game away when Baxter fouled out with 2:48 to play.

Two days later, Duke disposed of Arizona, 82-72 to wrap up the championship.

*Dickie V's View:* The one thing about Maryland under Gary Williams was that his players were never in awe of the four letters D-U-K-E.

I've seen a lot of teams over the years come into

Cameron and be intimidated by the Cameron
Crazies. You can see it in their body language. But
ever, ever Gary's kids. They thought they were as
ood as, if not better than, Duke – especially in 2001.

Maryland looked like they couldn't play any
etter in this NCAA semifinal game that year. They
ere playing brilliantly, absolutely dominating in
very phase of the game as they jumped out to a
2-point lead in the first half.

Then Uncle Mo swung drastically in Duke's favor
d the Blue Devils were on their way, rallying for a
5-84 victory.

I was sitting in the stands right behind Elton
and – who came in the same year as Shane Battier,
orey Maggette and William Avery and left after his
phomore year in 1999, when he was the first pick
the draft. And you could see the emotion and the
 in his face when Duke fought back. His buddies
Battier, Jason Williams and company – just kept
hting and scrapping like you couldn't believe. They
entually took over the game after Carlos Boozer,
eir big guy who had been hurt, came off the bench
 score 19 points.

Even though Elton Brand looked like a million
llars in his new suit, my gut feeling was that he
uld have preferred to be on that court jumping for
 with all his buddies. You had to believe that he
uld have loved to be on the stage and in the win-
's circle with Coach K and his former teammates as
y celebrated winning the national championship.

**D**uke coach Mike Krzyzewski embraces players Jason
Williams (22) and Shane Battier after a tremendous comeback
in the 2001 NCAA Tournament semifinals. The Blue Devils rallied
to stun conference rival Maryland, 95-84.

# LEN BIAS *leads Maryland to the 1984 ACC title*

## Lefty's Legacy

MOMENT NUMBER 38

Maryland 74
Duke 72
March 11, 1984

*Profile:* This was the late Len Bias' coming-out party.

Maryland's 6' 8" sophomore forward was just starting to come into his own. He had spent the summer after his freshman year working as a custodian and security guard at an elementary school near his Landover, Md., home – using the school's gymnasium to work on his shooting and ball-handling.

Bias, playing with growing confidence, averaged 15.3 points and shot 56.7 percent his sophomore year. But even though the Terps finished second in the regular season, he couldn't even crack the All-ACC second team.

So Bias simply took out his frustrations on his rivals in the annual ACC Tournament in Greensboro, leading the Terps past North Carolina State, 69-63, and Wake Forest, 66-64, and into the championship game against Duke.

Bias was unstoppable, making 12 of 18 shots and scoring 26 points as Maryland defeated the Blue Devils, 74-72. He took advantage of the fact Duke was emotionally drained from a gut-wrenching victory over North Carolina the day before, to lead the Terps to their first ACC Tournament championship since 1958.

"I came here with something to prove," Bias said after being awarded the MVP trophy. "I wanted people to know I could play and that I could do it in big games."

Actually, Bias felt teammate Herman Veal, who shut down forwards Lorenzo Charles of State, Kenny Green of Wake and Mark Alarie of Duke, should have received the award.

But there was no denying Bias' brilliance. Over three games, he scored 56 points on 26-for-43 shooting and had 18 rebounds.

The game had special meaning to Maryland's veteran coach, Lefty Driesell, a master recruiter whose teams averaged 20 wins but struggled to gain respect on Tobacco Road. Driesell had always insisted he wasn't obsessed with winning the granddaddy of all conference tournaments.

"Back when I first started out I wanted to win that thing real bad", Driesell told the media. "I said, 'If we win that thing, I'm going to get that trophy and screw it on the top of the hood of my car and ride around the state of North Carolina for a week.' I was really going to do that. Now I'm too old for that. I've got to get home and get some sleep."

*Dickie V's View:* When Lefty Driesell took the Maryland coaching job in 1970, he said he wanted make the Terps "the UCLA of the East."

His career will always be defined by his desire to win an ACC Tournament title. He used to get all fired up about it. He was always upset about playing

he games in North Carolina. The Terps reached the
ournament finals six times, losing five times by three
oints or less.

Well, on this day, the second-seeded Terps had a
hance. Why? Because they had one of the greatest
ver to wear a Maryland uniform – Lenny Bias.

Bias and four guys like me would have a chance
o beat anybody. That's how good this guy was. In
ct, when they talk about the greats ever to play at
aryland – guys like Len Elmore, Tom McMillen,
hn Lucas, Albert King and Juan Dixon – Bias might
ave to be at the top of the list.

Bias scored 26 points as the Terps defeated
uke, 74-72, in the ACC championship game at
reensboro. He helped Maryland rally from eight
oints down with 14:50 to play, igniting a 24-3 run.

Bias was the MVP of the ACC Tournament.

But this was Driesell's big moment and he was
bsolutely beside himself with joy. But he never
d ride around the Triangle with that gold trophy
rewed on the hood of his car.

**Lefty Driesell once called
Maryland, "The UCLA of the
East." He had Len Bias on
his team and that helped
the Terps earn an ACC
championship.**

# UNDERDOG

*LSU upsets top-ranked Kentucky in the 1986 NCAA Southeast Regional finals to make the Final Four as an 11th seed*

## A Tiger's Roar

MOMENT NUMBER

**39**

LSU 59
Kentucky 57
March 22, 1986

*Profile:* Dale Brown's second trip to the NCAA Final Four was totally unexpected – which may be why LSU fans still refer to the former Tigers' coach as the "Master Motivator" down in the Bayou.

Brown's team looked like it was headed toward a disastrous 1986 SEC season.

Before the season ever began, Jerry "Ice" Reynolds turned pro early. Center Tito Horford was thrown off the team two months later; starting center Zoran Jovanovich suffered a season-ending knee injury in December; and forward Nakita Wilson was declared academically ineligible after the fall semester, forcing Brown to move 6' 6" sophomore Ricky Blanton from off guard to center. In addition, several LSU players – including 6' 8" All-American forward John "Hot Plate" Williams – contracted chicken pox during the regular season.

In spite of all that, Brown was able to rally the remnants of his roster to a 22-11 season. And the Tigers, who had lost eight of their previous 13 games, sneaked into the NCAA Tournament as an 11th-seeded, at-large selection.

What happened the next two weeks was nothing short of miraculous, as the Tigers became the only team ever to defeat the No. 1, 2 and 3 seeds to win the Southeast Regional finals and advance to the Final Four in Dallas.

Sophomore forward Anthony Wilson scored a career-high 25 points as the Tigers opened the tournament by defeating Purdue in double overtime, 94-87. Then Wilson hit a game-winning jumper at the buzzer as LSU defeated third-seeded Memphis,

83-81, in the second round. Senior forward Don Redden, the team captain, scored 27 points and Williams added 23 as LSU knocked off second-seeded Georgia Tech, 79-64, in a Sweet 16 game in hostile Atlanta. Then they stunned mighty Kentucky, 59-57, in the regional finals.

Kentucky was a clear favorite entering the game. The top-ranked Cats were 32-3 and had won 21 straight SEC games. They had already beaten LSU three times that season, twice in the regular season and once in the SEC Tournament semifinals. But the Tigers, who had played the Cats close in a pair of two-point losses, came up huge when it counted.

Redden, who was selected Most Outstanding Player in the Southeast Regional, scored 15 points and grabbed eight rebounds for LSU while Williams added 15 for the balanced Tigers, who put four players in double figures.

But it was Blanton's role in Brown's "Freak Defense" against Kentucky's 6' 8" first-team All-American forward Kenny Walker that made the difference.

Walker scored 16 points in the first half but had only four in the final 20 minutes. The Tigers, who scored on eight of their last 10 possessions, were holding a 57-55 lead with 44 seconds left when Brown went to a spread. Kentucky coach Eddie Sutton waited too long to foul, and Redden found Blanton open for a layup with 17 seconds remaining to seal the deal.

Sadly, two years after one of the greatest moments in LSU basketball history, Redden died of heart disease at age 24, bringing back memories of LSU legend Pete Maravich, who also died too early at 40.

*Photo Courtesy of Louisiana State University Sports Information.*

*Dickie V's View:* Kentucky had beaten the Tigers three times before that game – twice in the regular season and again in the SEC Tournament. That was Kenny Walker's team. They were really a dominant club. They were No. 1 in the country.

But when Eddie Sutton knew he had to beat LSU a fourth time in the Southeast Regional finals to go to the Final Four, it must have been Nightmare City. Four times.

But LSU coach Dale Brown – "The Preacher Man" – found a way to make his LSU players believe in his gospel: that they were good enough to pull off the upset. He had them all motivated.

It didn't take much, man.

After LSU defeated Georgia Tech in the regional semifinals in Atlanta, Kentucky fans mobbed the Tigers in the hotel lobby, thanking them for beating the ACC team they thought would be their toughest competition.

That thought was still in the players' minds when they took the bus over to the Omni. Brown was a great psychologist. He was always talking about slowing teams down with his "Freak Defense." Whenever the subject came up, I would simply say, "Hey Dale, come on now. That's just a psychological ploy. It would be a freak if you had seven men on the floor and the other team had five."

But look what happened.

Kentucky looked like it was on its way as it was dominating early; but Brown, fighter that he found a way to get LSU back in the game. The Tigers contained Walker in the second half and eventually won, 59-57, when center Ricky Blanton, who had been on the bench most of the second half, stepped up and scored on a game-winning layup off a bounce pass from Don Redden.

When the ball went in, Blanton took off, flying down the court, pumping his hands in the air. In Louisiana, that victory dance became known as "The Blanton" and was rebroadcast on state-wide TV hundreds of times the next week before LSU left for Dallas.

And on that night, baby, his dance routine was better than the one John Travolta did in "Saturday Night Fever."

**1986** was a special year for Dale Brown and his LSU Tigers. This team made the Final Four as a No. 11 seed. The Tigers stunned Kentucky in the regional final.

# DAN DAKICH

*holds Michael Jordan in check as Indiana upsets top-seeded North Carolina in the 1984 NCAA East Regional semifina*

## Defensive Gem

MOMENT NUMBER

40

Indiana 72
North Carolina 68
March 22, 1984

*Profile:* Dan Dakich seemed an unlikely candidate to become part of Indiana folklore.

The Hoosiers' 6' 5" junior guard from Andrean High in Merrillville, Ind., had started only four games that season and was considered a tough, but not quick, role player. The night before Indiana played powerful, top-ranked North Carolina in the 1984 NCAA East Regional semifinals in Atlanta, Hall of Fame coach Bob Knight told Dakich that he was going to start and have the defensive assignment against Michael Jordan – the National Player of the Year.

Dakich, plagued by a stomach bug, immediately went back to his room and threw up.

In the locker room before the game, Dakich flipped open a game program to the tournament record page. The most points scored by one player in the East Regional was 61 by Austin Carr of Notre Dame against Ohio in 1970.

"Honest to God, no way I'm letting this guy get 60. I don't want my son to say someday, `Didn't you play for Indiana when Michael Jordan got 72 points?'" he told the Atlanta Constitution.

Then Dakich did exactly what Knight instructed. Knight wanted Dakich to allow Jordan to shoot the jump shot and keep him off the backboard to eliminate easy offensive rebounds.

Jordan picked up two early fouls. Then he disappeared for long stretches of the game, scoring just 13 points on six-of-14 shooting, and grabbed

only one rebound in 26 minutes during a stunning loss in Atlanta. Dakich took away a lot of his favori shots, and Jordan went 13 minutes of the second h without a point.

Dakich fouled out with four minutes to play. Bu he had done his job.

The best player in the game that night was sophomore guard Steve Alford, who scored 27 points on nine-of-13 shooting. Indiana, which shot 65 percent, controlled tempo and jumped out to a 12-point lead with 5:22 left. Carolina rallied to within two points on a pair of Jordan field goals wi 2:07 left, but Alford put the game away from the foul line.

Jordan acknowledged afterwards that Dakich di a good job, but he got all the shots he wanted. "I w trying not to think about it," he said, "but I never shoot well in the Omni."

As it turned out, that was Jordan's final college game. Ironically, Indiana lost its next game to the ACC fifth-place team, Virginia, in the Elite Eight.

*Dickie V's View:* Dan Dakich didn't grab many of the headlines when he played for Bob Knight at Indiana. He was a role player – a tough, physical ty of guy who got the most out of his ability with hus and scrappiness.

But he made a trip to the spotlight the night Indiana beat No. 1 North Carolina, 72-68, in the

94 NCAA East Regional semifinals in Atlanta.
ight gave Dakich the assignment of guarding
chael Jordan. Dakich did a good job containing
n, too, keeping him away from the glass, never
ing him break loose.

Jordan finished with just 13 points and got off
y 14 shots.

After that game, people used to joke that the only
son capable of holding Jordan under 20 points
s Dean Smith. But that was never the case. Jordan
s a scoring machine on the NBA level when teams
d to defend him man-to-man. On the college level,
ith taught him how to be part of the team concept.

Besides, in that particular game, Jordan picked up
early fouls and had to come out – so he couldn't
y big minutes.

Still, it was another big coaching achievement
Bob Knight, and the name Dakich became an
portant part of Hoosier basketball tradition.

**T**alk about a defensive
stopper! Indiana's
Dan Dakich upheld his
reputation by putting
the clamps on
the one-and-only
Michael Jordan in the
1984 NCAA Tournament.

*Photo Courtesy of Indiana University Athletics Media Relations.*

# DUKE RALLIES *from a 10-point deficit in the final minute en route to an overtime victory over ACC rival Maryland at Cole Field House in 20*

## The Miracle Minute

*MOMENT NUMBER*

**41**

**Profile:** The rivalry between Maryland coach Gary Williams and Duke coach Mike Krzyzewski has always been intense. But the atmosphere seemed particularly bitter in 2001 when the Blue Devils visited hostile Cole Field House and the two best teams in the league battled for supremacy in the ACC.

Many Maryland fans wearing obscene T-shirts greeted Duke players. And Krzyzewski's players were showered with ice and aluminum foil from hot dog wrappers as they sat on the bench.

It looked like the Blue Devils were going to get their lunch handed to them, too. Maryland dominated play for almost 39 minutes of the game, taking a 90-80 lead with 1:01 to play.

Duke's sophomore All-American guard Jason Williams, who had been effectively neutralized by his nemesis, Steve Blake, did not have a three-pointer. He had committed an unsightly 10 turnovers. Then just when Maryland fans began screaming, "Overrated, overrated," during a timeout and it looked like the Devils were about to be swept out of College Park, Williams took over. Taking advantage of the fact Blake had fouled out, he scored on a driving layup with 51 seconds remaining, then stole the inbounds pass and made a deep three-pointer, his first of the game. Eight seconds later, he made another three to

cut the Maryland lead to 90-88.

Williams had scored eight points and picked up a steal in 14 seconds to change the momentum, and the Devils forced overtime when forward Nate James made a pair of free throws with 21.9 seconds left.

It was forward Shane Battier's turn to take the game over once the overtime began. He hit a three to give Duke the lead for good, at 96-95, and Duke went on to win, 98-96, when Battier blocked a 10-foot jumper by Juan Dixon on the Terps' final possession.

In Durham, the wild comeback will be known forever as "The Miracle Minute."

Williams finished with 25 points after a poor start. And he left a huge scar on the Terps' psyche. Maryland fans left unhappy and mad. After the game Carlos Boozer's father stormed into the pressroom and claimed his wife had been hit on the head by a water bottle. Chris Duhon's mother said water bottle hit her twice.

*Dickie V's View:* I didn't do that one for ESPN. I had another big game in the afternoon, then flew back to Florida to host a pre-Super Bowl party at my home. We had the Duke-Maryland game on TV and I thought Duke was R.I.P. City.

Maryland was in total control, and the game was

**Duke 98**
**Maryland 96 (OT)**
**January 27, 2001**

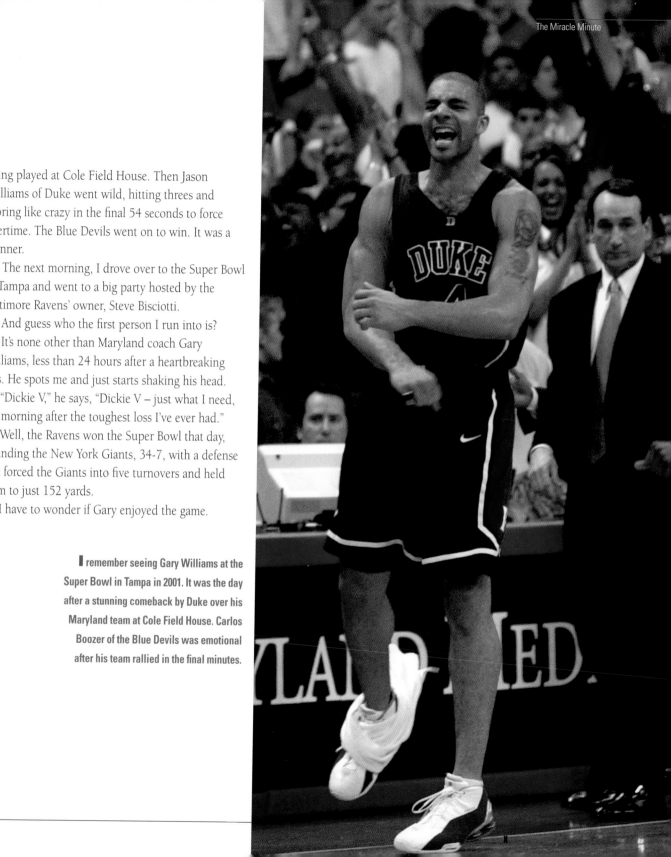

being played at Cole Field House. Then Jason
Williams of Duke went wild, hitting threes and
scoring like crazy in the final 54 seconds to force
overtime. The Blue Devils went on to win. It was a
stunner.

The next morning, I drove over to the Super Bowl
in Tampa and went to a big party hosted by the
Baltimore Ravens' owner, Steve Bisciotti.

And guess who the first person I run into is?

It's none other than Maryland coach Gary
Williams, less than 24 hours after a heartbreaking
loss. He spots me and just starts shaking his head.

"Dickie V," he says, "Dickie V – just what I need,
the morning after the toughest loss I've ever had."

Well, the Ravens won the Super Bowl that day,
pounding the New York Giants, 34-7, with a defense
that forced the Giants into five turnovers and held
them to just 152 yards.

I have to wonder if Gary enjoyed the game.

**I** remember seeing Gary Williams at the
Super Bowl in Tampa in 2001. It was the day
after a stunning comeback by Duke over his
Maryland team at Cole Field House. Carlos
Boozer of the Blue Devils was emotional
after his team rallied in the final minutes.

# SECOND-RANKED

*Georgetown defeats top-ranked St. John's in a 1985 Big East blowout at the Garden*

## The Sweater Game

MOMENT NUMBER 42

Georgetown 85
St. John's 69
February 25, 1985

*Profile:* Who would have thought a sweater could have affected the outcome of the 1985 season?

Before the start of preseason practice, a coach from Italy visited St. John's coach Lou Carnesecca on campus. It has always been an Italian tradition to exchange gifts, and Carnesecca received a brown sweater from the Italian coach. "It was an ugly sweater," Carnesecca recalled. "No style, no composition."

Carnesecca tossed the sweater into his closet and forgot about it until January 14, when he came down with a cold. St. John's had a game that day. His wife, Mary, felt the arena might be drafty and it would be a good idea for him to wear a sweater. So Carnesecca went into the closet and got out the gift.

That day, St. John's defeated Pitt on a last-minute jump shot. In Carnesecca's view, the sweater brought him good luck. "After that," he said. "I had to wear it. If I didn't, I'd hear all these St. John's kids yelling, `Hey, coach, where's your sweater?'"

Twelve days later, on January 26, St. John's broke Georgetown's 29-game winning streak, defeating the top-ranked Hoyas, 66-65, in Landover, Md., to take over the No. 1 spot in the AP poll.

The next time the two giants met – a month later in the Garden – St. John's, which had won 19 straight games and was 24-1, was still No. 1. Georgetown was No. 2. It was a classic Big East showdown, the biggest regular-season game in Garden history. Tickets were impossible to get.

Carnesecca had on his lucky sweater.

But Georgetown coach John Thompson brought

along a lucky charm of his own.

He had a T-shirt made up with the same design. And moments before tipoff, he opened his suit jacket and revealed the shirt for everyone to see. The sellout crowd at the Garden went wild. Even Carnesecca was laughing.

But no one from St. John's was laughing after the game started.

Sophomore forward Reggie Williams scored 25 points and All-American center Patrick Ewing had 20 points, nine rebounds and six blocked shots as Hoyas shot 60 percent in the first half and romped 85-69, to retake control of the best league in the country.

*Dickie V's View:* Yes, Looie Carnesecca's sweater was hideous.

But it was all part of his colorful personality. Looie had so much fun with that particular St. John's team probably because it had such a great New York City flavor with stars like Chris Mullin, Walter Berry and Mark Jackson. He once told his assistant coach Ron Rutledge, "You don't need a car to recruit. You can get on a subway and get five guys to win the national championship."

Only Georgetown stood in the way of the enthusiastic Carnesecca and St. John's being the best of the best.

The Hoyas sent a message loud and clear they were still the Beast of the Big East in that highly anticipated game at the Garden. And John

John Thompson had something special in store for Looie Carnesecca and St. John's before their showdown at Madison Square Garden in 1985. Thompson donned a special T-shirt in honor of his opponent.

ompson showed he had a nice sense of humor
t night when he showed up wearing that T-shirt
ock-off of Looie's sweater.

The Big East coaches were bigger than life back
n and these might have been the two best teams in
country. The Hoyas got St. John's a second time
the Big East championship game and then again in
national semifinals after both teams reached the

Final Four. And the games weren't that close.

Afterwards, Carnesecca was philosophical about
not winning a championship, saying he wasn't
bitter. "For my ego, it would have been great," he said
afterwards. "But it wouldn't have changed me any. It
wouldn't have changed St. John's."

I wonder what Looie did with that brown sweater.

*Photo Courtesy of Georgetown Sports Information.*

## SCOTTY THURMAN *makes the game-winning shot as Arkansas defeats Duke in the 1994 NCAA championship gar*

**Beam Me Up**

MOMENT NUMBER

**43**

Arkansas 76
Duke 72
April 4, 1994

*Profile:* President Bill Clinton was a huge Arkansas basketball fan and couldn't resist attending the Hogs' 1994 NCAA championship matchup against Duke.

As he sat in his luxury box at midcourt, he knew exactly who he wanted to take the biggest shot in school history.

"I kept screaming to get the ball to Scotty Thurman," Clinton said later. "He's a tremendous clutch player."

Thurman, a 6' 6" left-handed smooth-shooting sophomore guard, put an end to the Devils' dreams of a third national championship in four years when he launched a high-arching three-point shot over the outstretched arm of Duke's 6' 8" Antonio Laing that ripped through the net with just one second left on the shot clock – and only 51 seconds remaining – to give Arkansas a 73-70 lead. The SEC champions went on to a 76-72 victory at the Charlotte Arena.

Thurman arrived in Fayetteville from Ruston, La. He learned how to shoot in West Side Park from his father, Levell, who played for Grambling in the late 1960s. Levell once told his son he was the best jump shooter ever.

Thurman adopted some of that cockiness, although there was a time when it appeared his gift for making big shots might go unnoticed. LSU and Louisiana Tech never recruited Thurman, but then Arkansas assistant Mike Anderson, who was looking for a shooter after Todd Day and Lee Mayberry left,

discovered him on the AAU circuit and convinced him to sign with the Hogs.

Thurman entered school with 6' 7" forward Corliss Williamson, who went on to become a two-time SEC Player of the Year. Thurman was a two-ti All-SEC player himself. Together they led the Hogs two Final Fours in 1994 and 1995.

The Hogs advanced to the 1994 championship game by defeating Arizona, 91-82, on the strength 29 points from Williamson.

The final was, as Arkansas coach Nolan Richardson liked to say, "40 Minutes of Hell." Duk almost stole the Hogs' intensity, going on a 13-0 ru to take a 48-38 lead with 17 minutes to play.

But Williamson, who finished with 23 points and was selected Most Outstanding Player of the Final Four, would not let the Hogs get butchered.

They battled back to take a 70-67 lead before Duke All-American Grant Hill hit a three to tie the score at 70 with 1:29 to play.

But Thurman had the final word, making the biggest shot of his career.

Thurman and Williamson teamed up the next year to lead Arkansas back to the Final Four where they lost to UCLA in the championship game.

Both players declared for the draft after that season. Williamson was taken in the lottery. But Thurman, who was told by both his agent and Richardson he would be a first-round pick, wasn't selected at all and wound up playing in the CBA and in Europe.

*Dickie V's View:* President Bill Clinton is a huge Razorback fan. He loves his Hogs. When he was the governor of Arkansas, he once went to see their star forward Corliss Williamson – "The Big Nasty" – when he was in high school. And he visited Nolan Richardson's team in the locker room during the 1994 season.

So you knew he had to be there at the Charlotte Arena to see them play Duke that year in the national championship game.

Talk about traffic jams when that presidential motorcade rolled in.

Arkansas played its "40 Minutes of Hell" and Scotty Thurman made the President's night when he hit that jump shot in the last minute to rob Mike Krzyzewski of another national championship.

The next year, when Arkansas got back to the finals, Digger Phelps, my colleague in the studio, used his political contacts to arrange for us to hook up with President Clinton to discuss the championship game. Digger and I interviewed Clinton on a conference call at a party he was attending on the night of the championship game against UCLA.

Digger and I were shooting the breeze during a commercial break and all of a sudden we hear the President relaying to the crowd: "We're golden. Dickie V says he likes our chances because Tyus Edney isn't going to play."

You can't get 'em all right, I guess.

**P**ig Sooey...Arkansas was able to cut down the nets in Charlotte, North Carolina. Scotty Thurman hit the game-winning shot against Duke in the 1994 NCAA championship game.

*Photo Courtesy of Getty Images*

# RAY ALLEN'S *shot beats Georgetown in the 1996 Big East Tournament championship game*

## The Shot

MOMENT NUMBER

**44**

Connecticut 76
Georgetown 75
March 9, 1996

**R**ay Allen helped
Connecticut win the
Big East championship
in a hard-fought battle
against Allen Iverson
and Georgetown.

*Profile:* The 1996 Big East championship game between Connecticut and Georgetown didn't need much hype.

The Huskies were 30-3 and ranked No. 3 by AP. The Hoyas were 26-7 and ranked No. 6. Each team had a great player. Ray Allen of UConn and Allen Iverson of Georgetown were both first-team All-Americans.

"This one is not for children," Georgetown coach John Thompson announced. "The boys are gone. The men are here."

Though neither Allen nor Iverson distinguished himself with his shooting, this intense matchup between these two titans will always be remembered for its dramatic finish.

The 6' 5" Allen wound up being the star, scoring 17 points, grabbing 12 rebounds and nailing an acrobatic hanging 13-foot jumper with 13.6 seconds left to give the Huskies a 76-75 victory that sent the sellout crowd at the Garden into a frenzy. Ironically, it was the only field goal of the second half for Allen, who shot just five for 20 after being suffocated all night by freshman guard Victor Page and forward Boubacar Aw.

Georgetown, which had broken UConn's 23-game winning streak with a 77-65 victory in Landover, Md., and jostled Allen into a poor shooting performance during the only regular-season meeting between the two teams, looked like it had the seque under control.

The Hoyas, who made up for the fact Iverson sh just five for 18 and scored only 13 points by getting 20 from Page, appeared to have the game safely under control – taking a 74-63 lead with four minutes to play.

But UConn, getting heroic efforts from forward Kirk King and guard Ricky Moore, closed out the game with a 12-0 run. King had eight of his 20 poi during that rally.

With Georgetown clinging to a 74-73 lead, Page missed the front end of a one-and-one, and Allen

bbed the rebound. UConn called a timeout to set
its final shot. "It was designed for me to come off a
k," Allen said. "I jumped up, faked a pass; then on
way back down, I took it up. I got a lucky roll."
Despite all of Allen's heroics, the media – whose
es were collected before the end of game –
arded the MVP trophy to Page, who had set a
rnament freshman scoring record with 34 points
inst Villanova in the semis.
But Allen seemed more than happy with the only
East Tournament championship ring of his career.

*ckie V's View:* The Big East Tournament
mpionship game has always been one of the
st glamorous events in sports. Saturday night at
Garden – the Big Apple, Broadway. Connecticut
Georgetown. No. 3 vs. No. 6. You could feel the
tricity.
It was like going to a Sugar Ray Leonard-Tommy
rns fight or a Billy Joel concert. Only the stars
his show were All-American guards Ray Allen of
onn and Allen Iverson of Georgetown, two dyna-
e players you knew were going to be huge at the
t level.
The Big East has had its share of big-time
ments: like the time Walter Berry blocked Pearl
shington's last-second shot to give St. John's a
69 victory over Syracuse. Or the week in 2006
en Gerry McNamara owned the Garden when
acuse, which was a ninth seed, won four in a row
arn an automatic bid to the NCAA Tournament.
But this one ranks right at the top of the list.
The speed in the game was incredible. Every time

the ball was in Iverson's hands, there was a buzz. The
same with Allen. The funny thing was, even though
the game turned into a classic, neither one played a
big role in the outcome until the end, although Allen
was there to supply the finishing touches. He made
the game-winning jump shot on UConn's last
possession to give his team a 76-75 victory.

**A**llen Iverson fought
and scrapped every time
he took the court as a
Georgetown Hoya. His
team fell short in the
Big East title tilt against
the Connecticut Huskies.

# UTAH'S *Keith Van Horn steps into the hero's role during the 1997 WAC Tournament*

## Honk Your Horn

*Profile:* Utah's 6' 10" forward Keith Van Horn piled up a list of honors during his senior year in college. The Utes' all-time leading scorer was a consensus first-team All-American and the Western Athletic Conference Player of the Year for three straight seasons.

But nothing topped the spectacular nature of his three-game performance in the 1997 WAC Tournament in Las Vegas.

Utah entered that tournament as a heavy favorite, but the Utes almost made an early exit against SMU – a team they had beaten twice by 19 points in the regular season – in the quarterfinals. The Mustangs surged to a 15-point lead and still had a 58-57 advantage with just seconds left. Van Horn missed a potential game-winning shot, but the rebound went out of bounds off SMU. With just 0.3 seconds left, it appeared the Utes would need a miracle.

They got one.

When point guard Andre Miller set up under the basket to inbound the ball, Majerus designed a play on the spot.

He placed one player in each corner, another at the three-point line and Van Horn near the basket directly in front of Miller. Originally, SMU had two players on Van Horn. But one split off to guard one of the Utah players in the corner. Van Horn spun free, took a lob pass and tapped it in as the buzzer sounded.

MOMENT NUMBER

45

Utah 59
SMU 58
March 6, 1997

*Photo Courtesy of University of Utah, file photo.*

The next night, Van Horn scored just 10 points ng a 72-70 semifinal victory over New Mexico, he provided more last-second heroics. With the e tied at 70, Van Horn grabbed the rebound after ssed shot by Miller and put up an off-balance, e-winning 13-foot jumper that went in at the zer.

Again.

Van Horn dominated the championship game, shing off a magnificent week by scoring 37 points grabbing 15 rebounds as Rick Majerus' team v away TCU, 89-68, in front of an adoring crowd 0,101 at the Thomas and Mack Center to win a d straight title.

With four minutes left, the crowd began chanting name: "Keith Van Horn. Keith Van Horn." It was a ng tribute.

*kie V's View:* Talk about Midnight Madness. had to be an insomniac to watch some of these y finishes on ESPN. But it was worth it if you did. Keith Van Horn was the best player ever to play Rick Majerus at Utah. And Majerus had a few – Michael Doleac, Alex Jensen and Andre Miller, point guard who outplayed Mike Bibby when Utes ran a clinic on Arizona in the 1998 West onal finals. But no one dominated the WAC like Van Horn, led Utah in scoring and rebounding for four

straight years and had a knack for making big plays.

After he won the WAC Player of the Year award as a junior, Majerus actually recommended Van Horn leave early for the pros. Van Horn was married, with a daughter, and figured to go high in the first round of the NBA draft. But he stayed in school for a final year and had some special moments – especially in the 1997 WAC Tournament – making two game-winning shots at the buzzer and scoring 37 points in the championship game, which was held on the campus of UNLV.

That was a performance worthy of any headliner on the Vegas strip that week. Van Horn belonged as a marquee headliner, a la Vegas stars like the incomparable Danny Gans, Cher or Elton John or whoever else your heart desires.

When Van Horn did move on, the Nets selected him with the second pick in the 1997 NBA draft.

**U**tah's Keith Van Horn
had a flare for the dramatic.
He hit buzzer-beaters on
back-to-back nights in the
1997 WAC Tournament.

## FRESHMAN *phenom Pervis Ellison lifts Louisville to a victory over Duke in the 1986 NCAA championship ga...*

### "Never Nervous" Pervis

MOMENT NUMBER
**46**

Louisville 72
Duke 69
March 31, 1986

*Profile:* Pervis Ellison was appropriately nicknamed "Never Nervous" Pervis and he came to define Louisville's dominance in the early 1980s when the Cardinals went to four Final Fours in seven years and won two national championships.

When the slender, 6' 9" Ellison arrived at Louisville from Savannah, Ga., in the fall of 1985, he was a McDonald's All-American center. But 6' 10" Danny Ferry of DeMatha Catholic, who signed with Duke, was considered the best prospect in the country.

But Ellison dominated play during the Cardinals' 72-69 victory over Duke in the 1986 NCAA championship game, scoring 25 points on 10-of-14 shooting, grabbing 11 rebounds, picking up two steals and blocking a shot.

Ellison's 6' 8" junior teammate, Billy Thompson – part of the "Camden Connection" out of Jersey that also included All-American guard Milt Wagner – played superbly in a supporting role with 13 points on six-of-eight shooting, four rebounds and two assists.

Ellison gave his teammates a taste of what was to come in fall pickup games. Louisville coach Denny Crum, facing a huge hole in the middle after Barry Sumpter left school with academic problems, plugged Ellison into the starting lineup immediately. Ellison responded by averaging 13.1 points, 8.2 rebounds and 2.4 blocked shots. He was selected national freshman of the year for a resurgent team that finished 32-7 and won 20 of its last 22 games.

Louisville athletic director Bill Olson was so

confident his school would win, he had the player[s] sized for championship rings two days before they left for Dallas.

But Crum, a John Wooden protégé, was more cautious. He made sure his newest star stayed focused, keeping Ellison sequestered in his hotel room prior to the game so he wouldn't have to dea[l] with any media distractions. Ellison, who played t[he] piano, trombone and tuba, played his sweetest mu[sic] against Mike Krzyzewski's first Final Four team.

The Cards needed him to be at his best.

They were down by as many as eight points in the second half before Crum went to a game-alteri[ng] high-low post offense with Ellison and Thompson[.]

Duke, which got 24 points from its senior All-American guard Johnny Dawkins, attempted to pl[ay] Jay Bilas, Ferry and Mark Alarie on Ellison, with li[ttle] success. Louisville was clinging to a 66-65 lead wi[th] 48 seconds left in the game and 11 seconds left on the shot clock when Crum called a timeout to set [up] a play that would allow guards Wagner or Jeff Hal[l] to go one-on-one. But Hall threw up an off-balanc[e] air ball. Ellison rose above the crowd to grab the b[all] and lay it in. Then after rebounding a miss by Da[vid] Henderson, Ellison calmly deposited two free thro[ws] to push the lead to 70-65 with 25 seconds left and lock up the victory.

Ellison became the first freshman since Arnie Ferren of Utah in 1944 to be named the tourname[nt] Most Outstanding Player. "Oh, I get nervous some[-] times," he said afterwards. "But you got to go off t[he] court for me to get nervous."

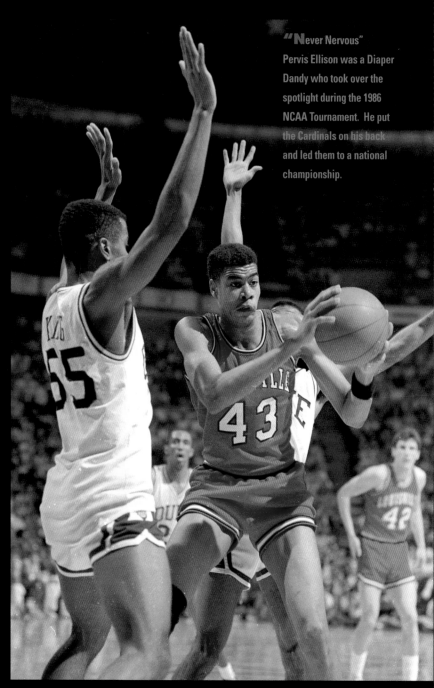

*ckie V's View:* I really thought this might be the
rt of the Pervis Ellison era in college basketball.
But it never happened.

Ellison never got back to a Final Four. The Car-
als were eliminated by Oklahoma and Illinois in
eet 16 games his junior and senior years. Ellison
s a consensus first-team All-American that
son and was the first pick in the 1989 draft
en he was selected by the Sacramento Kings.

Interestingly, Crum, who coached 23 teams
he NCAA Tournament and was inducted into
Naismith Memorial Basketball Hall of Fame in
94, never got back either.

As for Crum, he utilized the high-low post of-
se he learned when he was an assistant to the
zard of Westwood, John Wooden, at UCLA.
um produced some great big men. From 1989
ough 1996, four of Crum's post players – Ellison,
ton Spencer, Cliff Rozier and Samaki Walker –
re selected in the top 16 picks of the NBA draft.

"Never Nervous" Pervis. He was a Diaper Dandy
d he carried the team to the national champion-
p in 1986. He would not let them lose against
ke in the finals. Ellison made every big play
wn the stretch and wanted the ball, especially at
nch time.

Then, again, he was part of the Denny Crum
gram, which was so dominant in the '80s. In
rness to that team, Ellison had some great people
und him like Milt Wagner and Billy Thompson
he Camden, New Jersey, connection – who went
to play in the NBA.

Before the season started, I must be honest.
adn't heard much about Pervis Ellison.

Trust me, when the NCAA Tournament was
completed, Ellison had become a flat-out PTPer
(Prime-Time Player).

# THE BIG EAST *puts three teams in the 1985 Final Four*

## Block Party

*MOMENT NUMBER*

**47**

Georgetown 77
St. John's 59

Villanova 52
Memphis 45

March 30, 1985

*Profile:* When Providence AD Dave Gavitt sat down with the athletic directors of Boston College, St. John's, Georgetown, Connecticut, Syracuse and Seton Hall to form the Big East in 1979, he knew the frustrating history of college basketball in the region.

Before the formation of the league, the last team from the East to win the NCAA Tournament was La Salle in 1954. Between then and 1979, 12 teams from the East made it to the Final Four – La Salle again in 1955; Temple in 1956 and 1959; West Virginia in 1959; NYU in 1960; St. Joseph's in 1961; Princeton in 1965; St. Bonaventure in 1970; Villanova in 1971; Providence in 1973; Syracuse in 1975, and Rutgers in 1976.

But all had gone home disappointed.

Gavitt figured if he could put together a made-for-TV basketball conference of traditional powers located primarily in major markets in the Northeast corridor of the country, that would change.

Gavitt proved to be a visionary.

A year later, the league added Villanova; Pitt joined in 1982, thus creating a league that had the recruiting power to compete with anyone, even the powerful ACC.

Georgetown became the first Big East team to crack the glass ceiling – advancing to a Final Four in 1982 and winning a national championship in 1984.

But nothing topped the 1985 season when the Big East held its own block party at the NCAA Final Four.

Three of the four teams in Lexington's Rupp Are – Georgetown, St. John's and Villanova – were from the fledgling conference. A fourth – Boston College – almost got there, too, losing to Midwest Regional champ Memphis in the Sweet 16, 59-57.

Georgetown and St. John's came as no surprise. They were powerhouse teams that had jockeyed for the No. 1 spot in the AP poll all year. The Hoya defeated Georgia Tech, 60-54, to win the East Regional finals. St. John's defeated North Carolina State, 69-60, to win the West.

Villanova was more of a surprise. But the Wildo earned their way there by defeating a third ACC representative, North Carolina, 56-44, in the Southeaest Regional finals in Birmingham.

Surrounded by three urban Catholic schools, Memphis coach Dana Kirk jokingly declared his te the secular national champions.

Before St. John's played Georgetown in the first game of the national semifinals, the crowd began to chant, "Big East, Big East." The sound reverberated throughout Rupp Arena.

Villanova, as we know, became the Cinderella winner of that year's tournament, playing a near-perfect game to stun Georgetown, 66-64, in the finals. Since then, all of the first nine members of the Big East – with the exception of Pitt – have ma Final Four appearances.

And Dave Gavitt, the genius behind it all, is no in the Naismith Memorial Basketball Hall of Fame.

*Dickie V's View:* I wasn't really shocked that the heavyweights – Georgetown and St. John's – made it to that Final Four. I was a little more surprised about Villanova. I was familiar with the league, but I still took a lot of heat at the time for singing the praises of the Big East. But I didn't have to be an Edward Bennett Williams – a superstar defense attorney – to defend that conference.

College basketball runs in cycles.

This was a time when the Big East was really starting to flex its muscles. The league had some great jockeys – guys like John Thompson, Looie Carnesecca and Rollie Massimino – who were all about winning and producing great teams. And it had solid gold All-American players.

Give Dave Gavitt credit here. He put this league together, got it national TV exposure for guys like Patrick Ewing, Chris Mullin, Ed Pinckney and Pearl Washington and then got to sit there in Lexington, enjoying the fruits of his labor of love.

**V**illanova's Rollie Massimino celebrated a Big East party in Lexington, Kentucky, in 1985. His Wildcats were one of three Big East teams at that Final Four, and he had the luxury of cutting down the nets as national champions.

# A TRIO *of Flint, Michigan superstars leads Michigan State to the NCAA title in 2000*

Meet the Flintstones

MOMENT NUMBER 48

Michigan State 89
Florida 76
April 3, 2000

*Profile:* Tom Izzo's Michigan State program was a regular at the NCAA Final Four between 1999 and 2001, winning the national championship in 2000 when his Spartans defeated Florida, 89-76, at the RCA Dome in Indianapolis.

The bedrock of those teams, which filled a vacuum in the state after the Ed Martin booster scandal at Michigan, were three stars from the economically depressed, crime-riddled city of Flint, Mich. – senior point guard Mateen Cleaves, senior forward Mo Peterson and junior guard Charlie Bell.

Collectively, they became known as "The Flintstones" and they – combined with senior power forward A.J. Granger – led the Spartans to the Big Ten school's biggest victory since the Spartans won their first national championship in 1979, defeating Indiana State in the now-fabled matchup between Magic Johnson and Larry Bird.

Magic was part of the crowd of 43,116 who watched as the 6' 2" Cleaves made the Gators disappear. The three-time All-American, who was named the tournament's most outstanding player, overcame a sprained foot and helped the Spartans maintain their poise when Florida threatened to make a run.

The Spartans had been on a mission ever since Duke eliminated them in the national semifinals the previous year.

But this had been a difficult season for Cleaves.

The Spartans' inspirational leader turned down big money from the NBA to come back for his final season and wound up missing 13 games with a stress fracture of the right foot.

Taking advantage of the fact Florida did not use its trademark press early in the game, Cleaves scored 13 points as the Spartans jumped out to a 43-32 le with 16:12 remaining.

Then disaster almost struck. Cleaves was shove out of bounds and came down hard on his right ankle, forcing him to leave the game with the Spartans clinging to a 50-44 lead.

"When I got hurt, I almost wanted to cry," Clea said later. "I told the trainer that unless he was goi to amputate my foot, there was no way they were going to keep me out of the game."

Bell, who moved over to the point when Cleave was out during the regular season, held things together until he returned with 11:51 left. Peterson and Granger combined for the next 16 points as th Spartans took a 71-58 lead and cruised the rest of the way. Peterson, playing for his grandmother, Clara May Spencer, who had died the previous wee led the Spartans with 21 points. Granger had 19. Michigan State hit 11 three-pointers and shot 56 percent.

Cleaves, on crutches, returned for the playing "One Shining Moment" and he, Peterson and Gran took turns hugging Johnson.

This was a special, uplifting moment for the citizens of Flint, who saw three local superstars accomplish their dreams of an NCAA championsh

*Dickie V's View:* Don't you just love storybook endings?

Mateen Cleaves was a nationally recruited poin guard who followed his good friend, Antonio Smit from Flint, Mich., to Michigan State – opening the door for Tom Izzo to start a pipeline from that city Then Cleaves helped Izzo achieve his ultimate goa

The Flintstones were a special part of Tom Izzo's legacy at Michigan State. Mateen Cleaves was a true leader in the backcourt and he celebrated many big Ws in East Lansing.

...aves was a three-time Michigan State captain, ...ree-time All-American and a two-time Big Ten ...yer of the Year. He could have gone pro after his ...ior year. But he stayed around, overcoming all ...ds of physical problems during the regular season ...ead his team to the national title.

...Cleaves was a great leader, and his team rallied ...und him, picking up the slack after he got hurt in ...championship game against Florida. But Cleaves ...s back on the court for the end of an 89-76 victory. ...d he was there, on crutches, for the celebration.

Afterwards, Tom Izzo said that Cleaves had the heart of a lion.

And Cleaves never forgot where he came from. When he was addressing the crowd at Spartan Stadium, he made sure they knew it, too. "People called me crazy for not going to Michigan, Kentucky or North Carolina, or for not taking the NBA money," Cleaves said. "But Michigan, Kentucky and money, they can't buy this.

"You got to earn it."

Talk about a leader. Talk about a captain. He was Awesome with a capital A.

# MARQUETTE'S *Dwyane Wade lights up Kentucky in the 2003 NCAA Midwest Regional finals*

## Wade-ing Thru

MOMENT NUMBER

**49**

Marquette 83
Kentucky 69
March 29, 2003

*Profile:* Marquette basketball history will always be measured by the accomplishments of the late, great Al McGui and All-American guard Butch Lee – a pair of New Yorkers who playe such a huge part in that Milwaukee-based Jesuit university's magical 197 NCAA Tournament ride

But for one golden afternoon in 2003, Dwyane Wade was as g as anyone who ever wor Golden Eagle uniform. anyone in the country, f that matter.

The 6' 5" junior All-American guard went in the ultimate zone agains top-ranked Kentucky in the NCAA Midwest Regional finals. He scor 29 points on 11-of-16 shooting, grabbed 11 rebounds and contribut 11 assists, a game-high four blocks and one steal i 35 unforgettable minutes, as the Eagles hammered the Wildcats, 83-69, before a stunned crowd of 28,383 at the Minneapolis Metrodome, to advance to the Final Four.

It was only the third triple double in NCAA his-
y – the others coming from Magic Johnson of
chigan State in 1979 and Andre Miller of Utah in
98.

Wade scored at will in a dazzling individual
play against a great program that had won 26
aight games and had been favored to win it all
en the brackets were drawn up. "We didn't have
y answers for him," Kentucky coach Tubby Smith
mitted.

The Wildcats, who were crippled without a
althy All-American guard Keith Boggans, tried to
w down Wade with three different defenders –
pendable forward Chuck Hayes and guards Cliff
wkins and Antwain Barbour.

But it was an exercise in futility.

Wade dunked over Kentucky center Marquis
till and then made a free throw to complete a three-
int play. Then he hit a three-pointer from the top
the key, had another dunk from the baseline and
red on a layup and free throw for a second three-
int play in less than three minutes in the second
If as the Eagles took a commanding 72-54 lead.

"You never want to leave anything on the floor,"
said afterwards. "Once I got going, my teammates
l a great job in finding me. Once anybody gets
ing, they're tough to guard."

But Wade was not the only giant killer that day.

Senior center Rob Jackson, a transfer from
ssissippi State who felt disrespected because Estill
d the local paper he didn't remember him from
e SEC, introduced himself with 24 points and 15
ounds. And forward Steve Novak came off the

bench to hit five of eight three-point attempts and
score 16 points.

But no one radiated more heat than Wade.

*Dickie V's View:* You want to know why Dwyane
Wade is such a great pro?

Join me in a trip down Memory Lane, my friends.
Reflect back to his days at Marquette.

I remember Rick Pitino telling me Wade was
going to be a special pro. Hey, let's not forget he
was sensational in the 2008 Olympic gold medal
game as he scored 27 points to lead the USA to the
championship. He said Wade was going to be a mega
star at the next level – and he should know from his
days in the NBA. He was right on target.

At Marquette, Wade learned from Tom Crean – a
coach who was tireless, energetic and motivated. If
you've ever watched Wade work out, you would
understand. It's not only his skill, versatility and
talent, but also his basketball IQ that makes him
special. He is so cerebral, a coach's dream.

Crean must have thought he was dreaming,
watching Wade take apart Kentucky, which had won
26 straight games going into that game, sending out
a message loud and clear about how good a player
he was.

A triple double? You must be kidding me.

Long before Marquette played the Cats, Crean
ordered an enlarged picture of the Louisiana Superdome, where the Final Four was played that year, and
made every player sign it. It went everywhere with
them during the season as motivation.

Wade made sure they got to see the real thing
in person.

**D**wyane Wade of
Marquette put on an
amazing show against
Kentucky in the 2003 NCAA
Midwest Regional final.
He put up a triple-double
as the Wildcats were sent
packing. Marquette went
to the Final Four, baby!

# WAKE FOREST *guard Randolph Childress puts on a show at the 1995 ACC Tournament*

**Wake Up Call**

MOMENT NUMBER 50

**Wake Forest 82**
**North Carolina 80 (OT)**
**March 12, 1995**

*Profile:* For all of the legends to pass through the Atlantic Coast Conference, no one has ever put together a more sensational three-game run in the conference tournament than Wake Forest's 6' 3" junior guard Randolph Childress did in 1995.

Childress was unstoppable, scoring 40, 30 and 37 points as the Demon Deacons won their first ACC Tournament championship in 44 years in Greensboro.

Wake, behind the dangerous Childress and emerging 6' 11" sophomore center Tim Duncan, finished the regular season in a four-way tie for first place with North Carolina, Virginia and Maryland. Wake won the tiebreakers and got the first seed in the tournament. This was the year of the infamous Duke meltdown – when coach Mike Krzyzewski missed most of the season with a back injury – and the Blue Devils finished in last place at 2-14.

The Deacs drew Duke, which had won the eighth- vs. ninth-place game against North Carolina State, in the Friday quarterfinals. Childress torched the Blue Devils for 40 points (the fifth-highest in ACC Tournament history). He had eight three-pointers and seven assists to help the Deacons rally from a 20-point first-half deficit for the victory.

Wake played Virginia on semifinal Saturday. And Childress continued his tear, leading the Deacs to the title game with 30 points. He made six three-point field goals and had seven assists.

Childress saved his best for a North Carolina tea that featured Jerry Stackhouse, Rasheed Wallace, Donald Williams and Jeff McInnis, and eventually made it to the Final Four.

Childress seemed unfazed, going off for 37 poin making nine three-pointers and contributing seven assists. He also scored the game-winning jump sho with seven seconds remaining, as the Deacs defeate the Tar Heels, 82-80, in overtime. Childress scored nine of Wake's points in overtime and the Deacs' la 22 of the game.

The lasting memory of that game was Childress making North Carolina guard Jeff McInnis lose his balance with a crossover dribble, then motioning fo McInnis to get up and guard him. As McInnis made it to his feet, Childress launched a three that sailed through the net.

"I told my teammates to give me the ball and ge out of the way. If we lost, blame me," he said later.

All told, Childress smashed the tournament scoring record with 107 points – an average of 35.7 points per game. He also made 23 threes and added 19 assists. Ironically, he was not a unanimous selection for MVP. He received 174 of 177 votes. Joe Sm of Maryland earned two votes and Donald Williams got the other one. He wasn't even the leading vote getter on the all-tournament team, finishing second to Rasheed Wallace, who scored just nine points in the championship game.

Go figure.

*Dickie V's View:* Randolph Childress from Wake Forest put on one of the greatest exhibitions ever during ACC tournament play. Mike Patrick, ESPN's standout play-by-play man who has covered the ACC for years, claimed it was as good a three-game performance as he'd ever witnessed in ACC tournament history. Oh, I wish I would have been seeing those games, but I was at another tournament.

People claim that Childress was bringing fans to their feet with his performance, hitting jumpers from all over the place. Look at the numbers: 40, 30 and 37 against Duke, Virginia and North Carolina, en route to the title.

Give me a break.

Patrick claims that he was looking into the eyes of defenders with body language that said, "You can't guard me. You flat out just can't guard me." YouTube still has a video of him breaking down Jeff McInnis of North Carolina with a crossover in that title game. And it was just amazing the way he took Wake Forest to the winner's circle, draining the game-winning jumper as the clock was running down in overtime.

That was a really good Wake Forest team. Childress averaged 20.1 points and Tim Duncan led the conference in rebounding and blocked shots. A lot of people thought Wake would get to the Final Four for the first time since 1961 that year, but they lost to Eddie Sutton and "Big Country" Reeves from Oklahoma State in the Sweet 16.

Randolph Childress was virtually unstoppable in the 1995 ACC Tournament. Basketball fans everywhere were in awe of his performance.

*Photo Courtesy of Wake Forest Athletic Media Relations.*

206

# FABULOUS STARS *in the College Basketball Galaxy*

## Fifty More

I've been privileged to broadcast games throughout the last 30 years at ESPN of so many incredible players. Although I've selected my fabulous 50, I couldn't stop there. Following are 50 more superstars in chronological order that I think deserve some props too, baby.

| Player | School | Vitals | Years |
|--------|--------|--------|-------|
| Danny Ainge | BYU | 6-4 guard | 1977-1981 |
| Rolando Blackman | Kansas State | 6-3 guard | 1977-1981 |
| Terry Cummings | DePaul | 6-9 forward | 1979-1982 |
| Sleepy Floyd | Georgetown | 6-3 guard | 1978-1982 |
| Dale Ellis | Tennessee | 6-7 forward | 1979-1983 |
| Charles Barkley | Auburn | 6-4 forward | 1981-1984 |
| Keith Lee | Memphis | 6-10 center | 1981-1985 |
| Karl Malone | Louisiana Tech | 6-9 forward | 1982-1985 |
| Ed Pinckney | Villanova | 6-10 center | 1981-1985 |
| Mark Price | Georgia Tech | 6-0 guard | 1982-1986 |
| Walter Berry | St John's | 6-8 forward | 1984-1986 |
| Chuck Person | Auburn | 6-8 forward | 1982-1986 |
| John Williams | LSU | 6-8 forward | 1984-1986 |
| Mark Jackson | St John's | 6-1 guard | 1983-1987 |
| Kenny Smith | North Carolina | 6-3 guard | 1983-1987 |
| Reggie Miller | UCLA | 6-7 forward | 1983-1987 |
| Reggie Williams | Georgetown | 6-7 forward | 1983-1987 |
| Mitch Richmond | Kansas State | 6-5 guard | 1986-1988 |
| Stacey King | Oklahoma | 6-11 center | 1986-1989 |
| Pervis Ellison | Louisville | 6-9 center | 1985-1989 |
| Chris Jackson | LSU | 6-0 guard | 1988-1990 |
| Gary Payton | Oregon State | 6-3 guard | 1986-1990 |
| Hank Gathers | Loyola Marymount | 6-8 forward | 1985-1990 |
| Dikembe Mutombo | Georgetown | 7-2 center | 1988-1991 |
| Billy Owens | Syracuse | 6-9 forward | 1988-1991 |

| Player | School | Vitals | Years |
|---|---|---|---|
| Stacy Augmon | UNLV | 6-8 forward | 1987-1991 |
| Jamal Mashburn | Kentucky | 6-8 forward | 1990-1993 |
| Penny Hardaway | Memphis | 6-7 guard | 1990-1993 |
| Allan Houston | Tennessee | 6-6 guard | 1989-1993 |
| Donyell Marshall | Connecticut | 6-9 forward | 1991-1994 |
| Corliss Williamson | Arkansas | 6-7 forward | 1992-1995 |
| Ed O'Bannon | UCLA | 6-8 forward | 1991-1995 |
| Randolph Childress | Wake Forest | 6-2 guard | 1990-1995 |
| Joe Smith | Maryland | 6-10 forward | 1993-1995 |
| Tony Delk | Kentucky | 6-6 guard | 1992-1996 |
| Raef LaFrentz | Kansas | 6-11 center | 1994-1998 |
| Paul Pierce | Kansas | 6-7 forward | 1995-1998 |
| Keith Van Horn | Utah | 6-10 forward | 1993-1998 |
| Michael Bibby | Arizona | 6-1 guard | 1996-1998 |
| Elton Brand | Duke | 6-8 center | 1997-1999 |
| Mateen Cleaves | Michigan State | 6-2 guard | 1996-2000 |
| Troy Murphy | Notre Dame | 6-11 forward | 1998-2001 |
| Nick Collison | Kansas | 6-9 forward | 1999-2003 |
| T.J. Ford | Texas | 6-0 guard | 2001-2003 |
| Dwyane Wade | Marquette | 6-4 guard | 2000-2003 |
| David West | Xavier | 6-9 center | 1999-2003 |
| Jameer Nelson | St Joseph's | 6-0 guard | 2000-2004 |
| Chris Paul | Wake Forest | 6-0 guard | 2003-2005 |
| Sean May | North Carolina | 6-9 forward | 2002-2005 |
| Adam Morrison | Gonzaga | 6-8 forward | 2003-2006 |

Alford, Steve, with John Garrity. *Playing For Knight.* Simon and Schuster, 1989.

Basketball Reference.com Statistics.

Brill, Bill. *Duke Basketball: A Legacy of Achievement.* Sports Publishing, 2004.

Calipari, John, with Dick Weiss. *Refuse to Lose.* Ballantine Books, 1996.

Chansky, Art. *The Dean's List.* Warner Books, 1996.

Clark, Ryan. *Game of My Life: Kentucky.* Sports Publishing, 2007.

Cooper, Scott Howard. *The Bruin 100.* Addax Publishing, 1999.

Featherston, Alwyn. *Tobacco Road.* The Lyons Press, 2006.

Feinstein, John. *A Season Inside.* Villard Books, 1988.

Hunter, Bruce. *Don't Count Me Out. The Irrepressible Dale Brown and his Fighting Tigers.* Bonus Books, 198

Knight, Bob, with Bob Hammel. *Knight: My Story.* St. Martin's Press, 2002.

Lyons, Robert S. *Palestra Pandemonium.* Temple Press, 2002.

Majerus, Rick, with Gene Wojciechowski. *My Life on a Napkin.* Hyperion, 1999.

Morris, Ron. *ACC Basketball: An Illustrated History.* Four Corners, 1988.

*NCAA March Madness.* Triumph Books, 2004.

Olson, Lute, with David Fisher. *Lute! The Seasons of My Life.* Thomas Dunne Books, 2006.

Peeler, Tim. *When March Went Mad.* Sports Publishing, 2007.

Reynolds, Bill. *Big Hoops.* NAL Books, 1989.

Richardson, Steve. *A Century of Sports.* Missouri Valley Publications, 2006.

Shapiro, Leonard. *Big Man on Campus.* Henry Holt and Company, 1991.

Stauth, Cameron. *The Golden Boys.* Pocket Books, 1992.

Tarkanian, Jerry, with Dan Wetzel. *Runnin' Rebel.* Sports Publishing, 2005.

Vitale, Dick, with Dick Weiss. *Living A Dream.* Sports Publishing, 2003.

Vitale, Dick, with Dick Weiss. *Time Out, Baby!* G. P. Putnam's Sons, 1991.

Waters, Mike. *Legends of Syracuse Basketball.* Sports Publishing, 2004.

Weiss, Dick. *True Blue: A Tribute to Mike Krzyzewski's Career at Duke.* Sports Publishing, 2005.

Wikipedia.com.

**S**o many great players and coac
have gotten their marching orders f
The General, Robert Montgomery Kni
I feel privileged to have worked with hi
the studio during the 2008 NCAA Tourname

*Photo Courtesy of Dick V*